EX LIBRIS

VINTAGE CLASSICS

ANNA POLITKOVSKAYA

Known to many as 'Russia's lost moral conscience', Anna Politkovskaya was a special correspondent for the Russian newspaper *Novaya gazeta* and the recipient of many honours for her writing. She is the author of *A Dirty War*, *Putin's Russia* and *A Russian Diary*, and a collection of works, *Nothing But the Truth*. Anna Politkovskaya was murdered in Moscow in October 2006.

ALSO BY ANNA POLITKOVSKAYA

A Dirty War
Putin's Russia
A Russian Diary
Nothing But the Truth

ANNA POLITKOVSKAYA
THE ESSENTIAL ANNA POLITKOVSKAYA

TRANSLATED FROM THE RUSSIAN BY
John Crowfoot and Arch Tait

WITH A FOREWORD BY
Helena Kennedy
AND
AN AFTERWORD BY
Svetlana Alexievich

VINTAGE CLASSICS

1 3 5 7 9 10 8 6 4 2

Vintage Classics is part of the Penguin Random House group of companies

Vintage, Penguin Random House UK, One Embassy Gardens, 8 Viaduct Gardens, London SW11 7BW

penguin.co.uk/vintage-classics
global.penguinrandomhouse.com

Copyright © Anna Politkovskaya 1999, 2004, 2007
Copyright © *Novaya gazeta* 2007
English translation copyright © John Crowfoot 2001; Arch Tait 2004, 2010
Foreword copyright © Helena Kennedy 2026
Afterword copyright © Svetlana Alexievich 2026

The moral right of the author has been asserted

This collection first published by Vintage Classics in 2026

Penguin Random House values and supports copyright. Copyright fuels creativity, encourages diverse voices, promotes freedom of expression and supports a vibrant culture. Thank you for purchasing an authorised edition of this book and for respecting intellectual property laws by not reproducing, scanning or distributing any part of it by any means without permission. You are supporting authors and enabling Penguin Random House to continue to publish books for everyone. No part of this book may be used or reproduced in any manner for the purpose of training artificial intelligence technologies or systems. In accordance with Article 4(3) of the DSM Directive 2019/790, Penguin Random House expressly reserves this work from the text and data mining exception.

A CIP catalogue record for this book is available from the British Library

ISBN 9781784879730

Typeset in 11/13pt Bembo Book MT Pro by Six Red Marbles UK, Thetford, Norfolk
Printed and bound in Great Britain by Clays Ltd, Elcograf S.p.A.

The authorised representative in the EEA is Penguin Random House Ireland, Morrison Chambers, 32 Nassau Street, Dublin D02 YH68

Penguin Random House is committed to a sustainable future for our business, our readers and our planet. This book is made from Forest Stewardship Council® certified paper.

Contents

Foreword ix

A DIRTY WAR

Land of the Unknown Soldiers 3
Tainted Tins 12
Ingushlag 19
Bomb, Don't Save 28
Kalashnikov and the Old People's Home 34
Tell Them: This War Is Senseless 43
The Chechnya Reservation 52
Sentence Has Been Passed 60
The Ordinary Man Does Not Need Freedom 69
Netherworld 79
I Want to Stay Alive 88
Bread and Bullets 95
Murder or Execution? 99
Chronology 106
Biographical Notes 115

PUTIN'S RUSSIA

My Country's Army, and its Mothers 121
Tanya, Misha, Lena and Rinat: Where Are They Now? 135

More Stories from the Provinces	167
Akaky Akakievich Putin II	194
After Beslan	208

NOTHING BUT THE TRUTH

So What Am I Guilty Of?	221
Should Lives Be Sacrificed to Journalism?	226
The War in Chechnya	245
Nord-Ost	297
Russia: A Country at Peace	325
Planet Earth: The World Beyond Russia	333
The Other Anna	344

Afterword	357

Foreword

> 'Go to where the silence is and say something.'
> Amy Goodman, *Columbia Journalism Review*, 1994

In early 2005 I was invited by PEN, the organisation devoted to the promotion of literature and freedom of expression, to present an award to Anna Politkovskaya. I was delighted to have the opportunity of meeting her as I knew her work and greatly admired her courageous opposition both to the Chechen conflict and to President Putin's authoritarian regime. Her fearlessness in the face of grave danger made her one of the few international journalists whom human rights activists and lawyers held in awe.

My tribute to Anna saluted her uncompromising coverage of the horrors that had befallen the people of Chechnya; it recalled the torture and terrifying mock execution to which she had been subjected by Russian troops for documenting the atrocities perpetrated against the civilian population; likewise, her reports of the 2002 Moscow theatre siege and its bloody denouement, and her resolute defiance of threats from the state authorities and other shady operators within the Russian political firmament.

We owed her a debt of gratitude for helping the West reach a far better understanding of the emerging landscape in post-Soviet Russia and for shining a clearer light on the true nature of the occupation of Chechnya, a brutal conflict wilfully misrepresented as Russia's private front in the war on terror. No democracy is worthy of the name if freedom of the press is curtailed or writers and journalists are crushed; yet here was a writer who – at great personal risk – defied state intimidation to speak truth to power.

*

Anna received the reward with good humour and humility. As this collection of her writing shows, the reach of her journalism extended far beyond coverage of individual cataclysmic events. She frequently lifted the veil on more systemic inhumanity that did not attract as much international interest. Her tenacious investigations involved dogged correspondence and days sitting in court. Her coverage of the case of 'The Cadet', for example, reveals her staying power and commitment to reporting long trials that might have defeated others. Sergey Lapin – The Cadet – was a member of the Russian military in Chechnya believed to be responsible for many of the 'disappearances' of Chechens dragged from their homes, never to be seen again. He had a reputation as a torturer and extra-judicial killer but despite efforts to bring him to trial was able to manipulate the legal process by intimidation and covert influence. It was Anna's belief that the courts' failures to deliver justice must be documented and that it was the role of the press, on behalf of those who had suffered at his hands, to demand transparency and accountability. She had met the wives and mothers of The Cadet's victims, heard their stories and knew he bore responsibility. Her fight for them helped lead to his eventual conviction.

After the award ceremony we sat drinking wine and talking politics. Anna painted a haunting portrait of Putin's Russia, a country governed by an administration that bore many of the hallmarks of Stalin's; here was a land whose own secret services suppressed civil liberties and where fear stalked universities, newsrooms and every corridor in which democracy might have flourished.

Anna had been on the receiving end of death threats delivered over the telephone and posted on the internet. Articles had been published defaming her, she had been treated with derision and socially ostracised to the extent that some former friends and colleagues avoided contact for fear of becoming tarnished by association. She spoke with sadness about the toll on her private life, the effects on her family and children. Yet her isolation and aloneness, instead of diminishing her, appeared to have become a source of determination and strength, as though she had crossed some

Rubicon and was now beyond ordinary conceptions of fear or courage.

Shortly before the prize-giving she had been poisoned as she flew to Rostov-on-Don to cover the Beslan hostage crisis. Armed terrorists were holding over a thousand school children and adults captive, a siege that ended in massive loss of life. But Anna never arrived. As we sat into the night she described the episode with terrifying vividness: how she had made telephone calls to colleagues that must have been intercepted; how she had boarded the plane and accepted a small cup of black tea before take-off only to awaken in a hospital ward. Despite ourselves, we tend to nurture the fragile hope that heaping international honours upon those who make a stand, who defend freedom of expression, justice and liberty, affords them some cloak of immunity from retribution, however powerful, lawless or vengeful their enemies. In Anna's case such optimism was ill-founded.

She was shot dead on 7 October 2006, news that came like a physical blow. Yet whatever driving force gave her the strength to persist had stayed with her until the end. She was a truly exceptional woman, whose bravery in confronting oppression is her legacy to the world and remains a source of inspiration for us all.

I remember taking leave of her the night of the award and asking whether she might not think of leaving Russia, at least temporarily. She held my hand, smiling, and said, 'Exile is not for me. That way they win.'

Twenty years on, and Putin's rule has become synonymous with its brutal and sometimes murderous crackdown on dissent. The lawyers who stood beside Navalny and Vladimir Kara-Murza have been imprisoned. NGOs arguing for human rights have been banned. Large numbers of journalists have had to flee into exile for daring to call his war against Ukraine what it is – a war. And still, Putin's long arm of oppression reaches beyond Russia, with assassinations and poisonings, cyber wars and interference in institutions and elections worldwide.

Anna's murder was an augur of all that has followed. She saw it coming. And now Putin's attacks on independent journalism and media freedom are being emulated by every tinpot authoritarian across the world. The global death toll of journalists has never been higher. More and more, journalists are arbitrarily detained on trumped-up charges.

Speaking truth to power, exposing corruption, lies and disinformation, shining a light on gross violations of human rights – this is the animating spirit of great journalism. It has never been more vital. It is why Anna Politkovskaya is an iconic figure and why her writing remains an enduring testament to the importance of defending our freedoms before it's too late.

HELENA KENNEDY

A Dirty War

Land of the Unknown Soldiers
A New Delivery of 'Cargo 200'

23 August 1999

Senior Lieutenant (Medical Corps) Sergey Moiseyenko holds a glass laboratory dish between the palms of his hands and carefully raises it to his eyes. With a nod towards the corner of the office he indicates several bones lying on the floor, but keeps his eyes on the dish. Seven human teeth, discoloured as if they have not been brushed for a long time lie scattered there, together with small pieces of someone's lower jaw.

'Do you see?' says 25-year-old Moiseyenko, who, despite his youth, is considered one of the most gifted specialists at the renowned Rostov laboratory of forensic medicine. 'That's not a filling in this tooth here, but part of a bullet . . . Together the teeth and those bones are body No. 1007 according to our classification. An unknown soldier. He died in August 1996 in Grozny. My job is to establish who he was. There are already some indications. I think we'll get a result.'

'Lord only knows how! You've got nothing but scraps of bone and some teeth. And that bullet, of course . . .'

The conversation moves on. We talk about the frustration felt by all at the laboratory, and the reason why they are still swamped with work though the war ended three years ago. Soldiers in Chechnya carried no metal identity discs or documents. Their superior officers cared little what became of them once they were dead. As a result, body No. 1007 today fits into a small plastic bag.

'If they send back bodies from a new war without ID discs . . .' It was the evening of 17 August. Moiseyenko did not yet know that two days earlier, on a Sunday morning, the laboratory head

Vladimir Shcherbakov had already received a disturbing call from the Ministry of Defence in Moscow.

'How many "credo" bags do you have there?' someone shouted down the line.

'I'll find out immediately,' replied Colonel Shcherbakov.

'Send them all to Makhachkala.* Quickly! Can you get a hundred?'

Shcherbakov put down the receiver. His shoulders gave an involuntary shudder, as if from a chill, although it was 32°C in Rostov that day. For those who don't know, the 'credo' bag is one of those large black plastic envelopes, closed with a zipper (you've all seen US police films) in which they pack up dead bodies. The sort of container the army always needs when its men start getting killed.

Neither did Lieutenant Moiseyenko know that on 18 August, the very next morning after we talked, the bodies of soldiers killed in Daghestan would begin to arrive. They arrived in 'credo' bags, under the code name 'cargo 200', at the main reception and treatment centre in Rostov (which serves the entire North Caucasus Military District). And once again, they were without ID discs or documents.† Body 1007 would have to squeeze up and make space on the senior lieutenant's table for bodies 1015, 1020 and 1030. It looked as if the entire laboratory was fated to start from scratch all over again, although it still had 277 bodies to identify from the previous war.

Morgues are never cosy places, but wars are bound to happen

---

* Capital of Daghestan, one of 21 ethnic republics (including Chechnya) that with Moscow, Petersburg and the 66 predominantly Russian Regions make up the 89 'subjects' of the Russian Federation.

† In the 1990s Russia's armed forces adopted the Anglo-American ID disc or 'dog-tag'. Previously Soviet servicemen carried a capsule, resembling a spent rifle shell, in which personal details were sealed. For decades volunteers have searched for these on the battlefields of the 1941–5 war, providing confirmation of death and adding names to monuments.

and you need dissection rooms. There aren't any decent wars either. But they all leave us with a choice: we can either draw lessons from a war or ignore what it teaches us.

What lessons have been learned over the last three years, from August 1996 when General Lebed helped to negotiate an end to the war in Chechnya, to the present fighting in Daghestan? Why have ordinary soldiers again not left behind even a single drop of their blood to aid their rapid identification? What was Colonel Shcherbakov up to all that time? Why didn't he persuade the generals that they should never wage another war like that in Chechnya?

Body 549

'What was *I* doing?!' The colonel is indignant. 'I was telling them just that. It's the reason I was in such disfavour.' He explains:

'The more I pushed, the greater the pressure on me. I was accused of every failing in order to shut me up. Finally, when I could see no other way out, I drafted a law: "On Forensic Registration and Identification in the Armed Forces and Other Paramilitary Formations." And what do you think? It's been lying unheeded at the Duma for almost a year. Where was public opinion? And the human rights activists who are today shouting that the Daghestan campaign is a repeat of the Chechen war? They said nothing.'

'The Ministry of Defence, on the other hand, and the presidential staff, accused me of playing "political games" to the detriment of the job in hand. But I started to push things further, and demonstrate it was essential to have a database for the identification of all who are in the armed forces. Then they began a campaign to discredit me. Supposedly I was not fighting for identification, but only to create a nice cosy job for myself; I was exploiting these remains to push ahead scientific research. I was personally blamed because the laboratory was identifying no more than four or five bodies a month. But that was simply the reality!'

★

Body 549 reached Laboratory 124 from Grozny on 20 August 1996 with the label 'unknown' attached to the stretcher. It had also been set on fire after death (someone had burnt the soldier after he was shot). The tissue was already in a state of total disintegration. The corpse was therefore impossible to identify visually; it had evidently lain under the southern sun for several weeks. There was no ID disc or any information about his unit. Two distinctive features: the top joint of the left thumb was missing and, by some miracle, a tin cross of the Old Believers still hung around his neck.*

In September 1996 when the lab's officers could see that no one was coming to claim Body 549 – neither those who had served with him nor his relatives – they sent out thousands of letters, requiring military registration offices throughout Russia to track down any of 549's surviving fellow soldiers. (It was known which units had taken part in the August battles in Grozny, and so they had a good idea which military registration offices had provided their conscripts.) It was 18 months before they received any replies. That's how things work in our country. Only many months later did the following letter reach the laboratory:

'From 24 June 1996 I served in Chechnya with unit 21617. On 9 August we were ordered to advance. We went about a kilometre and, after the company in front of us had gone ahead, we came under fire from both sides. I was hit by shrapnel, first in the foot and then in the arm. I fell down and they fired at me again. When the shooting ended I got back to the armoured vehicle. Private Ozhigov was sitting there. Perhaps they would not have noticed him, but he began to make a tourniquet above my elbow to stop the blood. Suddenly he fell across my knees. A sniper had got him. Then our side gathered all the wounded and loaded them onto the armoured vehicle.

'Again the Chechens started firing at us, this time with mortars.

---

* The Old Believers, the 'Dissenters' of Russian Orthodoxy, broke from the Church in the mid-seventeenth century over its reform of texts and rituals.

I fell down and passed out. When I came to, the platoon leader and our driver-mechanic Khazanov were lying next to me. They said I should keep down because a sniper was watching us. We lay for four hours, pretending to be dead, until the helicopters started bombing the nine-storey building where the sniper was. Then we crawled into some cellar where our commander found us with one of the scouts. We were put in an armoured vehicle . . .'

Private Artur Kamaleyev, from the Volga republic of Bashkortostan, then spent many months in military hospitals: Vladikavkaz, then Rostov and Ufa. Only in spring 1998 did the district military registration office find him, at the laboratory's request, when he was discharged as unfit for further service. It was then that they discovered he had been saved by Private Ozhigov, who did not have the upper joint of his left thumb.

The laboratory sent a formal request to the military office in the Altai Region, for blood samples, plus thumb and palm prints from the parents of Ivan Ozhigov. His mother and father also sent a photograph of Ivan which Major Boris Shkolnikov, a forensic craniologist, compared to the skull of Body 549 – the same test carried out on the remains of the Romanovs. After five more major scientific investigations the experts could say without doubt: 'This is no longer an unknown soldier.'

On 3 August 1999, three years after he died, Ivan's family received his remains, and a short while ago the body of this 19-year-old private, who had died trying to save his wounded comrade, was buried in a village in Siberia.

A shocking story? Yes, but all the more so because it is no exception, but a typical and everyday example. The majority of cases at Shcherbakov's laboratory are of this type. He cannot help 'spinning out' the identification procedure.

Perhaps you imagine that Moscow – i.e. the Ministry of Defence and the presidential staff – drew the same conclusion from the history of Private Ozhigov? Nothing of the kind. 'For three years you've been messing around with one body!' That was the accusation thrown at Shcherbakov. The colonel's retort was just as sharp: 'Don't blame me for your mistakes; all those who could have been recognised by simpler methods have long ago been identified. From now on we can only work in this way. We shall be forced to continue doing so, moreover, until you take urgent measures to finally create a database of identification samples for all soldiers and officers who are sent to areas of conflict.' Keep your voice down, they told Shcherbakov: You're the one making a good living out of these corpses, it's your people who are writing dissertations and won't listen to anyone else. So now we are declaring war on you.

Slander

The campaign against Shcherbakov was headed by Victor Kolkutin, the chief forensic expert at the Ministry of Defence, and Konstantin Golumbovsky, head of the president's working group on the exhumation and identification of soldiers killed in action. They are highly respected and well-known people. However, it is difficult to describe the weapon they unleashed against Shcherbakov as anything other than public defamation. In Moscow, journalists, Duma deputies, and the Ministries of Health and Defence were supplied with deliberately distorted information about the colonel. It was claimed, for instance, that Shcherbakov was openly disrespectful towards the remains he worked with, separating skulls from bodies simply because that was easier for his research purposes.

How can you check? The only way is to sit there, among the skulls at the laboratory, in the section headed by Major Boris Shkolnikov and read through dozens of files on unidentified soldiers. Here are the bullet wounds in the skull and here is the file. As you read, it turns out that each of these skulls represents a body: at best a few, individual bones are added to the skull and even then it's not clear to whom they belong. Lengthy molecular-genetic investigation is needed before they can be proved to come from the same person. Something else of major importance became clear to me then – the soldiers were already in this state when their remains, delivered by Golumbovsky's team, reached the laboratory.

The other accusation was that, for the convenience of research and the writing of dissertations, the army privates who serve as lab assistants are forced to boil up the bones of the deceased soldiers in the laboratory courtyard in full view of the unfortunate parents. Mothers supposedly had to pass by bubbling cauldrons full of skulls before they could view the remains of their children. It's a blood-chilling scene and makes one want to demand the immediate arrest of Shcherbakov.

How do you check this story? You must venture yourself into that devil's kitchen. There it is, exactly as described. Surrounded by filth and an unbelievable stench, soldiers are boiling the bones until the rotting flesh falls off them. It is also quite true that they do this in large vessels more usually employed for boiling clothes. But you must ask why. The reason is that money to purchase autoclaves was not allowed for in the budget estimates. Even the laundry pans were bought only recently. Before that the bones were boiled up in large tins that previously contained jam or herrings. They have no choice. Genetic investigations with contaminated remains are strictly forbidden since they will give no results and damage the equipment. What were they to do? Warn Moscow that all identification work is henceforth halted until autoclaves are provided? They might wait for years. And how then could they look mothers in the eye when they came demanding, if not their sons then at least a coffin?

As a result, the six months before the present fighting began in Daghestan have been spent squabbling, not working. The laboratory got on with its job, but in Moscow they intrigued and spread rumours and Shcherbakov had to fight back. The idea of creating a database for identification of all soldiers sent to areas of conflict has not advanced one iota. The army entered the present war in the same barbaric state as the Chechen war of 1994–6, while Colonel Shcherbakov, a unique specialist whose knowledge is now desperately needed, is a thoroughly harassed and exhausted individual. He is bound, hand and foot, by numerous investigations that do not cease from one week to the next. He is a workhorse, he says, that Moscow has driven to its limit and will soon finish off.

Graves or Monuments?

Who benefits from this outrageous squabble over bones? The immediate and obvious causes are entirely traditional. People, as always, are fighting for wealth and fame. The Moscow authorities are determined that Shcherbakov must be neutralised so that they can decide who is in charge, throughout the country, of identification research and procedures.

Novaya gazeta has learned that very recently – just as they were preparing for the war in Daghestan, in fact – a decision was taken at the highest level by the government and the presidential staff: the unidentified 'Chechen' bodies still in Laboratory 124's refrigerators must be rapidly laid to rest. The reason? The soldiers' mothers were making too much of a fuss, and it was proving too expensive for the State to pay its respects by identifying and burying everyone. A site had already been chosen in the Rostov City northern cemetery and the builders were given until 25 August to prepare the monument. When, in future, the mothers complain that they wanted to bury their children themselves the blame will be shifted entirely to Shcherbakov. It was he, they will be told, who dragged out the identification process. Any future court cases should be brought against him.

This conveniently kills two birds with one stone. Our authorities hate to be held responsible by the living, whether they are the families of missing soldiers or that tiresomely demanding Shcherbakov. But they adore all kinds of ceremonies in commemoration of the dead – don't worry about feeding people, but be sure to place a wreath on their graves. Having proved unworthy of their soldiers and officers, politicians and military officials love annual visits to the Grave of the Unknown Soldier where they can shed a few restrained masculine tears for the benefit of the television cameras. As the Duma elections approach, the need is urgently growing for some kind of memorial to the unknown dead of the Chechen war. Politicians and the military need somewhere they can demonstrate their penitence in public. Today this is the most important and fundamental point of disagreement between Shcherbakov and the authorities. He will not hear any talk of such a monument and whenever he meets people in authority he does not fail to warn them that the State could not bring greater shame on itself than by this hurried burying of the problem. Each time he repeats the same quotation. It comes from the rules of the US Military Pathology Institute's medical examination directorate (the American equivalent of Laboratory 124):

> The goal that all of our employees strive to attain is simple. We must not permit any American serviceman or woman to be buried beneath the inscription: 'Here lies an American soldier who covered himself with glory and whose name is known to God alone.'

Shcherbakov follows these words with a demand for money in order to continue the expensive identification research. The more he insists, the more our authorities dream of the peace and quiet of the Grave of the Unknown Soldier.

20 August. Deliveries of 'cargo 200' from Daghestan are never-ending. Shcherbakov is worn out. The laboratory has no more resources than before. As we leave, Lieutenant Moiseyenko tells us: 'If they drive such people as Shcherbakov out of the army, I shall also resign.'

ROSTOV-ON-DON

On 7 August 1999 a convoy of vehicles and armed men crossed into Daghestan. It was led by the Chechen commander Shamil Basayev and a veteran opponent of the Soviet forces in Afghanistan, the Saudi-born Khattab. They had come supposedly in support of local Wahhabites. Army and police units were sent to repel them.

Tainted Tins
How the Soldiers are Fed

30 September 1999

If it had not been for the fighting in Daghestan the two of us might never have met: the tinned meat of the Semikarakorsk meat processing plant and my digestive system.

It was getting near suppertime and the men of the Lipetsk Region OMON [riot police] who were off duty invited me into their improvised kitchen. They are currently based in the Kazbekovsk district next to the Chechen border, and are guarding the approaches to Dylym, the main town in the area. I should have been warned by the mysterious winks and smiles they exchanged.

The kitchen turned out to be in a cellar, down two dark flights of stairs. The lower we descended, the greater my reluctance: the foul stench rising to meet us suggested that chemical weapons had been used not far away.

'May I offer you a gas mask?' a pleasant young man asked.

'You're most kind, but if you can take it, so can I.'

'Oh, you mustn't compare yourself with us, we're already used to it.'

At that moment we reached our destination and the dishevelled character in charge of the kitchen came into view. With a knife he was opening one after another of the latest rations from the Semikarakorsk plant. They had received them the day before from the OMON quartermaster at the food depot in Kizlyar. Plunging his blade through the pliable aluminium he counted aloud:

'... Tin 23, rotten. Tin 39, likewise. Tin 41, the same ... That's enough! Tin 42 is for you. Take it back to Moscow and show them what they feed us. Perhaps you'd like me to disembowel it here and now, so there's no mistake?'

'Better not,' jokes Alexander Pavlovich Ponomaryov, the lieutenant colonel in charge of these Interior Ministry forces (to them he is simply Pal'ich), 'everyone on the plane might die before the tin reaches the capital of our great country. Try a sample of what they regularly serve us.'

I sniffed and licked. What else could I do? My organism reacted instantly.

'We have stomach infections all the time,' concluded Pal'ich. 'And that's the condition we fight in.'

'But do you have enough to treat it? Did they give you anything?'

'Medicine, you mean? Not really. We're chronically short of everything here.'

I pulled out all of the anti-diarrhoea tablets I'd taken with me on the trip and handed them over to Colonel Ponomaryov. Then I decided to investigate local life and its chronic shortages.

Food Fit for Heroes

This unit of the Lipetsk OMON is already famous throughout Daghestan. They are in charge of the Kazbekovsk section of the *cordon sanitaire* that runs along the Chechen–Daghestani border and they recently performed a feat of heroism. In early September they were guarding the small town of Novolakskoe. With them were the town's fearless policemen and an army unit under the command of Infantry Major Zhenya (in Daghestan officers do not introduce themselves, even to fellow officers). At one point it became clear that things were going badly and the bandits would soon have the area completely surrounded. No one wanted to die. So while there was still a way out of the town, Major Zhenya grabbed an armoured personnel carrier and drove away from the fighting, leaving his own soldiers and the policemen to their fate, and to almost certain death.

'Why didn't you save yourselves and run?'

'We had wounded men with us.'

When resistance became almost futile and they faced capture or death, the Lipetsk OMON decided to break through enemy lines. Of course, they had almost no chance of getting through alive. It was simply a case of despair, resentment, and a desire to live. Guided by their senses, they crawled out at night, stealthily and silently, tracing a great arc across Chechen territory, beyond the surrounding fighters, where death waited behind each hill.

Discussing their feat of bravery in that stench-ridden kitchen only sharpened everyone's perceptions. How could people who have shown such bravery in impossible circumstances and, weeks later, continue to face mortal danger every day, now be living like stray dogs that no one cares for? Is this how the Motherland repays their valour?

The next subject proved highly sensitive for these resentful people whose nerves have been stretched to the limit. The Lipetsk OMON escaped from encirclement in worn and tattered clothes. What was left when they reached freedom could have gone straight on the fire. But did anyone hurry to issue them with new uniforms? The military quartermasters now running Daghestan did not even blink. Instead they had to rely on their well-disposed comrades to cover their nakedness.

Their heroism was not reflected in their pay, either. Prime Minister Putin may frequently offer the nation therapeutic TV sessions, but the OMON are still getting a mere 22 roubles a day [about $0.70, Tr.], and there's no hope of any more. Not for them the $1,000 the Chechen fighters are supposed to get each month! It makes no difference whether you're a hero, or a Major Zhenya. Pal'ich supposes that somewhere, perhaps in Makhachkala, at staff headquarters, some of the generals may already be doing quite nicely. On the front line, here in Dylym, where they expect the Chechen fighters to break through again at any minute, no one has seen any extra money.

Hence their hungry existence. They live little better than savages and our beloved country blows the smell of tainted meat in their faces. The Lipetsk OMON men are greeted by this stench in place of supper and can expect nothing else. There are no streetside kiosks here, only ravines and mountains, and even if they could buy something to eat they have no money. If it were not for the tins from Semikarakorsk then the Motherland would be offering its heroes nothing more than gruel. When the local women notice how thin the soldiers defending them are, they bring them food out of the kindness of their hearts.

Alexander Ponomaryov, their commanding officer, is 42, and 27 of those years he has devoted to the army. His shoulders constantly twitch and jerk, from the cold and from a nervous tic. He huddles up in his shapeless old sweater and is sunk in melancholy. His life, for the most part, has been wasted, he believes, fighting difficult military campaigns for which the country has never even offered a grudging 'Thank you'.

'Do you know why you're fighting here?'

'Because of someone's political ambitions. And for 22 roubles a day. Otherwise everything would be different. You can see for yourself. The furthest post where our men are on duty is 15 kilometres from this barrack. If anything happens there we don't even have a car or the money to buy petrol – they don't supply one, it's not standard issue. So we run out into the road, flag someone down and ask for a lift. And what if it's night-time? Who can you ask here in the village? It's a joke. But when something happens you feel nothing but hatred for the powers that sent us here. As you can see, they have created all the necessary conditions for feats of heroism . . .'

Pal'ich laughs. Our dear Pal'ich who knows from bitter experience that the brisk reports delivered by the generals from morning to night on all the TV channels are very far from the truth here on the front line.

At this point someone will certainly say to himself: What a green creature this Politkovskaya is! Just imagine, the tinned meat was off, and the colonel got emotional like some delicate college girl. Well, if you're sitting comfortably and safely in Moscow, then indeed there is little need to become overexcited. But if someone is aiming at you, every hour of every day down the barrel of a gun, and if you take your life in your hands simply by glancing out the window, then your nerves will be in quite a different state. The complaints about living conditions are entirely justified. If the country wants acts of bravery then it should give more practical expression to its rapture at such heroism. As long as the authorities think they can buy off their heroes with awards and decorations – and dozens are being proposed for decorations in Daghestan today – then the heroes will desert them.

Semikarakorsk

My two last phone calls were to Rostov-on-Don and Semikarakorsk. At supply headquarters for the North Caucasus Military District the answer was simple:

'The meat-processing plant in Semikarakorsk won the public tender. You can't hold us responsible. It's impossible to open every tin. When we made spot checks the results were good. All complaints to the producer.'

In Semikarakorsk someone who describes himself as the plant director answers the phone. He is very evasive and lengthily assures me that these rumours are lies, nothing more than the newspapers trying to concoct a sensational story.

'But how much were you paid for these consignments to Daghestan?'

The moment money is mentioned the director turns nasty:

'Get lost. I'm not telling you,' he snaps, 'it's a commercial secret. We're a private company.'

Then our Semikarakorsk butcher gets carried away. Like a real old-style Communist he tells me that the soldiers have become too demanding, they are asking for the impossible and should be more modest. The Motherland 'is in no fit condition . . . Do you understand?' And a lot of other nonsense.

Finally I reach the end of my patience:

'You're a real bastard, aren't you? Are you really too thick to understand that your rotten meat may be the last thing one of those young soldiers ever eats?'

There is an unpleasant, disparaging laugh:

'Fax us your questions and if we see the necessity, we'll provide answers.' Without a word of farewell he slams down the receiver.

You want to know his name, of course. The businessman I was talking to is called Igor G. Lisakonov. And if you wish to personally express your revulsion at a scoundrel who has been turning a pretty penny from these tainted supplies then you may ring him on the following telephone numbers: Rostov (886356-2) 13-94 or 14-94. Perhaps then he'll finally get the message.

At all times and under all regimes wars have been profitable business. While others carried the dead off the battlefield, the quartermasters and their kind in supplies were lining their pockets. The longer the war, the fatter their wallets. The more soldiers despatched to the front, the finer the Mercedes some ministry official can obtain.* You tell me that the Chechens are to blame for our troubles. Don't worry, we're doing quite well on our own.

A Minefield

Today more than a dozen unexploded bombs, dropped from the air, lie about the churned-up mess that is Novolakskoe. They didn't go off, unfortunately, because they were rather old; someone says they were made in the 1950s. Naturally people returning to their homes asked the military to remove these dangerous and unpredictable lumps of metal as quickly as possible. The soldiers replied that the bombs could not be safely moved and must be detonated where they are. The explosive force of each bomb, they

---

* Pavel Grachev, Minister of Defence during the first Chechen war, was famous for his acquisition of several Mercedes for himself and his leading officials.

added, lowering their gaze, is equivalent to that which destroyed the high-rise block in Buinaksk.* Did no one think of that before? Now Novolakskoe will acquire a dozen large craters and suffer extensive new destruction. People are horrified.

That's how our soldiers are living at the front. No one cares for their safety and they are forced to stroll past unexploded bombs all the time. One bomb waiting to explode is their semi-starved existence; another is the lack of normal warm clothing; a third is their miserable wages; a fourth ... Do the authorities really not foresee the consequences? Do they expect people who have served in these conditions to return home, calm and confident, convinced they are real heroes?

An armoured personnel carrier races through the maize fields along the road that borders the *cordon sanitaire*. It is full of soldiers. An officer leaps out and introduces himself: 'Colonel N.' All of them here say that: Colonel N., Major N. and so on. Among themselves the officers say that if they give their surnames the Chechens will find their families 'in Russia' and wreak vengeance on them. The colonel is in a highly nervous state. Restlessly he struts back and forth, twitching and sometimes breaking into a run; he gives an odd and unbalanced impression. At his command the soldiers point their weapons at everyone who isn't in uniform or riding in an army vehicle. No one trusts anyone else here and they're all afraid of each other.

That's how we now behave, yet the land around is part of our country, it's not a fascist, gangster-run republic. We created this situation. Only officers who are daily shown how little they count could behave in this way.

MAKHACHKALA—DYLYM

---

* On 4 September 1999, 62 soldiers and members of their families were killed when a residential building in their compound in Buinaksk was destroyed by an explosion. Over the next ten days there were two bombings of residential blocks in Moscow (see Chronology, p. 106).

Ingushlag
A New Concentration Camp

4 November 1999

A tragedy is today unfolding in Ingushetia. It has grown to such catastrophic proportions that, believe me, it is now hardly less terrible than the war in Chechnya. What difference does it make, in the end, if you die from hunger or from bombing? During the month that they have spent in the refugee camps – in these poultry and old stock-raising farms, in cellars, tents and out in the open beside campfires – thousands of people have become deeply embittered, with no regular food or place to wash, and without any occupation or work.

Hopes of returning home have finally melted away. Now people in the camps are desperately struggling just to survive. They await the first snows in November almost as though they were death itself. Each night their fear of bombardment is magnified a hundredfold by the roar of weapons being fired nearby. All the food they brought with them has now been eaten and there is a chronic shortage of humanitarian aid: the little there is, is totally inadequate for the number of refugees. Cold, hunger, sickness and everywhere pale children with blue lips. Adults squabble over each crust of bread. People ask only two questions: 'Why?' and 'How many more victims do you need?'

Death from the Skies

We are standing in the middle of the camp and even laughing, although it's no laughing matter. We're looking up at the sky where rockets fly over our heads. Insolently they rip through the air above us as though we are not standing below and, instead, this were some weapons testing site. Why the laughter? It helps us save face in front of each other and conceals the nervous trembling that has seized hold of us all.

27 October 1999. It's sunny and there is no wind. Soon it will be midday. We are on the outskirts of Karabulak, a town in Ingushetia. The camp – more than 3,000 refugees squeezed into 98 army tents – is in a shallow gully beside the River Sunzha. Most people are now gathered in the centre of the camp. Behind the hills to the right stands the town of Mozdok. To the left are more hills, and beyond them the capital of Ossetia, Vladikavkaz.

At last it's midday. We feel a shock wave of uncertain origin pass through our bodies, and pick up an inner rumbling of the earth through the soles of our feet. A 25-year-old from Grozny with a degree in Russian Language and Literature and the wonderful name of Mir* explains: 'They've just launched a rocket. Now we shall be able to follow its tail. We saw them yesterday as well.'

He's quite right. In a second two white trails stretch across the sky from the direction of Mozdok. At 12.10 there is a repeat performance. Only this time the missile has been fired from near Vladikavkaz and again there are two trails.

Mir Khadjimuratov thinks aloud: 'Doesn't all this remind you of the famous password: "The Spanish sky is cloudless"?† Are they deliberately provoking us? What feelings can you have, other than a desire for revenge, when you sit watching death fly towards your home town?'

Half an hour later it is as if those vile traces of the rockets had never been there. People are no longer laughing, nor are they trembling. Now their eyes are hard and dull, clenched teeth show through their jaws and their hands in their pockets are bunched

---

* It means 'Peace' in Russian.
† The signal for Franco's forces to begin their rebellion in 1936 was broadcast as part of the weather forecast on the radio.

into fists. No one even smokes. The men leave the square with the comment: '27 October, between 12.00 and 12.10 another 100 people died. None of them fighters.'

Mir Khadjimuratov asks: 'Why do they continue firing missiles into Grozny after the tragedy in the Central Market?* Each missile immediately hits a great number of people. That many fighters never gather in a single place, even our children know that. So it's genocide. And those who didn't want to fight are now ready to.'

Vakha Nurmagomedov is 40 years old and comes from Moscow. He had permanent domicile registration in the capital's Mitino district, but police harassment forced him to move. He returned first to his native Urus-Martan in Chechnya and then, with his family, left the republic. Vakha is very keen for his point of view to be heard – not by Putin (that would be a waste of breath, he thinks), but by the millions who today are ready to vote for a continuation of this cruel war in the North Caucasus. 'You don't win people over to your side by firing rockets. Missiles spell the end of a friendly attitude towards Russia, even among those who used to feel that way. You must understand, we can never allow ourselves to forget all this. Otherwise we are not the fathers of our children or the children of our fathers.'

'We could not forget and forgive deportation,'† I constantly hear this refrain from the crowd of refugees. 'We simply had no right to do so. The first Chechen war joined those memories and so will the present war.'

The main focus of their life in Ingushetia in the refugee camps

---

* On the afternoon of 21 October 1999 the Central Market in Grozny was struck by a rocket attack, leaving many dead and wounded. Despite denials it seems clear that this was authorised by the Russian government.

† In February 1944 the Chechens and Ingush, accused of intending to aid the invading German forces, were deported en masse to Kazakhstan. Many died on the journey. The survivors could not return home until 1957. (The Germans captured Mozdok in August 1942, but could never get close enough to take Grozny and Baku, then the Soviet Union's greatest centres of the oil industry.)

is the accumulation of hatred as they daily study the missiles flying overhead and observe the fighting which can easily be followed from here. By heading for Ingushetia in late September and early October the refugees were leaving the war behind them. Now it has caught up with them again, in their temporary refuge.

Children Fated Not to Survive

Above the Sputnik camp, not far from the village of Ordjonikidzevskaya, it is the Grad [Hail] missiles that swagger across the skies.

Here at Sputnik anyone who wants to can easily guess what the military are planning. The camp is roughly seven kilometres from the small town of Sernovodsk in Chechnya. In late September tents were erected here for the convenience of the refugees. Taken in by the Kremlin spokesmen, local officials believed that the 'anti-terrorist operation' would not last long nor affect Ingushetia. It would therefore be easier and quicker, the republic's Ministry for Emergency Situations decided, for the refugees to return home from here.

These good intentions have backfired on everyone. Today the tents sit directly in the zone of bombardment. If the officer aiming the weapon has had a little too much to drink (and the military do take to drink here – it's also bad for *them* to go on fighting this long) then a tragedy is inevitable. The refugees are in a shallow gully between mountains. On one hillside are the Russian forces, on the other, the town of Sernovodsk. From one hilltop they are firing at Sernovodsk and a stream of murderous metal flies over the heads of almost 5,000 people living in the camp, half of them children. The volleys produce an unpleasant hissing sound, like snakes, and they make the already hard life of the refugees unbearable.

Take, for instance, one half-hour around midday on 28 October: 12.45, volley; 12.47, another; 12.51 yet another . . . Then, there is a brief respite until 13.11, when the firing again resumes every two minutes.

'They're trying to catch Basayev,' decide the women in the weeping, worn-out crowd. 'Those officers up on the hill probably don't know that Grad missiles can't pinpoint a target, they're a weapon of mass destruction. But we know that all too well.'

Meanwhile some boys between five and seven years old are digging a trench beyond the furthest tents. Gradually they disappear below the ground, and pay no attention to what the adults are saying.

'What are you doing?' I finally ask them.

But the children look at me as though I'm from another planet. They don't speak Russian because they were born after the first war in 1994–6. It is their mother Toita Elimkhanova, from the Pervomayskaya village where 157 of their clan are living, who explains:

'The boys themselves took the decision. No one asked them. They say it's just in case: we left home under a terrible bombardment.'

It's interesting that the children a little older than two or three do not react at all to the Grad missiles. They are a very strange sight. 'Hunger makes them apathetic and lethargic,' says Hasan Tempieva from Gudermes. She is without her husband and has eight children. 'There is starvation here. Bread is handed out free, but there isn't enough for everyone. In my family, for instance, it is three days since any of us ate. We just drink hot water.'

Small children, still entirely dependent on their mothers, react quite differently. Their short lives are threatened by each volley. On the night of 25–26 October, when there was a particularly severe and unrelenting stream of Grad missiles and sparks from the sky burned holes in the tents, many refugees lost control of themselves. The screams of women rose over the Sputnik camp and drowned out the howl of the rockets. Seven months pregnant, Malizha Derbieva from the Ishchorskaya village in Naurskaya district (now she is in Tent 8, Block 6) was so frightened that by morning she gave birth prematurely. Her little baby girl died immediately. Malizha is still being treated in the Sunzhensk district hospital. The doctors cannot guarantee she will ever have children now, the shock was too great.

Aina Terekmurzayeva, from the small village of Betimokhk in the Nozhai-Yurt district, is 17 years old. Only a short while ago she married someone from Gudermes where she herself was born. When Aina arrived at the camp she already had Ibrahim her newborn son with her. He's now four months old. The skin on his face is transparent and his bluish but still smiling lips try to find something to eat. Aina herself has wasted away and is barely alive.

Aina's milk failed as soon as the Grad missile volleys began. A four-month-old cannot eat bread, so for a week now they have been giving him nothing but weak tea. If you've ever had children then you'll know that an infant cannot survive long like that. Aina went to the camp administration and asked if they could get hold of some baby food. So far they have found nothing. The warehouses of the republic's Ministry for Emergency Situations are empty.

You probably think I'm writing all this to stir your pity. My fellow citizens have indeed proved a hard-hearted lot. You sit enjoying your breakfast, listening to stirring reports about the war in the North Caucasus, in which the most terrible and disturbing facts are sanitised so that the voters don't choke on their food.

But my notes have a quite different purpose, they are written for the future. They are the testimony of the innocent victims of the new Chechen war, which is why I record all the detail I can.

The Warehouse

The measure of our present kindness is the warehouse for humanitarian aid on the outskirts of Ordjonikidzevskaya village. Officially it's a local depot of the reserve supplies of the Ministry for Emergency Situations. We arrive unexpectedly and accompanied by Major Tugan Chapanov. He heads one of the Ministry's departments, and on 23 October a decree issued by President Aushev made him commandant of the Sputnik camp (replacing the refugee leaders who had held the post).

Being a refugee is demeaning, not only because you are without a home and of no concern to anyone else. But for days on end there is nothing to do in the camps, apart from go out in the morning to collect sticks and twigs for the fire and chat with your fellows in misfortune. In these endless conversations a great many myths are born. For example, people said that the relatives of Shamil Basayev and Alla Dudayev* are living peacefully in the Ingush capital Nazran. The government pays all of their bills, no one is in pursuit of them and they have the best cottages the rich could buy. The conclusion? The war is not against the 'bandits', but against 'us' and they aim to exterminate 'us' completely.

Another persistent myth concerns the aid warehouse. The refugees are certain that it is overflowing with supplies and that those distributing the aid are to blame when it does not reach the right people. They are selling most of it at the market, goes the myth, and pocketing the money.

Alas, on inspection the 'supply depot' is almost empty. The local deputy director, Hasan Bogatyrev, shows us several metal beds that could not be issued because there were no mattresses, let alone pillows and sheets (they're waiting for a delivery). There were also some black olives that were well past their sell-by date, so they did not risk sending them to the camps. (They would certainly be eaten there, no one has any doubt about that, but who can tell with what consequences?)

Also standing idle in the warehouse were the military kitchens and mobile bath units. People are starving in the camps and they

---

* The Russian widow of Chechnya's first president, Dzhokhar Dudayev (see Biographies).

are lousy because they cannot wash. Why then are such valuable items left here? The answer is very simple. Ingushetia already has serious problems with its water supply and now is quite incapable of providing for the refugee camps as well. The camp commandants are afraid to take the bath units since they have no fuel to run them and their many urgent requests to the Moscow authorities to increase the water allowance in the republic's supply network have gone unanswered.

'But what about the kitchen?' demands Major Chapanov.

'What will they cook?' His question is met with a question. 'And who will take responsibility?' continues Bogatyrev. 'To begin with the federal Ministry of Labour was, apparently, ready to pay the services of cooks from among the refugee women as persons engaged in socially useful work. Now they're keeping quiet. It has all remained at the level of good intentions and the Ministry officials, after tossing out these promises, have gone back to Moscow. We have to sort things out for them.'

This is the honest truth. The refugees are extremely bitter. It must be said that they do not accept everything that happens with calm and understanding. There are constant quarrels and fights. Harsh measures are directed against every 'newcomer' to the camp. The Chechens are now almost certain that their brother Ingush* are brazenly cheating them. A dangerous feud between the two nations threatens, though when the refugee exodus began nothing of the kind was in the air. It must also be admitted that we came across people in the camps who were stirring up anti-Ingush feelings.

What will be the outcome? Only one conclusion is possible, that some dishonourable person of dubious sanity passionately desires to extend the war to Ingushetia.

---

* Until 1991 the ethnically close Chechens and Ingush were united in the autonomous republic of Checheno-Ingushetia. When Chechnya declared independence, the less numerous Ingush (135,000 in 1989) decided to remain within the Russian Federation.

What Can We Do?

All these passions will abate to reasonable levels if the refugees are clothed and fed. Warm clothes are urgently and desperately needed, for children and adults. The majority of women are still wearing only socks and need warm tights. Medicine is also in urgent demand. So are shoes, toothbrushes and toothpaste (families of ten or twelve members have been issued with two or three brushes). Most urgent of all is the need for baby food and milk.

The best thing would be not only to collect the abovementioned items, but also to hire and equip a convoy of trucks to drive to Ingushetia and hand out these goods ourselves. Where is our fellow feeling? If you want to know what is needed today in which camp, and its exact location, ring the author on her pager (232-0000, #49883). We must get the better of this appalling misfortune. And we must do so together. The last consideration is the most important of all, because we will only remain united in future if we act together now. Otherwise we shall become so many wild and hunted wolves each retreating to hide in its lair.

The refugees in Ingushetia are suffering inhuman deprivation. Despite everything, though, they dream of remaining human beings. They need not only our practical help but also our moral support. Where are all the actors of our great country? Where are its singers, musicians, performers and satirists? Don't tell me they're all too busy with the Ukrainian elections. Where are our own de Niros (remember how he flew to the refugees in the Balkans?) who are trying to reach out to these unfortunate people?

No one is visiting the camps in Ingushetia today, apart from the republic's equally exhausted officials from the Ministry for Emergency Situations who are responsible for their administration. No one is talking to the people or explaining what's going on. The information war has been won, but for the time being the battle for human souls has been completely lost.

INGUSHETIA

Bomb, Don't Save
The Old People's Home in Grozny

15 November 1999

The refugees in the camps in Ingushetia fall into one of two groups. Some hate the Russians and anyone from Moscow. Others cannot and don't want to imagine a future outside Russia. However, when they begin to describe the pitiful state of those left at the old people's home in Grozny they are all in full agreement. Almost 100 old men and women, 30 of them bedridden, remain in the Chechen capital with bombs falling indiscriminately all around. 'What can you [i.e. Russians, AP] do right, if you can't even save your own old folk from being bombed?'

It was painful and shaming to hear. Left without relatives, these elderly men and women were reduced to desperate begging, wandering the city in search of food. Those still able to walk brought food for the bedridden. The staff had abandoned them. There was no water, electricity or gas. And behind all these tales, alas, lies the issue of nationality: for the most part those spending their last years at the home are Russians and other Russian speakers,* 'your people'. Chechens do not usually send their old people to such homes.

And that was how the idea first arose. We had to get these unfortunate old men and women out of Grozny at any cost and find them somewhere decent to live. But how?

---

* Those assimilated to the dominant Russophone culture but not themselves ethnically Russian. The last Soviet population census in 1989 found 15 million people across the USSR who defined themselves as such 'Russian speakers'.

'What Can You Do Right?'

We made a start. All of Moscow officialdom, probably, received the same question. Who should help the Grozny old people's home? Whose responsibility is it? Tell us his name, patronymic and surname.

The answer, it turned out, was no one. During both wars, it is true, representatives of the Russian Ministry of Labour and Social Development came to inspect the home, supposedly to provide aid. But now? When bombs were falling? Political considerations and the 'struggle against terrorism' had made them forget all about their charges. Then the military added their contribution: all who had remained in Grozny, they declared, were accomplices of the bandits. That was an end of it. There was now no way of calling the Ministry of Labour to account: it was easier to bomb them than save them.

We could only conclude that the way our State is run today there is not one official who accepts responsibility for the fate of 100 old and lonely people, stranded on the front line of the great military and political venture in the North Caucasus.

At this point emotion took over. At first sight the rescue of these helpless old men and women was an almost impossible task. It only began to appear a reality once we started appealing directly to people's emotions. The first to take our idea to heart and bring his considerable personal connections into play was Yevgeny Gontmakher, who heads the Department for Social Development on the government staff. He did everything he could, acting as an individual, to ensure that the Minister of Labour and Social Development, Sergey Kalashnikov – who until then refused even to talk about the Grozny home (while fully aware of its terrible plight) – received the necessary order from Valentina Matvienko, the Deputy Prime Minister. Very soon Kalashnikov's deputy, Sergey Kiselyov, had found places for the old people in homes located in nine other regions of the country.

Here we committed a fundamental and fateful error. In order

not to dampen their stirring enthusiasm we ignored too much of what these federal bureaucrats were saying. We pretended not to hear, for instance, when those involved in the operation loftily declared that it was 'politically unwise' to evacuate the old people from Grozny. We even agreed to a compromise, promising not to publish a word until the happy end had been reached. When that moment came, we assured them, we would give a lyrical description of all the participants and forget every unpleasant moment there had been.

And there were more than enough of those. Kalashnikov, for instance, demanded our guarantee that there were 'only Russians' in the Grozny old people's home; a little later, when he found out there were 'also Chechens there', he accused us of deceit. We pleaded with certain politicians, battling to enter the new Duma, for money to buy warm clothes for the old people, and to pay for the bus to get them out of Grozny. Those aspiring tribunes of the people also insisted on guarantees: yes, they would do something but only if they were shown on all the main TV channels, greeting the helpless old people from Chechnya. Without a shade of embarrassment, these future parliamentarians mused aloud to themselves: 'Only 100? That's not going to bring in many votes . . .'

Our compromise with this cynical company served no purpose. We kept quiet about the story while the government officials and Duma candidates were just looking for a chance to avoid doing anything. Their main concern was to ensure that no one later learned how indecently they'd behaved.

'Who's She? Matvienko?'

While we continued trying to win over the political elite in Moscow the military completely encircled Chechnya. It was now 100 times more difficult to move the old people's home residents out to the frontier with Ingushetia. For hours I stood at the Caucasus checkpoint. I looked the commandant, Colonel Khrulyov, in the eye and I begged, pleaded and explained to him that the Deputy Prime Minister, Valentina Matvienko, had already issued the relevant order. His answer was simple: 'Who's she? Matvienko?' Or: 'What are they to you, these old people?' He hinted persistently that the enemy was vigilant and that 'terrorists could enter Russian territory' disguised as busloads of pensioners.

I asked colleagues who were working nearby, some of them very well-known TV journalists, to help. They listened attentively, but did not show the slightest inclination to get involved.

According to Sergey Kalashnikov's instructions Ruslan Tsetsoyev, the Minister of Labour for Ingushetia, was to help in transporting the elderly. However, Tsetsoyev was so engrossed in the preparations for his own birthday party that he shamelessly pushed me out of his office when I began speaking about the old people's home. Most important of all, he let us down whenever we needed his help. If we reached agreement that a bus should be at the checkpoint by 9 a.m. then it was not there at 9, or 10, or 11 . . . It took a while before we understood: he had been told by Moscow to do nothing.

We got in touch with the Chechen side. Perhaps the people struggling to hold on to power in Grozny would like to demonstrate their own magnanimity and themselves deliver the old people to the frontier with Ingushetia?

Alas, the Chechen reaction was indistinguishable from that of the federal authorities. There were a great many promises.

First from the lips of Mate Tsikhesashvili, Aslan Maskhadov's personal representative, who heads the department for intergovernmental relations of the Chechnya cabinet of ministers.

Second from Vakha Dudayev, a deputy of the existing parliament of Chechnya. He was especially insistent that his was the only legitimate representative assembly in the republic and so it was a matter of honour for the deputies to see that the old people were evacuated.

Third from the Red Cross representative in Grozny and from

dozens of private individuals. They swore oaths and gave us heartfelt looks.

These words all proved so much hot air. Gradually it became clear that those in charge of Chechnya today, or their close allies, wanted exactly the same as their opposite numbers on the federal side: as much blood and horror, as many deaths and bombs, as possible. The two were in direct and uncompromising confrontation and knew that neither could back down. We were repeatedly told by the Chechen side that the old people's home had been bombed out of existence and its inhabitants were now all dead. Not once did they offer the slightest proof. The federal side played the same game, assuring us that Chechen fighters had destroyed the home. And not once did they offer us a shred of evidence.

The well-informed in Nazran told us there was only one remaining chance: we should throw ourselves on the mercy of Valery Kuksa, who was Ingushetia's Minister for Emergency Situations, the all-powerful local equivalent of Sergey Shoigu. He was the only one who could help. Kuksa was closely linked to the generals leading the combined forces group and he had connections with the equivalent ministry in Chechnya. He had fought alongside Ruslan Aushev, President of Ingushetia, during the Afghan war – and he was not just a friend, but had been Aushev's commander. Kuksa would find out if the old people were still alive, he would get them out.

So we appealed to him. And Kuksa promised. He was surprised, though, at my persistence. I appealed to him a second time. Kuksa again gave his word. But asked me not to pressure him too much. I appealed to him a third time, and Kuksa promised yet again.

And that's as far as we have got.

Strong, brave, active and ambitious individuals have now gone into hiding to avoid facing the plight of the weakest, loneliest and most abandoned people. It does indeed disgrace the nation.

What now? They say you should live quietly and not go poking your nose into other people's business. They say that Putin's rating is growing because he has shown how tough he is. They say that Valentina Matvienko is his right hand and can do anything she wants.

Let me tell you, it's all lies. These heartless tough hands are signing death sentences.

INGUSHETIA—MOSCOW

Kalashnikov and the Old People's Home

29 November 1999

This should have been a profoundly optimistic report describing the successful evacuation, under bombardment, of the inhabitants of the old people's home in Grozny. For the last month and a half, our newspaper has spent every day preparing this complex operation. A permanent team was formed and it worked to gain the goodwill and assurances of the General Staff and the Ministry of Defence. Meanwhile readers helped us to collect enough money for guides and coaches. (No one would do a thing without payment – it proved quite unrealistic to expect that – and we discovered that government departments had no funds to spend on such activities.)

At long last, a date and time were agreed.

What then happened was shameful, and we can offer readers no words of consolation. The fighters defending the Chechen capital suddenly realised that the federal authorities placed a certain value on these old people. So they simply turned them into hostages. How and why will become clear from what follows.

Here and Now

The last week we had been full of hope. Leaving home and family, all our energy and determination went on ensuring that no later than 10 a.m. on 25 November, our long-awaited red Icarus coach would return from Grozny to the Chechen–Ingush border. There, at the 'Caucasus' checkpoint on the Rostov–Baku Highway, we would meet 'our old people'. Then we would escort these sick and lonely old men and women, whose lives began with a war and were closing with two more, back to a peaceful and quiet existence.

25 November arrived. At 10 a.m. so did our Icarus. But instead of the old people, the guides brought us a written note. It said, in effect, that the local authorities had forbidden the evacuation. The Chechen guides, who only a few days before had been so courageous and admirable, sat uneasily before us. They fidgeted. They gave muddled explanations about the people who had been there to meet them when they reached the old people's home. Finally they passed on the following verbal message: the journalists were expected at the home tomorrow morning and then, perhaps, they might let the elderly go.

'Who's expecting us there?'

'The people who didn't let the old ones leave today.'

Ruslan Koloyev's drawn face darkened. He had welcomed, and then nursed through, the entire operation, and in its final stages, as Ingushetia's Deputy Minister for Emergency Situations, he had shouldered the main burden. Powerless, he stood and silently left us. He was gone for a long time, at least half an hour. We were stunned. As we waited, our guides told us more of the fantastic tales they had been spun by those thugs. Finally Ruslan's absence became a reproach. I went to find him.

'Where's Ruslan?'

'He's praying,' his colleagues quietly replied.

Ruslan is a devout Muslim. But you'd never know it. Not a single word, look or movement betrays his inner faith, let alone demonstrative green bandannas or cries of 'Allahu Akbar!' Ruslan returned from his prayers to our room, sent out the talkative guides and said: 'Last night I already knew this was going to happen. Only a miracle could have changed things.'

And this, day by day, is how it came about.

On 23 November, following a carefully agreed route, the Icarus coach left for Grozny. It was to go to 194 Borodin Street in the city's Staropromyslovsky district, where the old people's home was located. We had already sent volunteers there several times before to investigate and test the ground. Each time the story was the same. The old people were exhausted and starving, all the staff had long ago run away, no one had any money and those who could still move went out in the streets begging. We must hurry. Since the end of September, while the Moscow bureaucrats idled their time away, twelve of the old people had died. There were now only 85 left.

Finally the evening of 24 November arrived. Anticipating a happy end, I could hardly wait. Then, like a bucket of cold water, at 9.30 p.m., following the main evening news, came the Channel One TV programme *Here and Now*. The presenter, Alexander Lyubimov, was talking to Sergey Kalashnikov, the Minister of Labour and Social Development.* Kalashnikov is in charge of homes for the elderly throughout Russia, and whenever we needed his support he had unfailingly obstructed us, doing everything to ensure that the old people in Grozny never crossed the border into Ingushetia. His greatest concern was about the issue's 'political aspects' and he was determined to ensure that no solitary *Chechen* pensioners would somehow be included in the mission.

The interview went roughly as follows (I'm reporting not the exact words, but the fatal message they sent). One, the elderly had been evacuated from Grozny. Two, the Ministry of Labour had been working long and stubbornly to achieve this goal. Three, the successful outcome was the result of an undercover operation by the Russian government on the territory of the Chechen Republic.

More of a public slap in the face for our operation would be hard to imagine. You already know the rest. The guides then came back and told us they had been forbidden to evacuate the elderly from Chechnya.

---

* Kalashnikov is a leading member of Zhirinovsky's nationalistic Liberal Democrat Party.

★

26 November. From early morning the following day, as informed army officers had repeatedly warned us, Grozny was subjected to the most powerful artillery and aerial bombardment of the present war. Moreover, the shells were falling precisely on the Staropromyslovsky district where the old people's home was. We had been in such a hurry because the military had told us: 'After the 26th it will be too complicated. Get a move on.'

But surely, you are saying to yourself, a government minister like Kalashnikov must have known as much as journalists and senior officers? Of course, he knew. That's exactly why, perhaps, he took the risk and, from midday on 25 November, began to issue quite false claims over the wires of the Itar-TASS news agency that the elderly had been successfully evacuated. As he knew only too well, it would be very dangerous to go and check whether these announcements were true or not. Later that day he repeated his cheap lies live on Channel One TV. Guided by the overriding principle that 'War justifies everything', Kalashnikov was evidently quite happy to abandon the old people's home to bombardment from the ground and skies. He also had reasons of his own.

The minister was covering his tracks using every means at his disposal. And, considering his status within the government, he had access to some significant means. Throughout 1997 and 1998 Kalashnikov's ministry had poured money from the federal budget into that same old people's home. Funds were transferred from Moscow, and no account of their expenditure was demanded. At the ministry they were well aware that not a rouble was being spent for the purpose intended. The money went on presents – not to the elderly, but to members of Maskhadov's government. As a result, the home was ruined and abandoned by its staff, with no one left to feed the elderly or give them essential medicine.

The money was siphoned off and Labour Ministry officials knew exactly where it was going, because they had punctiliously ensured it reached its destination. If the elderly left Chechnya, however, there would now be living testimony of this embezzlement of state funds. For Kalashnikov and those who actually made the transfers this spelled ruin. That's why he took the risk.

The following scenario is, in my view, highly probable. On the day the guides and our coach appeared in Grozny, Kalashnikov was alerted from Chechnya (despite all that people say, lines of communication remain open). He was warned that the evacuation was about to begin and was asked to take measures. And he acted. On the very evening the guides were in Grozny this fact was publicly announced on television. It was the equivalent of saying: 'At this very moment American intelligence agents have entered the Kremlin and are trying to steal top secret documents . . .'

The lives of these lonely and helpless old people finally lost any value of their own. They had become no more than a means to an end.

A Powerless State

The moral of this story is that the State does not exist in Russia. We have been hearing a great deal of talk from Prime Minister Putin, in the run-up to the forthcoming Duma elections. They are building a powerful State, he tells us, to take the place of the once great superpower. But the State led by this premier does not exist. The Russian Federation is a case-study in total and irreversible impotence.

That vacated arena is now filled with the ambitions of some, and the laziness and indifference of others; some publicise their ludicrous stupidity, others tell barefaced lies, while idiocy is raised to the level of government policy, and all are guilty of a slovenly inefficiency.

The evidence is here, before your eyes. This was a tiny and quite specific case that demanded specific and exclusively humanitarian action – it did not require the authorities to mobilise the army and send in tanks and armoured personnel carriers. But the State sets no value on such people. The situation has become quite intolerable. What earthly use to me is the Putin we see, prancing about on TV and telling us that he's going to 'wipe out' the bandits after they're cornered 'in the shithouse'?

I want a Putin who will defend the weak – according to the Constitution our State exists, first and foremost, for the good of the people. Give me a Putin who at least can control his ministries. Let's have a Putin who does not kow-tow to the army, police and security service, but instead appeals to ordinary citizens: to the people who are suffering and dying under bombardment, as though they are at the mercy of blood-crazed terrorists! I want a different Putin. Not the man who, in front of the TV cameras, climbed into the cockpit of a bomber wearing a pilot's helmet that was evidently the wrong size, but someone who will go to the Staropromyslovsky district and visit the Grozny old people's home.

Isn't it strange, though, that a newspaper whose job it is to provide information should so persistently shoulder the functions of the government? Why should journalists do the job we pay ministers to do? Obviously because the authorities with the same stubborn persistence refuse to carry out their duties. As soon as ministers are appointed they are cosseted and protected from popular pressure. Their power and privilege is all that interests them.

The only reason we started this operation was because not one official could be found in the entire State who would do the job for us or without our help. We acted because there was no alternative and because the State was immobile and indifferent. And, at the same time, we were perfectly aware that we could not take the place of those authorities and that this situation was public proof of the State's absence.

The end result was that, while we were doing Kalashnikov's job, he started doing ours. He suddenly became hyperactive and began posing as a journalist. He was convinced that anyone could do the job. He was mistaken. A journalist is above all someone who does not lie and will check facts many times before risking an error.

Our Colleagues

I also observed the behaviour of our colleagues in the media during this crisis. Their only interest in our operation was to capture some dramatic events. 'You create some news for us, and then we'll react,' was their principle. From morning onwards they came up to us in Nazran and asked: 'Are the buses going to come? You couldn't be more precise about the time so that we can be sure to broadcast live?' Not once did we hear an offer of help. The only news team that became truly involved and lived through the entire tragedy of the last few days with us as if it concerned them personally were the camera crew from Channel One TV, led by correspondent Olga Mezhennaya.

All attempts to interest Western (or our own) human rights organisations in the fate of these helpless old people from Grozny were also futile. Today such organisations are based in Ingushetia and mainly engaged in the theoretical defence of human rights. The practical side of things does not greatly worry them. The majority are enthusiastically collecting information about mass infringements of Chechen human rights. They can be seen every day in contact almost exclusively with representatives of the Chechen parliament and other similar organisations.

When it became clear that the elderly were being held in Grozny by Chechen fighters, people representing a powerful and influential organisation such as Human Rights Watch did not show the faintest desire to help. Every day they issued press releases about the Russian army's acts of genocide (also undeniable) against the Chechen people. There is a thorough filtering of information to serve a single point of view. If it's a question of a press release, based on Chechen accounts, about the shelling of the Samashki psychiatric hospital, then they are only too happy to oblige and very quick about it. They have no intention, though, of writing and despatching to New York a press release about the inhuman ban on the evacuation of elderly people from Grozny, a ban imposed by Maskhadov's followers who have long since sent their own families to Ingushetia. Sad as it is, that is the fact of the matter.

What Next?

Clever people, including some in the government, have told us that following Kalashnikov's public statements there is now almost no chance of evacuating the elderly from Grozny. The only hope of saving anyone is to make a personal appeal to Basayev.

And that says it all. Basayev has more influence over the fate of our fellow citizens than Putin. It's a vicious circle. The old people must forgive us, but we cannot bring ourselves to appeal to the Conqueror of Budyonnovsk, a man who held the mothers of the maternity hospital there hostage, and ask him to take pity on these lonely old men and women. In my mind the images of Kalashnikov and Basayev are now totally blurred and confused. (The latter's beard makes no difference.)

You can see where all this is leading. By tolerating such things on our own doorstep and allowing the State's officials to perform these acts of violence against us we shall very soon have our own Pinochet. We shall be so relieved, in fact, when he comes that we'll throw ourselves at his feet, and beg him to save us.

INGUSHETIA

Postscript

The editors would like to thank all who tried to help us perform this mission of conscience and duty. Their names are listed in order of the magnitude of their personal contribution, starting with those who did most: Ruslan Koloyev, Deputy Minister, Ingushetia Ministry for Emergency Situations (MES); Yury Shum, Head of the North Caucasus Regional Centre, Federal MES; Valery

Kuksa, Minister, Ingushetia MES; Tugan Chapanov, Section Head, Ingushetia MES; Marina Kurkieva, Deputy Minister of Labour and Social Development, Ingushetia; Anatoly Khrulyov, CO of the 'Caucasus' checkpoint; Ruslan Aushev, President of Ingushetia; Yevgeny Gontmakher, Department Head for Social Development, Russian government; Valery Vostrotin, Deputy Minister, Federal MES; and Valentina Matvienko, Deputy Prime Minister, Russian government.

Tell Them: This War Is Senseless

6 December 1999

Abandon all logic, ye who travel here. Shake off your Moscow stereotypes and conceptions. Forget all you have been told about this war. Then you will rapidly see that the army you were shown, confident in its sacred purpose and storming one enemy position after another with ease and no tangible losses, does not exist.

Instead you see exhausted men with unbalanced minds. Then there's the cold, the filth, scabies, rotting feet, drunkenness and hashish. And they all desperately want to come through this alive.

Fatal Confrontation with a Cow

'If those ★★★★★ in Moscow are not going to pay me then I'll . . .' – the General yelled with such gusto that the sound echoed around the hills and drowned the howls of the artillery salvos – '. . . go back to Moscow and demand my money! Why come here causing mischief?'

We were standing outside the village of Muzhichi, in the distant foothills of Ingushetia. For no reason whatsoever this army general had just shot dead a skinny, young brown cow that provided the milk for one Ingush family. It's not far from the border with independent Georgia and no distance at all, across the pass, to rebellious Chechnya. So the troops and howitzers have long been billeted in the village and the children sleep badly at night, disturbed by the crash of the artillery.

The cow met its end as follows. She was ambling back from

the pasture through the twilight with the other cattle towards her familiar shed. She could already see the fence, where she enjoyed scratching herself, and her owner, Khadizhat, whose warm hands would gently pull at her stubborn teats each evening. Suddenly the path to her familiar and understandable world was blocked by the General. (We know his first name and surname, but are not publishing them because he has children of his own, and they are not to blame.)

He was young and handsome, a striking figure. A real fighter. Bare-chested, camouflage hat at an angle, he had fury in his eyes and was as full of testosterone as any teenager after three months at the front. Leaving his men behind him he placed his (by local standards) Very Important Person in the middle of the path and faced the herd. The General was obviously selecting a target. Then, he rapidly fired his machine-gun one-handed and from the hip. Khadizhat screamed and the village shuddered. Tomorrow they would be burying someone else they thought.

First the General shot the cow with his own gun. Then he lifted the body onto the armoured vehicle and, to the wails and laments of the cow's owner, ordered his men to drag it back to the field-kitchen.

'You had nothing to eat?' I asked.

'No, I'm not hungry. It's just that those ★★★★★ aren't paying me any money!'

'Who? The Ingush from Muzhichi?'

'No, the Muscovites in Internal Affairs.'

The soldiers listen very attentively to this conversation.

'What's your name?'

'It's a military secret.' The cow-conqueror smelled of stale alcohol. 'We are forbidden to associate with journalists. One more question and I'll arrest you for spying.'

In the given circumstances our General has evidently lost 'the ability to analyse events and understand his own thoughts and actions'. It is that capacity, supposedly, which defines the professional war-worthiness of our senior officers – just as those with warm and gentle hands are chosen to milk the cows. Perhaps, though, you are consoling yourself with the thought that this was a regrettable misunderstanding. It only reflects, you say to yourself, the tolerable percentage of monsters that somehow have found their way into the disciplined ranks of those who defended the Motherland from international terrorism. Before I answer, let me show you the second picture in our North Caucasian military exhibition.

A High the Size of an Ammunition Box

Yura's tongue had obviously got the better of him and Volodya also felt an excessive and strange urge to chatter. It was clear they were both mildly stoned. Their thoughts became confused and tangled, and constantly turned back on their tracks but they each have one endlessly repeated, muddled and obsessive theme. Anyone who has smoked grass can tell what the problem with Yura and Volodya is.

They are both serving with the OMON [riot police], a lieutenant and corporal respectively, and we met them at their post near the Chechen village of Assinovskaya. Both were proudly showing off their new sleeve badges: the OMON are no longer snow leopards or lions they're TEAM SPECIAL (the words are written in English). Our specialist, Lieutenant Yura, could not stop talking about the blood and dismembered flesh of 'persons of Caucasian nationality'* and several times repeated his fantasies of how 'yesterday they slashed a *dukh*† to pieces in the drainage channel, just

---

* A euphemism, widely used by the police and other Russian officials, to legitimate a common racial stereotype applied to anyone from the post-Soviet states of Armenia, Georgia and Azerbaijan or the seven North Caucasian republics within Russia.

† 'Dukh' (lit. 'spirit'), Soviet army slang for their opponents in Afghanistan (1979–89).

over there'. Volodya was just as obsessed with his wages, which were too low in his view.

Volodya felt deeply offended; Yura saw himself as a hero in some American action film. He described more revolting scenes, watching to see how his listeners reacted. The FSB distributed videos among the soldiers in the North Caucasus, he said, and they watched them every evening to 'get in the mood'.

'What do they show?'

'How they kill and rape. Don't you know how they raped Shamil Basayev's brother, Shirvani, in Nazran? A whole gang of them. Well, I saw it.' Yura is very pleased with the nauseating effect this has.

'Did you enjoy that?'

'Not bad.' Yura is satisfied. It doesn't take long to realise he is mentally unbalanced. All that's lacking is a formal confirmation.

People are now so used to seeing mentally ill men clutching Kalashnikovs at the front line in the North Caucasus that they might not notice it any more. It would be foolhardy of them, however, to ignore it. One curious detail. Standing next to Yura is his unit's staff psychologist. He's also a little strange, if only because Yura's behaviour seems to have no effect on him.

By December these men are worn out by the war. Around Yura and Volodya we see the faces of their fellow-OMON men tormented by gunfire in the night. Further off are the army soldiers who are hungry and dirty, and all with athlete's foot because they never take off their rubber boots, even at night. Before their eyes flows a constant stream of misery and grief, as the refugees shuffle across Assinovskaya through all the shortening hours of daylight: weeping women and children, scowling old men. The wounded fighters are carried through from Chechnya, men with amputated limbs and oozing wounds.

'I wouldn't wound them,' comments Yura. 'I'd just finish them off.' Think for a moment, and you're likely to go mad at the thought: they are taking men for treatment in Russian hospitals who were crippled by Russia's own soldiers, and the same budget is today financing the murderous bombing attacks and the treatment of their victims.

The landscape before the man with a gun is too doleful for him not to brighten it up somehow. By the end of the autumn, thoroughly commercial relations had been established on the border between Chechnya and Ingushetia, not far from the 'Caucasus' checkpoint. The soldiers drive up in armoured vehicles from the nearby 'liberated' villages. They are met by the black marketeers from the Ingush side.

Policemen from the Ingush OMON man the first post on the road to the 'Caucasus' checkpoint. They tell us the going rate for 'intensive care'. For two zinc cases (i.e. boxes of ammunition) you get either 20 bottles of locally produced vodka (at 10 roubles each) or one glassful of hashish. Usually the deal works as follows. The soldiers bring the cases in the evening or at night, whenever it's dark (and always accompanied by an officer), and by that time their partners with the vodka or hashish are already waiting at the Ingush post. The police are convinced that all the participants in these exchanges have earlier reached agreement on the time and place and that the whole system runs very smoothly.

Why then do these well-informed Ingush policemen simply sit and watch? Where are the seizures of contraband, the arrests and widely publicised investigations into these cases of corruption?

'We've received no order to act,' say the valiant OMON, averting their gaze.

If you believe them, I don't. But it's impossible not to think about the other side of this coin. The military have become so mercantile that they are selling the very bullets that, sometime later, will almost certainly fly in their direction.

100-Rouble Gateway

Picture No. 3 from our exhibition. There is one more very curious checkpoint in this war. The 'October' checkpoint allows you to travel from Chechnya to Mozdok (where the headquarters of the combined forces in the North Caucasus are to be found). Refugees at the Sputnik camp near the Ingush village of Sleptsovskaya (Ordjonikidzevskaya) have extraordinary tales to tell. The soldiers at the checkpoint supposedly tell women from north Chechen villages who are taking food to sell at the market in Mozdok: 'You're not allowed there! Mozdok is a prohibited city for you.'

But as with all else in Russia, never be in a hurry to go away. After a little while the town becomes quite open and the soldiers tell the most persistent women how much they must pay. One person on foot must pay 100 roubles; a light vehicle costs about 500–600 roubles, depending on the mood of the bribe-taker. To cross with a body (forgive this cynicism!) costs 1,000 roubles. 'If you pay the soldiers they don't even look at your passport,' the refugees assure me.

Can you believe such assurances? Of course not. Or not until you've tried it yourself. I travelled there, driving about two hours by car from the Sputnik camp. The refugee women were quite right. I paid 100 roubles and got past without showing my passport, with its 'permanent resident' stamp from the Moscow authorities, or any other details of my life and work.

At which point a treacherous suspicion entered my head. What if you offer them 200, 300 or 500 roubles? Could you then carry back arms and ammunition into Chechnya without any hindrance? And then leave the republic again without showing up on their computer? All this talk as though it is the frontier with Georgia that matters!

Cleaning Up

And what are we to make of the military trucks that drive back and forth across Ingushetia? Suddenly their interiors are hung with carpets to make them warmer. It's unheard of. I hope no one imagines that our generals, like modern-day Suvorovs,* have indeed taken the comfort of their men so much to heart that they added carpets to warm the interiors of the trucks.

There is as much plundering in this war as there was last time. Stories about 'cleansing of property', at the same time as 'liberated population centres' are 'cleansed' of real and suspected fighters, are some of the commonest tales among the refugees in the tent camps. Of all that I have heard I have chosen the monologue of Yazirat Dovletmurzayeva, an 85-year-old grandmother from the village of Samashki. Today she lives in Tent 3, Block 13 of the Sputnik camp. She is illiterate, and all her life she has worked on the land, tending her cows, never getting involved in any political events. She finds it hard to understand the motives behind the wars that have raged around her for the last five years. She's quite clear about one thing, though. She has never acquired any wealth during her life and has no possessions in her home.

'Yesterday [21 November, AP] I walked over to Samashki to see if I could return home at last. I want to go back very much. When I got there some soldiers were climbing out of the windows. The house had been plundered. They had taken away everything they could find, all my pickles and conserves. They took the cow. They even took the door. I'll never save enough to buy a mattress as good as the one I had.'

If the military can listen calmly to this tale, then I think they'll agree with me: when such things happen the war could go on for ever and each new trainload of troops for Chechnya will be very happy to be transferred to the North Caucasus.

And how can we leave out the vile story about the Interior Ministry soldiers in Sernovodsk? Berlant Magomedova describes what she saw:

'The soldiers walk around the market demanding vodka.

---

* Russian Generalissimo Alexander Suvorov (1729–1800) insisted that his soldiers have cool heads and warm feet.

Sometimes they bring sacks full of tinned meat and exchange it for vodka. Once they're drunk they begin shooting. On 15 November they shot our neighbour Mohammed Esnukayev. He was a very good man, an orphan who had been looked after and brought up by the entire street, but when he told the soldiers "I don't have any vodka" they shot him dead.'

It was from Sernovodsk, remember, that a platoon of soldiers came in their armoured vehicle to the village of Sleptsovskaya (Ordjonikidzevskaya) on 25 November. Led by their commander, they demanded that same accursed vodka and, in similar circumstances, shot dead a young female shop assistant. All Ingushetia was stunned by this event. But it is a natural consequence of everything that has happened to the army in the North Caucasus. Something of this kind was bound to happen sooner or later.

The Costs of War

Inevitably someone will say: 'That is the cost of war. It always carries with it a certain element of evil and unpredictability.' And he or she will take comfort in the thought. Those who have actually been there know that things are much worse than anyone could imagine.

As winter progresses the mood in the army is changing rapidly. Too many feel themselves caught in a dead end. They're confused and uncertain. After the soldiers have sat for weeks in a dugout that is more like a swamp, wearing rubber boots day in, day out, and their commanding officer is forced to wander around collecting enough money to go to the baths in the next village, then the war ceases to appear a sacred feat of liberation – even supposing they arrived in the Caucasus with such feelings.

The men in uniform are today physically exhausted and psychologically worn out. They can no longer tolerate these inhuman conditions and begin, as a consequence, to behave inhumanly themselves. They're not supermen, but ordinary people like you and me. So we must stop lying to ourselves: what is going on in Chechnya is not at all what many in Moscow dreamt of!

I'm not reporting these particular offences to encourage the staff officers in Moscow and Mozdok to immediately track down those who committed them. That would be stupid and inefficient. They must act quite differently, either focusing the war within clear limits or a local arena, or else halting it altogether. The present 'struggle with the terrorists' is spreading across the entire country and is becoming a deadly danger to many who have not the slightest connection with the terrorists.

Dusk began to fall rapidly at the checkpoint near the Chechen village of Assinovskaya. We could stay no longer. Night-time was when the trade in bullets and vodka began. Lieutenant-Colonel Gubich, head of the Kursk OMON stationed here, despairingly drove away all non-military personnel, in accordance with his orders. As we were leaving, however, he told us: 'Pass this message on to Moscow: "This war is quite senseless." And that,' he added, 'is the most important truth of all.'

INGUSHETIA

The Chechnya Reservation

27 December 1999

Tragic news has reached Moscow. Refugees living in railway carriages have been attached to a locomotive and shunted, against their will, six kilometres into Chechnya. At first sight, this is nothing special. We might be inclined to agree with Vladimir Kalamanov, head of the Federal Migration Service: 'What's the fuss? It's only six kilometres. And nearer home.'

However, half of those in the carriages grabbed their children and belongings and leaped out as they moved off. They preferred to become illegal residents in Ingushetia, although that republic is gradually ceasing to be a welcoming host. Those living in the tent camps who do not want to go back are deprived of their daily ration on orders of the commandant: they no longer get their half-loaf of bread and plate of hot soup.

A notice hung up in Aki-Yurt village in the Malgobek district of Ingushetia reads as follows:

ALL REFUGEES FROM THE CHECHEN REPUBLIC IN AKI-YURT! WE INFORM ALL REFUGEES FROM THESE DISTRICTS IN CHECHNYA: NADTERECHNAYA, SHOLKOVSKAYA, NAURSKAYA, ACHKHOI-MARTAN AND THE TOWN OF SERNOVODSK, THAT THEY ARE TO RETURN TO POPULATION CENTRES IN THOSE AREAS. IN ACCORDANCE WITH THE DECISION OF THE MINISTRY FOR EMERGENCY SITUATIONS AND FEDERAL MIGRATION SERVICE OF THE REPUBLIC OF INGUSHETIA THEY WILL NOT HENCEFORTH BE GIVEN HUMANITARIAN AID.

THE ADMINISTRATION

Why are refugees being shunted from one place to another like so much unclaimed luggage? Why so little respect for people's feelings and desires? We are continuing to create a nation of outcasts who lack all civil rights. Is it deliberate? I'm afraid so.

Why They Don't Want to Go

The refugees don't want to go home because they know very well what awaits them. 'We shall go back only after the troops have completely left,' says Kulady Aidayev, a 53-year-old from Grozny. He used to live at 2 Tovarny Street and run the depot for the Chechen Bus Company, but now he lives in a tent at the Bart camp near Karabulak.

Kulady is adamant and his words are supported by all around him. He found himself at the camp in early November when his 25-year-old son Adam was killed during one of the bombing raids. The body was so disfigured that they could not find the head, and buried him without it. The father says he cannot look at the soldiers strolling around Grozny. The others are all in agreement with him. The majority have similar distressing experiences to recount concerning their relatives and friends.

'But what if they send you back to Chechnya by force?'

'Force will get them nowhere,' comes the immediate and uncompromising reply, fast as a sniper's bullet. The speaker is Adlan Tepsayev from Grozny.

Obstacle No. 1: none of them wish to live next to the soldiers on principle. Indeed, it would be better if the majority of men here do not come across any of the federal forces: they must avenge the dead members of their family or be shamed as men without honour.

Looters

Abdurashid Aduyev is *yut-da* of the Chechen town of Assinovskaya, 45 kilometres each way from Nazran and Grozny, and 12 kilometres from the 'Caucasus' checkpoint. *Yut-da* means *father of the village*. On such people depends the decision whether fighters are allowed into the village or not, which young men go away to fight and which stay at home. I should remind readers that federal forces entered Assinovskaya at the very beginning of the 'antiterrorist operation' and met almost no resistance. *Yut-da* Abdurashid is an old man, a pensioner, who has lived most of his life under the Soviet regime and carries his title with pride. He did not flee the town, and he did not want to go to Ingushetia or any other Chechen village. He had nothing to fear, this old man decided. However, in the first days of December he was to experience for himself all the 'pleasures' of sharing the town with the soldiers.

One evening five hefty and already drunk men in masks burst into his house on Zelyonaya Street. They were contract soldiers with the Interior Ministry, whose job it is to maintain law and order in the town. They beat up the *yut-da*, then locked him in his cellar for more than two hours. What were these degenerates after? First they demanded all the gold ornaments in the house. Then they wanted $1,500! They beat up Abdurashid because he would not meet their demands immediately.

Two hours later the conquering heroes relented: 'Get the gold and collect the money from the neighbours, you're elder of this town, aren't you? We'll be back tomorrow. If you don't have it ready we shall send you to the filtration camp as a supporter of the fighters!' That morning the insulted and demeaned *yut-da* went to the military administration of the town and lodged a complaint, detailing all that had happened. It had only a limited effect. No military prosecutors appeared to pursue such criminal activities and no security men were there to protect him, but, nevertheless, the bandits in uniform did not return that evening to rob him. They didn't even shoot him down in the street, as his neighbours had predicted.

Unrestrained and open plundering is one of the main features of life in Chechen villages 'after liberation'. The most frightening figure in this war remains the contract soldier hired by the Interior Ministry: a law unto himself, he is desperately feared not only by the refugees and the 'liberated' Chechens, but even by soldiers serving with units of the Ministry of Defence. If the soldiers and the contract men are assigned to man the same post, the army digs itself trenches at a reasonable distance from the 'police' and unless there is fighting keeps well away from them. The contract men beat up the conscript soldiers, humiliate them, take their food and personal belongings, and send them into the village for vodka, which is strictly forbidden under present circumstances.

To the north of Assinovskaya is Sernovodsk, the very place where the 36 carriages full of refugees ended up. It is indeed not far from Ingushetia, but the two might be on different planets. Peacetime laws do not apply in Sernovodsk and 'cleansing' of property by the Interior Ministry's units has become a normal and everyday occurrence. They took everything they could find on Lermontov Street and Mazayev Street, Ivet Bashigov tells me:

'We didn't have anything fancy at home, we're very poor people. But the contract men carried off an electric alarm clock before my father's very eyes. They didn't say a word and walked past as if he did not exist. If they'd asked us, and said they needed an alarm clock, we would have given it to them . . .'

Sixteen-year-old Ramzia Kharachuyeva cries as she listens to these words. Today this orphan is already back in Sernovodsk. I talked to her when she was still at the Sputnik camp. Like the rest she was simply dumped in Chechnya, after being denied her ration and effectively driven out of Tent No. 7, Block 10.

Hers is a tragic tale. During the first war, the federal forces killed her father, then buried him themselves, not permitting the relatives to follow Muslim funeral customs. Afterwards – and she witnessed it all – they drove a tank back and forth across his grave several times in a fit of hatred. Those same soldiers then took everything out of the house and set it on fire. Her relatives helped Ramzia to build herself a 'cosy dugout', the girl's own description, in Sernovodsk. This November when there was a new 'cleansing' of the town, the dugout was pillaged and then destroyed.

Ramzia tells me: 'I went back to see where I could live now. Soldiers were wandering around the market asking for vodka. If they don't get it for free then they bring sacks of potatoes or tinned meat and exchange it for vodka. Once they're drunk they start shooting. That's how Mohammed Esnukayev died, because he didn't give them vodka. But he didn't have any, he was a very religious man.'

Ramzia clenches her fists: 'The time will come.'

Adam Aduyev, nephew of the humiliated elder Abdurashid from Assinovskaya, is living for the time being in Nazran with his family. Adam, 38, was director of the school at the Assinovsky collective farm, just outside Assinovskaya, and then deputy director at the technical college in Sernovodsk. He likes talking about their beautiful farm, the wonderful people who worked there, and how bright all the children were. This is his verdict on recent events:

'I shall only go back if they observe one fundamental condition: the local authorities must be in control, not the military. I'm an educated man. I don't need their insults. I cannot live where the federal forces are. I don't want my sons to grow up under the barrel of a gun, humiliated from the very first simply because they are Chechen.'

The overwhelming majority of refugees say the same. Only perhaps ten per cent of those I talked to were totally indifferent to what was going on and simply wanted to shut themselves up in their houses and take no notice. Their argument: 'Let whatever will happen, happen. We might as well die there as here.'

Obstacle No. 2 to their return is that they also want to avoid the unparalleled pillaging and humiliations that living with the federal forces would bring. Chechnya has been handed over to the 'victors' for plunder and pillage and the generals are wallowing, with enjoyment, in these mediaeval practices. Their only disappointment now, it would seem, is that most of the villages are half-empty and there are too few people about. If only there were crowds, crammed and squeezed together, that they could now command and dominate! Then the adrenaline and blood would pulse through their veins. Like a diabetic in need of insulin, the generals acutely feel the lack of the Chechen population: too many of them are over the boundary in Ingushetia and there you cannot have much fun, because peacetime laws are still in force.

This explains the announcement to be found in Nazran, in the republic's own migration service, of a 'list of population centres in the liberated districts of the Chechen republic allocated for the reception of those who were forced to leave'. This numbers two dozen villages and towns throughout lowland Chechnya. It is signed by Colonel-General Kazantsev, commanding officer of the combined forces, and is further authorised by 'Lieutenant-General Babichev, Commandant of the Security Zone; Chekalin, First Deputy Commander of the Russian Interior Ministry; Lieutenant-General Palkov, Deputy Commander of the Interior Ministry's Internal Forces; and Major-General Bayramov, Deputy Commander of the Russian Ministry for Emergency Situations'.

Nobody cares that this is an open lie, since there is nothing left to return to. Samashki looks little better than a sieve; Valerik from the air resembles a moth-eaten old coat; the camp at Znamenskoe is inaccessible for the majority; and the authorities still refuse to investigate the tragedy at Alkhan-Yurt. (We were the first to write about the events in Alkhan-Yurt, but the Kremlin only turned its attention to the punitive nature of the 'cleansing' operation there after President Clinton was informed of events by the Western media. They, in turn, got the story from us.) But the authorities could not care less about the old people, pregnant women and homeless children. It is time, they've decided, to put the collective punishment of the Chechens on a different footing. Now they intend to make everyone pay, even those whom they first accepted and saved in Ingushetia. It will be much easier, however, if all these citizens are returned to their historic Motherland and then locked away there. Every journalist who has been working in the area knows that it will be much harder to find out what is going on in Chechnya than to visit the camps in Ingushetia. If the forcible return of civilians to the 'liberated' areas continues, they will find themselves trapped and in close proximity to forces that behave as occupiers without a care for the consequences.

The Laws are Powerless

The Independent Expert Legal Council in Moscow, at the request of the Memorial Human Rights Centre, has recently provided its analysis of certain aspects of events in Chechnya. This voluntary group of lawyers, headed by Mara Polyakova, has spoken out firmly and clearly, as international law and Article 2 of our own Constitution ('the rights of the individual take priority over all other values') demand.

There can be no talk of a guilty nation that must answer for the actions of certain of its members. The Criminal Code and Russia's law 'On the Struggle against Terrorism' both define a terrorist action as a specific event. An antiterrorist operation is therefore an action taken against specific individual criminals. Any restrictions on the rights and liberties of the population as a whole can only be imposed by the law 'On the State of Emergency'. In this case, that law has not been invoked. Additional Protocol No. 2 of the Geneva Conventions (to all of which Russia is a signatory) is expressed in even more uncompromising terms: 'collective punishment for a specific crime is categorically prohibited'.

Are we witnessing an anti-constitutional putsch? Without a doubt. When you carelessly congratulate yourself that we have just had democratic elections to the Duma, stop and think for a moment. We are living under a Constitution that has in part been revoked and now functions only in those parts that continue to receive the approval of the Kremlin. If they then take a dislike to other articles they will toss them aside, just as they will quickly deal with any of us. Yet what will Chechnya look like in the year 2000? We are moving towards the creation of some anti-constitutional territory, a reservation jointly controlled by the harsh military rule of the federal authorities and the so-called police force of the Gantamirov band.* This reservation has been set aside for people of an inferior status, Russia's Red Indians of the late twentieth century, who are guilty of having been born in the Chechen Republic. Russia, it seems, cannot live without a Pale of Settlement.† At the end of the last century the Jews were thus confined and, as a consequence, they provided many of the young revolutionaries and terrorists of Bolshevism. By creating a reservation for the Chechens we are preparing an inevitable rebellion, led by the hot-headed youths who will grow up there.

INGUSHETIA—MOSCOW

---

* A Dudayev ally until 1993, Beslan Gantamirov then aligned himself with the federal authorities and returned with them in October 1999 (see Biographies).
† The nineteenth-century Pale of Settlement restricted Jewish residence to the Western provinces of Tsarist Russia (modern-day Ukraine, Belarus and Lithuania).

Sentence Has Been Passed

6 February 2000

Before I wrote the following report I wondered whether I shouldn't now spare the reader. Perhaps it would be better to leave you all thinking that the army and the new authorities were settling down and we could be optimistic about the future. However, when the intensive psychotherapy of political expediency to which the Russian authorities have subjected us wears off, it will already be too late. Hundreds of decent people will have died because we lacked compassion. And we cannot avoid the consequences or return to our pleasant and carefree existence.

The Sernovodsk Nightmare

A stout, elderly woman in filthy rags crawls with great difficulty on her hideously swollen legs along the stinking narrow corridor. It is crowded with people in old clothes. She is wailing and imploring everyone who catches her eye to help her die: 'I can't stand it any longer! There's nothing to eat, nowhere to live! Nowhere to die even . . .'

'Who are you?'

'I'm no one. Valentina Yefimovna Silova from Grozny. All my life I taught the youngest classes in the school at Cheshki. What did I ever do wrong?'

The old woman falls on her side. People make room for her, but no one has the strength to lift her up and help her to a bed. The crowd just weep over her body. Indifferent to everything apart from pain, hunger and cold, she clambers upright against the wall and moves on – though where she is going no one knows. Her thickly matted vagrant's mop of hair shakes above her trembling back, covered by a coat several sizes too large. Valentina is in Ward 6 (just as in Chekhov's story of madness!) of what used to be the Sernovodsk agricultural college. She has a temperature of 40°C and it shakes and tosses her from one wall of the narrow corridor to the other.

Sernovodsk is a small Chechen town. It has long been within the 'zone of security', supposedly, and as a consequence there are thousands of people here who fled from the pogroms and fighting. They have all been forbidden to travel on to Ingushetia. No one has any money. They are in the grip of cold, flu, lice, heart attacks, TB and psychiatric illness.

'Do you have any children, Valentina Yefimovna, who might take you away from here?'

'I shan't tell you. I just want to disappear.'

Finally it becomes clear that she actually has two sons, one in Bryansk and the other in Rostov-on-Don. Like a partisan being interrogated, she refuses to give their names so as not to make things more difficult for them.

'But you're dying!'

'Yes. Thank God, I am.'

That is the most horrifying reality of the refugee camps in Russia today, that people who have been driven to extremes of despair are now readily pronouncing their own death sentence. (I call on her nameless sons to ignore Valentina Yefimovna's wishes and to quickly get in touch!)

A diminutive old man runs up. He has a crazy look in his eyes, he is dirty and dishevelled, and the ear-flaps of his hat wave about. No, he isn't an alcoholic, there's been nothing to drink here for a long time and no money to buy anything. He's just another demented person.

'Valya,' he calls her, 'I've found it.' Paying no attention to anyone else he prods the indifferent body of Valentina Yefimovna with a small book he's carrying. He was looking for something about Stalinism in the college library and has found it. His name is Nikolai Semyonovich Sapunov, but it is pointless asking him any questions. He doesn't answer or even look your way. His elderly mind has been so oppressed by months of hunger, cold, anarchy and shooting that it is kinder not to insist and overexcite him. The only thing that interests Nikolai Semyonovich now is a comparison between the present killing of those who live in Chechnya with Stalin's similar activities in the 1940s.

Suddenly he returns from his own imaginary world to the present and reality: 'I want to eat. Nothing else. I don't want to hear or know about anything else and I don't want to see anyone. I just want to eat! If you can't feed me then get out of here!'

So I left. An impoverished country which I, in some sense, represent started this war and now it is unable to feed the elderly who have worked for it all their lives. By irresponsibly unleashing this war, the authorities have condemned Valentina Yefimovna and Nikolai Semyonovich to almost certain death. The Kremlin issued those orders. As I hope you've noticed, the former schoolteacher and her husband are both Russian. Perhaps that detail will help some people to show a little feeling.

Ward 5

I leave the corridor and go into the wards where dozens of refugee families are squeezed together. Finally I reach Ward 5. Here the crowd is made up of people who are lying down or can barely walk. Squashed in side by side, 39 people lie there without any consideration of infection or privacy. Twenty grown-ups and nineteen children, from infants to grim-faced teenagers. A very handsome man stands out against this background.

'My name is Saikhan Bazayev. I'm 44 and I have four children. I come from the Shatoy district. I have TB. They've removed my left lung and it's actively spreading in the right lung. There's no medicine and even if there was . . . In my condition I need to eat properly six times a day. Here all I get each day is half a tin of corned beef and two pieces of bread.'

Saikhan is not at all nervous. He is very calm and thoughtful, with no sign of excitement. He doesn't long for death like Valentina Yefimovna, he simply knows that it is not far off and that he will achieve nothing more in his life. His children will be left destitute, since his house and orchards were destroyed by the war. Even if they could escape this nightmarish refuge, they have nowhere to go.

'It's hardly decent for me to complain, you know,' Saikhan continues, his shoulders shuddering with the fever that does not leave him for one moment. 'I just feel so sorry for those around me. I'm passing on my infection to the children all the time. Our living conditions here make it impossible to isolate me from the rest. Even if they survive the camps and go back to some kind of home in Chechnya they have little hope, I've signed their death sentence. For instance, I pleaded with the people from the Migration Service to give me a separate basin. They said that was against the rules.'

His wife Malika is weeping next to him: 'Just look at us, we're real terrorists.'

'What are you hoping for in life?' I ask. 'Everyone in order to live, must have something to hope for.'

'We have no hope.'

It may seem to you, my readers, that your continuing support for the war gives you the right to pass sentence on another human being. Yet when you imagine that you can obtain if not happiness then at least peace of mind at the cost of another's life you are making a tragic mistake. I can only say that no one's peace of mind is worth the death of another human being. Retribution is sure to come. Moreover, it does not come to us together, which would be easier to bear, but to each individually. Then we have to face a single choice: either we end this war or it will be the end of us.

Into the Carriages!

On the far outskirts of Sernovodsk there is one more appalling place. To the right of the railway track is a military compound and to the left is another. This means that every night there are gunfights, drunken soldiers, disturbances and uncertainty. On the night Yeltsin abdicated, for instance, rounds of ammunition were joyously fired straight at the carriages and everyone lay on the floor, not daring to make the slightest movement. For between the two compounds sits a train of 47 carriages in which 2,250 refugees are living. It was shunted here from Ingushetia under strong pressure from Deputy Prime Minister Nikolai Koshman. It is crucial, he thinks, for the future of Russia that those who fled to Ingushetia from Chechnya must be forced to return as quickly as possible, and he has persuaded acting President Putin and Minister for Emergency Situations Sergey Shoigu to support his policy. The rationale is that finance for the refugees will then flow directly from Moscow to Gudermes and pass through his hands only. There must be no more diversion of funds to Ingushetia. The results of his policy can be seen only on the ground. From ministerial offices in Moscow you see very little of what is really going on.

Roza Djabrailova from Carriage 16 and Yakhita Dudayeva from Carriage 15, both from Grozny, insist they are only 40 years old. The two women look nearer 60. Circumstances have forced them to forget about themselves, but they beg us, for the sake of the children and old people, to pass a message to someone at the top, and to take them back to Ingushetia. There is no water and nothing but hunger, lice, filth, and a desperate cold in the carriages. Since early January there has been no fuel for heating their miserable refuge. Roza clings to my sleeve and begs me not to leave. It's easy to understand. As soon as the carriages were moved to Sernovodsk journalists were forbidden to go there, so that the complete elimination of the refugees could proceed in profound concealment from the world. The decision was taken at the headquarters of the forces in Mozdok, by those same generals who are implementing a policy of mass liquidation of the civilian population.

However, we must keep working, even when access to information has been totally denied. Journalists secretly reach the carriages by employing all the guiles of the partisan: wearing different clothes, lying their heads off, and, in some cases, giving various forms of bribe to those at the federal checkpoints. It's very unpleasant to behave in this way, but people are begging for help. How does this square with the numerous assertions in Moscow that Chechnya is a part of Russia and that Russia supposedly wants it to live in peace? I think you know the answer.

As I am talking to Roza Djabrailova, a young woman, Dina Saldalieva, crawls out to us. A week ago in the freezing carriage, on the filthy bunk, she gave birth to her daughter, Iman. Dina is sure her little girl will not live. In front of everyone else, and with no shame or embarrassment, Dina and Roza tell of their gynaecological afflictions – the constant haemorrhaging, pain and inflammations they suffer. I ask them, why don't you at least lower your voices, as is usual when talking of such matters: it makes an extraordinary impression. They look at me with incomprehension and say, 'When you're facing death you cease to fear such things.'

I remember the dormitory at Sernovodsk. It was the same there. The women told me of the uterine growths and tumours, inflammation of the Fallopian tubes and the absence of obstetric stools without lowering their voices, standing in the middle of a crowded ward next to their own apathetic husbands and, most shocking of all, the husbands of other women.

Clutching her stomach, Liza Elbieva, 42, from Grozny, staggers over to speak to us. She stayed till the very last moment, when even the basement had been destroyed. In early January the soldiers came and told her: 'You have 40 minutes, run in that direction. After that the bombing will begin.'

'What if someone can't get out?'

'That's their bad luck,' the soldiers replied.

On Pitomnik Street, for instance, the Vagapovs, father and son, remained behind at No. 16. The son was handicapped and confined to a wheelchair. In 40 minutes you could get nowhere safe with him.

As a result of all the shock and stress, Liza is now suffering a massive haemorrhage and it's noticeable, but I'm the only one to pay any attention to the spots of blood on the back of her coat. In the Kirov suburb of Grozny, an Uzbek soldier called Ural, who was at the checkpoint, also saw these blood spots. No one wanted to let the people fleeing from Pitomnik Street go any further, although they had been told to abandon their homes (so much for those imaginary 'safe corridors' out of the city). The Uzbek came up to Liza and quietly said: 'I'm also a Muslim. Let me help.'

And he did. He was able to get her through the checkpoint and when Liza reached Sernovodsk she went to the local hospital, a small and poorly equipped place. The gynaecologist there refused to examine her and said indifferently: 'Go to the market and buy me some gloves. Then I'll examine you. But in any case I have no medicine.' Liza had no money at all.

I give her some money and beg her to spend it on herself, to buy the gloves and the medicine. She grabs the banknotes as if she were delirious. She has forgotten about her pain, she says, now she can provide for her children for many weeks if she uses all of the money to buy millet and prepares no more than 100 grams a day.

Walking past the carriages towards the crowd are four people of Russian appearance. They are the carriage conductors, it turns out, who were also shunted back into Chechnya in the carriages with the refugees without their knowledge or consent. Now they are virtually hostages. The Railways Ministry has forgotten all about them. The Migration Service and other government departments, of course, have no time to worry about their plight. They have even been forbidden to walk back into Ingushetia and phone home: the checkpoints are no more ready to let them through than they are the refugees. Lilya Bayazitova, Larisa Gavrilova, and Zhenya Kukushkin are all from Chelyabinsk.

'Remind them in Moscow that we're down here,' they request, and comment: 'Why are *we* here? We're totally bemused. Are we still at work? Or are we participating in some experiment in survival, together with the Chechens? Whatever for? We also have nothing to eat. All the medicines we had we gave to the children in the carriages.'

Ruslan Koloyev, First Deputy Minister in the Ingushetia MES, is not used to showing his emotions. He is of a profoundly practical turn of mind and takes a rather sceptical view of the reality he faces today. He is not inclined to overreact to the horrors of the refugees' existence. At the same time, he cannot calmly observe what is going on:

'Sernovodsk is in the Chechen republic, it is not part of Ingushetia. Who should be in charge there? Who should be caring for those people? The answer is quite clear: the government of Chechnya, headed by Russian Deputy Premier Koshman and his people. I can't understand why they're doing nothing! Why are we the ones who have to take the most basic food to Sernovodsk every day? – which, strictly speaking, is an infringement of the rules. I'm ashamed to admit it, but we're sending dried milk and baby food to Sernovodsk and thereby depriving the refugees who are actually in Ingushetia. Because we can see what's going on there. Supposedly, the Migration Service is functioning again in Chechnya and they have put a certain Mr Kaplanov in charge and given him the responsibility for feeding "his" refugees. But nothing has happened. We don't know where Kaplanov is or what he's doing. We merely see the results of his "activities". The tins of meat that very occasionally are sent to Sernovodsk for "Kaplanov's" refugees are bought for 20 roubles, when they should cost only 8. It's barefaced squandering of funds. Remember, the budget is paying out 15 roubles a day to feed each refugee. If a can of meat is sold for 20, then all that person will get is two-thirds of the contents. Naturally, no one bothers about the regular transfers of funds and the result is nothing less than a tragedy.'

A hungry person, who has no way of earning a living for months, endlessly waits for some aid from the authorities. Finally he gets one tin of meat to last him a week. Can you imagine what that means?

CHECHNYA-INGUSHETIA

The Ordinary Man Does Not Need Freedom
Chechnya's New Leader

24 July 2000

On 8 June 2000 Ahmad-Hadji Kadyrov was appointed by President Putin to head the provisional administration of the Chechen Republic. Born in 1951 in Karaganda, Kazakhstan, he studied at the agricultural college in Sernovodsk (Chechnya) and at the construction institute in Novosibirsk, but failed to graduate from either. In the 1980s he received a religious education in Central Asia, attending the *medresseh* (Koranic school) in Bukhara and the Tashkent Institute of Islam. Since 1991 he has lived in Chechnya, becoming the republic's deputy Mufti in 1993 and Mufti in 1995.

Q. **There have been many different leaders in Chechnya over the last ten years – someone, you might say, to suit everyone's taste: Dudayev, Zavgayev, Khadjiev, Maskhadov and Koshman. Now you. Every time a new leader arrived, the people heard enticing words about the happy future that was just round the corner. But it never came. Instead, they faced poverty and violent death. What are the main tasks of the new Kadyrov regime?**

A. My task is to save the Chechen nation from the path that it has repeatedly been deceived into following for the last 300–400 years. Each imam who came to our land, once every 50 or 100 years, would incite the Chechens to begin a jihad.* He'd promise them paradise on earth, then abandon the nation before it

---

* An allusion, in particular, to the Imam Shamil, a religious and military leader from Daghestan, who led a protracted guerrilla war (1817–59) against Tsarist forces in the Eastern Caucasus. The Chechens rebelled in 1825–6 and joined forces with Shamil in 1839.

ever reached this goal. I speak from experience. I was drawn into such a jihad. We shall gain our freedom, I thought, develop our republic and start to live well.

And at first everything indeed seemed to end in victory for the Chechen people. In 1996 the federal forces withdrew, we held elections and President Maskhadov had all the power in his hands.

I did a great deal to ensure this happened and consider his election to be my personal achievement. Without me the elections would never have taken place. After that all Maskhadov had to do was preserve the reputation the Chechens had won after the first war; the Arab and Muslim world were then simply in raptures over us. But Maskhadov failed in this, as in so much else. Gradually people lost confidence. He allowed ordinary people to be robbed. He should have sent away all the mujahedin who had come from abroad, but he didn't.

Q. **How could he? If you fight in a war you always expect your share of the booty.**

A. It's very simple. He should have told them: 'If, as you say, Allah led you to join us then we are very grateful. We owe you nothing, and you've already stored up enough wealth in paradise. Off you go.' Instead we let them take enormous liberties, gave them oil wells and they brought criminals here from all over the world. Finally, the assault on Daghestan began and the federal troops entered Chechnya. Once again Maskhadov did nothing to stop the war, though he was given the chance: I appealed to him, and so did Moscow.

I personally witnessed the phone conversation between Voloshin, the Head of the Presidential Staff, and Alsultanov, then Chechnya's Deputy Premier, who was actually in Maskhadov's office. 'If you make an announcement that you condemn terrorism,' said Voloshin, 'then a meeting with Yeltsin can take place.' Maskhadov replied: 'I won't say any such thing. It's only the Russians, only Moscow, who need me to say it.' It is my conviction that Maskhadov abandoned the Chechen nation after the first war.

Hence my main goal today: the nation must no longer be left stranded half-way; no longer must it be deceived by this 'independence' and 'liberty' that no one has ever actually given us and never will. Freedom, in fact, is something the ordinary man – and I count myself one, I come from a very modest peasant family – does not need. He needs work and in return a wage and security.

Q. **That's just what no one here, apart from yourself, possesses at the moment. You have a job, you're paid a salary for doing it and your personal security is assured by your own bodyguards, supplemented by members of the Alfa group** [elite FSB commandos, Tr.] **disguised as Chechens. You're taken by helicopter to work in Gudermes from your home in Tsentoroy village and then flown back again. Meanwhile Grozny is stricken with hunger and infectious diseases; there is no water, gas or electricity but a great many mentally disturbed people. In the villages entire families are now suffering from tuberculosis.**

A. That's the price you pay for phoney freedom.

Q. **You're saying that as long as you're in power the idea of an independent Chechnya will never be discussed?**

A. There will be no discussions, no ideas of that kind. Today all that people want is an end to the shooting. Simply not to be robbed or killed. Of course, when everything settles down they'll want to get back to work. And they'll need jobs and wages. That will be freedom for Chechnya. I take Ingushetia and Daghestan as an example. They're also Muslims and they're in no hurry to go anywhere else; they don't let themselves be deceived. But we Chechens, I wouldn't say we're stupid, but we are more warlike than other nations and have allowed our warrior instinct and ourselves to be exploited. Now I want to obtain a document from Moscow that guarantees that we'll be left alone for 40–50 years.

Q. **You want some kind of 'safe conduct' from the Kremlin?**

A. That's right. All we have been doing for the last 300–400 years is to devalue our worth as a nation. The best and bravest people, after all, the most honourable, the real patriots, are the ones who go off to war. They are offered ideas, deceived by them, and they perish. I must stop all that. In this document it must state that our people are the main treasure of the nation and no ideas should be allowed to lead them off to war. This document is necessary so that, at any moment, any new leader who wants to start a war could be told: 'You mustn't get us involved, we have lost so much already.'

Q. **But you're hardly a pacifist, are you? You yourself declared a jihad against Moscow. What now? Are you revoking it? Are you going back on your vow to Allah?**

A. I declared a jihad during the last war. And it finished of its own accord with the Khasavyurt Agreements in 1996.* That's my view. When the war ended and we decided to build an Islamic State we had no right to fight with anyone else and infringe the rights of neighbouring nations. However, we invaded Daghestan, thereby going against Sharia law. That's why I have said we are guilty of starting this war. And in 1999 I did not declare a jihad. So there is no jihad today.

Q. **In the future Chechnya for which you now bear responsibility, what place is allotted to Islam?**

A. All Chechens are Muslims. But Chechnya should not be an Islamic republic. I consider that Islam should occupy the same place with us as it does in Ingushetia and Daghestan. They have as many *medresseh* and mosques as they need and no one is oppressed. To call it all an 'Islamic republic' is unnecessary. We once described ourselves in that way and did everything that goes against Islam. What good did it do us, marching under a green flag? Did we help Islam? No, in fact we were driving Muslims away from Islam! We were pushing the nation towards extremism. All these Taliban, Wahhabites and other tendencies are against Islam. They were deliberately encouraged by those who wanted the world to equate Islam with terrorism.

---

* See Chronology.

Q. **Have I understood you correctly? You're saying that what Aushev has done in Ingushetia is a model for you?**

A. Yes. At a recent meeting with the governors from the Southern Area, attended by both Kazantsev and Aushev,* I said just that in front of everyone: 'Aushev is a very clever lad. When he understood in 1991–2 what Dzhokhar [Dudayev] wanted to do in Chechnya, he broke away. Today Ingushetia is flourishing and we're a catastrophe.'

Q. **Do you see Aushev and talk to him?**

A. Not since the beginning of this war.

Q. **Public opinion considers you to be fiercely opposed to Aushev. You are always running him down in public statements.**

A. Aushev must understand me. I want to save my nation.

Q. **But Aushev is also saving the Chechen nation. When do you think those several hundred thousand refugees now in Ingushetia will have enough confidence that you are really in control to return to Chechnya?**

A. Some figures, first. Aushev constantly talks about 214,000 refugees. But I sent my own commission to Ingushetia and they found no more than 115,000 refugees there.

Q. **Does that really make any difference?**

A. Before winter I want to move all refugees to my own territory and set up temporary tent settlements for them in the Sholkovskaya and Naurskaya districts. I'm confident that Moscow will provide serious and rapid aid. Not the present kind of support. Every day for us, after all, is like a year.

Q. **How are you going to deal with what people call the 'Wahhabite' problem?**

A. There is no alternative but to root it out.

---

* In May 2000 Putin appointed seven presidential plenipotentiaries to each supervise a group of regions within the federation. General Kazantsev was put in charge of the group embracing the ethnic republics of the North Caucasus and the predominantly Russian regions to their north.

Q. **But you can't destroy a single idea in someone's head, except by decapitating him.**
A. Exactly. Anyone who will not admit that he is wrong and will not turn back, will meet such an end. Anyway there are no convinced ideological Wahhabites in Chechnya, only people who have been misled or have sold their support.

Q. **What about the suicide-bombers? They're not ideological?**
A. They aren't fundamentalists but zombies. They've simply been hypnotised and stuffed full of drugs. No normal person would do such a thing. Islam strictly forbids suicide. Unending punishment by Allah awaits the suicide-bombers until Judgement Day: every time they blow themselves up, they will be brought back to life so as to be blown to pieces again.

Q. **Who is explaining this to people today after a series of such terrorist attacks?**
A. I told the nation this on television. [The television broadcasting station in Gudermes, where Kadyrov's official residence is located, broadcasts only to the population of that small town, AP.]

Q. **What are you today? A mullah or an official?**
A. I would like to consider myself a human being. But since I now head the administration of the Chechen Republic, I am an official.

Q. **Who is the present Mufti of Chechnya?**
A. No one as yet. I have already summoned all the imams and said: 'I cannot be both Mufti and head of the administration. Choose someone new.' For the time being they have not agreed on a single candidate. Personally I would like to see Ahmad Shamayev, the imam of the Shatoy district, as Mufti. His greatest merit is that he will tell everyone the truth. If need be, Putin himself. Every day he says what he thinks to those who walk past him, fully armed, knowing quite well that they could kill him as they murdered the imams in Urus-Martan and Alkhan-Kala.

Q. **Are you trying to talk to Maskhadov now, to make him change his mind?**
A. We don't talk directly: he fires a missile, I fire one back. We don't meet face to face.

Q. **What's stopping you?**
A. He wouldn't understand my reasons even if I asked him to meet. But if he wants to meet me, I shall not refuse.

Q. **Why don't you take the first step? What's the problem?**
A. What good is he to me? He controls nothing. Basayev acts on his own, Khattab acts on his own, and so does Maskhadov. He's got money but no power. The field commanders are a law to themselves. They come to me and we talk about them giving themselves up.

Q. **But when will Turpal Atgiriev give himself up, for example? It's now two weeks since you supposedly agreed that he and his 200 followers would lay down their arms.***
A. I heard that I'd reached such an agreement from the television. Turpal's people certainly came to me and suggested a meeting, but I refused.

Q. **Why?**
A. I don't trust him.

Q. **What should he do to make you trust him and include him in the amnesty?**
A. He must not turn people against me.

Q. **Which other field commanders, if not Atgiriev, have already surrendered to you?**
A. Brigadier General Ali Sultanov from Shali. At one time he was Maskhadov's deputy premier. Ali was seriously wounded and went abroad for treatment.

Q. **How many fighters did he bring with him?**
A. There was no surrender of weapons as such by his group. He simply came, we talked and he made an official announcement.

Q. **So his detachment continues to fight?**
A. Today there are only very small detachments. Only the big names remain. Even Mohammed Khambiev, who was

---

* Turpal-Ali Atgiriev and his men took part in Salman Raduyev's January 1996 raid on Kizlyar (see Chapter 3). He also headed Maskhadov's election campaign in 1997.

Maskhadov's Minister of Defence, has less than a dozen men. If Khambiev announces that he's surrendering and we tell him to bring in his fighters he'd have no one to bring. And Khambiev himself has hardly left home since the fighters withdrew from Grozny. Atgiriev does not have anyone either. Yesterday evening people from Vedeno came to see me at home and said: 'A detachment of 50 men in our district wants to surrender.' I said, 'Let them come.' Because I know they're not Wahhabites.

Q. **They're part of Basayev's brigade?**

A. Of course. At the moment many of our fighters are waiting for a guarantee that if they surrender the federal soldiers will not infringe the amnesty.

Q. **However, there should be a guarantee on both sides, not just from the federal forces. Can you guarantee that the fighters will not go back to war again?**

A. There are no guarantees. Only words. Only trust. We have to trust people.

Q. **But no one wants a bullet in the back!**

A. What do you suggest, that they should sign something? Even if they gave me such a document it would solve nothing. For instance, I know that Atgiriev very much wants to end this war, he's tired and has been weary for a long time. He did not make any announcements of this kind earlier because then it was Koshman's administration here. Atgiriev and the others will be drawn by the name of Kadyrov.

Q. **If you are so sure of yourself then why do you fly home to Tsentoroy every night from Gudermes? Who are you afraid of?**

A. No one. It's just that my home's there, and I like it.

Q. **Are you hoping for a mass reaction to the amnesty and that many will surrender their arms to you?**

A. Yes, many will surrender because of me. But I won't intercede for some with the federal authorities. There are about 20–30 per cent that can only be destroyed. I can name them: the Akhmadovs from Urus-Martan and the Tsagarayevs.

Q. **And Maskhadov?**
A. Maskhadov is quite a different matter. He is neither a Wahhabite nor a Sufi. He's no one. Maskhadov must officially renounce his post. That's all we ask of him. If only he'd say: 'Forgive me, I could not cope' – and then go and live with his son in Malaysia for good.

Q. **And they'd let him go?**
A. I think so, yes.

Q. **But who wouldn't they let go?**
A. All those whose names are constantly being mentioned. I don't want to repeat them and give them another free advertisement. They are in the media all the time, as it is. But they're just like the rest of us, they're mortal. They show Khattab with long black locks, armed to the teeth, and apparently invincible, but he fears death as much as any of us. He's not made of iron. Khattab also wants to live and that makes him weak.

Q. **What do you think will happen to him in the near future?**
A. I think he'll run away.

Q. **And Basayev?**
A. He'll stay, I think, and fight to the last. If he decides to take up arms again then it will be his last uprising.

GUDERMES

Postscript

This interview left a strange feeling. On the one hand, it all made sense: Kadyrov is on the side of the truth and ordinary people. On the other, literally every word was tinged with petty untruths. This is clear to anyone who has spent a couple of days driving round Chechnya as it is today and talking to people. Ask anyone in any part of the country, 'Who is in charge round here?' and no matter whether you're in Chiri-Yurt, Argun, Shali, Grozny, Oktyabrsk or even Gudermes, the answer is the same: 'No one is in charge.' 'But what about Kadyrov?' 'If he were in charge we would at least have seen him.'

Having taken Koshman's place in Gudermes, Kadyrov never leaves there. He is afraid to. He does not drive or walk anywhere. It is pointless to ask him anything about the economy. He cannot answer the most elementary question of that kind – for instance, how many enterprises there are in Chechnya and which of them are working today. Kadyrov is wholly engrossed in political feuding, in his hatred for Maskhadov and his urge to show that he has won and can draw the field commanders to his side. And he displays a fatal absence of ideas about how to ensure the most important thing of all, a peaceful existence for his republic.

Once you realise that, you can no longer accept his fine words about the 'Chechen nation' and how it 'must not be deceived any more'.

Netherworld
Tales from Grozny

27 July 2000

The Courtyard

Klavdia Anufrieva, 73, is blind and lives in apartment 85 at No. 46 on International Street. She has not washed for a long time, and her hair is uncombed. Today is a happy day for her, she tells me: there were two pieces of bread for lunch.

'But where do they take you to wash?'

The old woman does not want to say that she is not taken anywhere to wash. And the toilet is out among the anti-personnel mines. Going there several times a day is like playing Russian roulette.

'Why don't your relatives come and get you? Where are they?'

Klavdia tries from memory to repeat the Moscow telephone number of her one and only son who, it turns out, is in charge of the fire brigade at Mytishchi near the capital: 'But you must say that everything is fine.'

'I'll tell him what I saw.'

'Not under any circumstances! He'll be upset. And he's a very important man, always at work and that's why he can't come to get me.'

Klavdia Anufrieva's fate is typical of Grozny today. Tens of thousands remain here because no one has come to take them away or even invited them to leave. Our old woman is living on what is a most typical courtyard in contemporary Grozny. (Just round the corner is Minutka, the city's famous central square. These days it's like a firing range.) In the courtyard they let down a bucket on a rope through an inspection cover into a hole where everything liquid gathers in such a heat wave, and they use what they find there as water.

In the middle of their courtyard is an enormous pit. It appeared several days back when unknown people dug up a body there. Now the children swarm at the edge of the open grave. For them it's like a sandpit. They make mud pies there and their parents are not shocked.

Unexpectedly Klavdia turns harshly: 'O do shut up, Volodya! I'm fed up with your whining.'

Vladimir Smola, a tiny dried-out figure on stiff reedy legs, stands on top of a pile of rubble. Above him the sky and under him, his mother. Seven months ago that heap of bricks was apartment 24, his apartment. 'Don't shoot!' he yells. 'I'm 51, I want to live!' He looks up into the sky above Grozny and just as we might wave away persistent flies from a pot of jam he tries to bat aside the military helicopters flying overhead. Back and forth energetically, left to right . . .

Mad? Yes, Vladimir no longer remembers that helicopters are not flies. He used to be an electrician. He gradually went out of his mind, beginning on 15 January 2000 when the third staircase on which he lived was directly hit. He survived, but his mother and two of her old women friends were buried in the rubble. Since then Volodya has lived on this common grave.

At first he searched everywhere for an excavator to dig them out. Then he went mad.

'Don't get the wrong idea, before this war our Volodya was quite normal.' Maryam Barzayeva from 55 Lenin Street, is talking. 'Let's go and pay our respects to Auntie Amina, Auntie Katya and Auntie Roza.'

We set off and behind us runs a crowd of the local children. They listen to this talk about graves and dead people and do not show any reaction at all, as if it were normal that the corpses of three old women lie only a short distance away and no one has dug them out; with the temperature around 50°C the smell is predictable. The children whisper to one another: 'Go and call Yura.'

Here he is. Yury Kozerodov. Swollen from hunger, his age is uncertain and if he did not carry his passport opened in front of him (as everyone who wants to stay alive here has learned to do) you could not tell his sex. In order not to go mad at the beginning of the siege of Grozny Yura thought up the fairy tale that he was guarding the city's MacDonald's.

'Where is it then,' I ask, 'the MacDonald's?' It's hard to imagine that this ploughed-up corner of the earth has room for a fancy fast-food outlet.

'Over there,' Yury points at a door. He didn't even go down in the basement but remained guarding the door he had chosen. It is still intact, but leads nowhere. Yura, though, is now just another crazy person in the courtyard.

'Yura was quite normal before the war. He was a very good man. But it was hell here,' explains Zinaida Mingabieva. She was once an 'Honoured Stockbreeder' in the USSR and lives in the same courtyard. Zina is convinced that her mind, at least, has not been affected at all by the war, but three times she repeats exactly the same story: what records of milking production she achieved at the collective farm and how many times they sent her abroad to learn from the experience of milkmaids in the GDR, Czechoslovakia and Hungary. 'I grew to hate eating meat then. Now I don't remember when I last ate some meat. How I want to eat, all the time.'

I turn to Yury Kozerodov. 'Yura, do you have any relations?'

'Near Tikhoretsk, but they call me a "Russian Chechen" and don't want to take me in.'

'And you, Volodya?'

'Near Smolensk, but they won't take me either.'

'What about you, Zina?'

'I'm even less welcome.'

That's just one courtyard in Grozny. I picked it at random, by chance. It was to ensure that this courtyard lived in peace that they began the 'antiterrorist operation'.

The Factory

Before the [1994–6] war there were 34 large industrial enterprises in Grozny. Some of them were working very well and employed thousands of people. What's happened to all that activity today? Where are the workers?

'I want to make steel, like I've been doing for the last 25 years. Tell that to Moscow. I'm no bandit. There's nothing I want apart from to make steel again, and then go home, tired after a day's work.'

Said Magomedov heads the trade union committee at the machine-building plant, Red Hammer, one of those 34 enterprises I mentioned, none of which is now operational. Red Hammer was a State-owned enterprise, so it still exists only because the workers have taken the initiative and are determined to preserve it whatever happens.

Today Said is on duty at the plant. With him are two cheerful old men, Medi Saidayev and Selimon Tokayev, respectively a turner and a milling-machine operator. Each has worked for more than 50 years at Red Hammer.

'Lady!' asks 70-year-old Medi flirtatiously, tipping his pale blue skull-cap at a jaunty angle, 'what is an honest Chechen to do? There's no one in charge, apart from the thieves, that is. So we're on guard here. Ourselves.'

Said shows me the duty rota. Since 3 April this year, 80 of the 5,000 formerly employed here take it in turns each day to protect the plant from looters. Until last summer its eleven workshops were turning out heavy equipment for the oil industry. On Stakhanovites' Street in the Lenin district where Red Hammer is located, the fighters came on 1 November and the workers dispersed to their basements. Then, for several months, the military bombarded the workshops with predictable results.

'Has anyone in authority talked about the prospects for getting the plant working again?' I ask.

'No, of course not. No one shows the slightest interest.' Said becomes exasperated. 'The plant belongs to Moscow, but they've not shown their noses round here. We demanded to know, "Tell us, is it yes or no?" Hopeless. No reaction. Up there they're only concerned about who gets into power and controls the money for rebuilding the country. But we want to have a clear idea what's happening in the near future. So far it's our impression that the authorities don't realise that without jobs there's no way of saving Chechnya. The plant must work and that will be the best cure for banditry.'

Said likes to speak his mind and find out the truth. But is there anyone today who still believes that what has happened here has done anything to stop the bandits? Strolling through Grozny quickly convinces you of the contrary: everything is being done to make the bandits feel at home and make life unbearable for everyone else.

Said strides along like a real worker, proud, strong, at ease – just the way workers were shown in Soviet films about the proletariat. Each morning he walks round the remains of the eleven workshops. But before anything else he visits his own steel-making shop at the heart of the plant.

'Look at this and remember it all your life.' If Said knew how to cry he'd probably howl. 'There was kilometre after kilometre of industrial estate here, packed with equipment. Dynasties of workers who won medals and decorations; it was all alive. Now, there's nothing. We're digging out the ruins by hand and making an inventory of all that's survived.'

'What for? Did someone ask you to do that?'

'No. We know it should be done.'

And this is also typical of Grozny today. Nothing now is being rebuilt in the city. Absolutely nothing. It is a silent ruin. All that talk in Moscow about restoration work and rebuilding is no more than an extravagant PR exercise, put on for the rest of the country. No one here has seen it. 'Work is proceeding,' the TV assures us, but there is no work. Or only to the extent that a TV report requires, in order to convince the 'necessary people' in Moscow that 'everything is in hand'.

Do you remember at Easter they showed us the generals standing in front of the Orthodox church in Grozny, which 'had been restored in record time'? If you could only see that church today. All the 'repair work' stopped as soon as the cameras turned away. And if, driving past the endless ruins of the city, you were not told, 'There's that church the generals promised to rebuild,' then you would not even realise it was a church building. And do you remember those stirring images on 9 May when a Victory Day parade was organised in the Grozny sports stadium? The rest of the country was told: 'The stadium has been restored.' The stands were full of invited spectators. Hoorah!

Now here they are, those same stands. And here we are with Mohammed Khambiev, a former construction-site foreman who, like everyone else, has to beg in the city to survive.

'We were all herded in here the day before and they said, "If you work, you'll be paid. Start with the stands," they ordered us. Then we put some paint on the main building. The TV cameras came and they filmed. The day after the parade everything went into reverse. The builders came to the stadium, expecting the work to continue, but no one was interested any more. The military didn't show up. Work stopped. With only a few days notice we had been asked to work round the clock and afterwards they didn't pay us one rouble.'

It's hard to conceive today that the stadium was recently repaired. It looks more like it was plundered. After the parade, those inhabitants of Grozny who are trying to rebuild their homes before winter, without any assistance from outside, came in and took what they could for building materials. Foreman Mohammed is one of them. There are nuts, hinges, bolts and other fixtures in his bucket. First he screwed them in and now he has ripped them out. Do as you have been done by.

The Hospital

Nothing can compare, however, with the powerful PR surrounding City Hospital No. 9 in Grozny. Every leading official of the health service has given numerous press conferences about the hospital's restoration after the storming of Grozny and the provision of the very latest in medical equipment.

Hospital No. 9 is the only accident and emergency hospital in Grozny. You come here to be saved or to die. All emergencies end up here, from appendicitis to a stab-wound in the chest. Most of its patients, though, are people wounded by mines. Not a day passes without an amputation, because the main scourge of the city are the anti-personnel mines that were scattered everywhere and today turn up in places where they were not to be found yesterday. During June there were 41 amputations, not counting the patients who did not survive. Ilyas Talkhadov in Ward 3 was blown up on a route he had safely used the day before, driving to collect hay from the '60th October Revolution Anniversary' collective farm. The six neighbours travelling with him were torn apart. Both Ilyas' legs are broken and his hip joints were smashed to pieces. The only hope for him is Hospital No. 9. However, there is nothing here today apart from healing hands and souls. Nothing that could distinguish a hospital of the early twenty-first century from a rural dispensary of one hundred years ago. The only modern equipment is an X-ray machine that works one day in two because the electric current is unreliable and the machine itself is old.

A diesel engine roars fiercely outside the office window. The military donated it so that the hospital could occasionally have some electric light. Abdul Ismailov, deputy chief surgeon of the hospital, explains why the engine has just started: the relatives of a patient have finally found some fuel and the doctors have begun to operate.

Another way of operating is described by Salman Yandarov, a middle-aged and highly qualified specialist. Today he is the chief traumatologist and orthopaedic surgeon of the Chechen Republic, having recently returned, after appeals from his colleagues, from St Petersburg where he had everything: a professorship, students, respect and a very good position in a famous clinic (not to mention a salary).

'This is my native country, so I gave up everything. But what can I offer people who are blown up by mines every day? The hospital is not functioning, it simply exists,' he says. 'For instance, they often bring in someone who has lost both legs and needs urgent amputation if they're not to die. I carry in the battery from my car, connect it to the X-ray machine and take an X-ray. Only then do we operate. When the relatives don't have any money to buy diesel I again go and get my battery, rig it up to my car-lamp and operate. It's shameful . . .'

'But they've surely been bringing you some equipment from Moscow?'

'Yes,' replies the doctor, who has the hands of a pianist and the manners of a gentleman. 'They donated three operating tables. I can tell you, they are so out of date that no self-respecting hospital in Russia would accept them today.'

To begin with I thought how senseless everything happening here was. If you look at it from the State's point of view, why scatter a vast number of mines around the city and receive in return an astronomic growth in the number of disabled people, who require tons of medicine, artificial limbs and so on? And then scatter more mines. And again ferry in medicine, etc. Now it's clear what the State is up to. Its concern for the situation is purely virtual; the only reality is the scattering of mines. No matter how much we want to believe the reverse, or attribute everything to our chronic disorder or thieving, the reality is that the inhabitants of Grozny have been sentenced to this fate. Evidently, the ultimate aim is to ensure that as many people in the city as possible are either left without legs – or dead. Perhaps this is a new stage in the 'anti-terrorist operation', an unhurried punitive mission directed against one ethnic community, which now requires hardly any more ammunition, just the patience to wait for the inevitable outcome.

It all fits together. Why bother to rebuild if there is no fundamental need to rebuild? Why feed people if there is no fundamental reason for them to be fed? The only working excavators in the city I was able to find were those digging out deeper trenches around the army posts.

GROZNY—MOSCOW

I Want to Stay Alive
How the Soldiers Survive

3 August 2000

Locked Up

Fortification work is furiously under way at an army post in one of the most dangerous parts of Grozny, not far from Minutka Square. Military trucks energetically deliver one load of brand-new concrete blocks after another. The crane rumbles and the excavator squeals. The inhabitants of the neighbouring ruins quietly gather round, but no one approaches the army post. They prefer to keep their distance, sitting in silence on mounds of broken brick and distorted building panels.

Everyone feels uncomfortable: the soldiers working under the mute gaze of the onlookers; the people among the ruins as the barrels of automatic weapons point their way.

'I've only got one task here,' says Yury Sidorov, the post commander from the Petersburg OMON, 'to protect the lives of my lads.' As he directs the work to strengthen their position he casts a weary glance at the gaping windows of the half-ruined buildings opposite.

'There's nothing else you're trying to do?' I ask.

'Nothing else. I've no wish to die.'

Who does?

Evening descends. I must find somewhere to spend the night – there isn't a single hotel in Grozny now. We ask to stay at the post at the end of Staropromyslovsky highway, on the city outskirts. It turns out the Archangel Rapid Response Unit is based there. To begin with the commander is welcoming, but soon he has second thoughts and categorically refuses to shelter or feed us. He doesn't need any extra responsibilities.

'Fine,' I say, 'in that case give us somewhere in one of the protected houses nearby.' The post is located on raised ground and below it stands a group of private houses that have not all been destroyed.

'We have no control at all over those buildings!' he answers. 'How could I put you up there?'

Why did they fight this war then? It is now a year since the 'antiterrorist operation' began. Thousands of combatants have been killed or crippled. Tens of thousands of civilians have died or fled and vanished.

You can spend a long time discussing the logic of all that has occurred in the North Caucasus, but this is what it has come down to: each post in Grozny only controls its own immediate 'territory'.

Every army and police post must keep going independently and rely on itself alone, like a tiny State surrounded by enemies. All the posts taken together are like the water-tight bulkheads of a submarine. Camaraderie is all very well, but if one compartment catches fire the others must seal it off and have no right to come to the aid of their neighbours if the rest are to survive.* After seven or eight in the evening, every post in Grozny is locked up as tight as a bank vault.

Then the city stops pretending. Unidentified armed men come out onto the streets. There are a great many of them and they are everywhere, in their tracksuits and running shoes, without uniforms but carrying automatic weapons. Who are they? Whose city is it?

Well, some are the newly created 'Chechen police', for the most

---

* The *Kursk* submarine sank on 12 August 2000, nine days after this report.

part self-appointed. There are also the looters who now dominate Grozny's summer nights. Yet this is not the most important thing in a situation that is already difficult enough for an outsider to fathom.

'Why don't you catch them?' I ask the policemen from Vyatka who now man the post on 8th Street in the Staropromyslovsky district.

'I've no wish to die,' says one.

There it is again, the catchphrase of the present war.

You will hear those words everywhere, like a password, a dozen times a day in Chechnya. From military men of any rank, with every award and medal, at any post and in any branch of the armed forces. That is the true Constitution for people in uniform who find themselves in Chechnya. That is the unwritten Statute that guides their actions from A to Z.

Do people think that way when they feel safely at home? No. Chechnya is not a part of the same country. And it won't be for some time.

So, you ask, what are we to make of those impassioned streams of patriotic rhetoric that assert the contrary? Don't pay them any attention. Let him who is not afraid to lie say such things. However, when you fly from Chechnya to Mozdok, back to headquarters and to peace and quiet, the officers meeting your helicopter joyfully greet you: 'Welcome back to the Motherland.'

That is the truth. And we must get used to it.

The Argun 'Ministry of Foreign Affairs'

'We're foreigners here, aren't we?' many federal soldiers serving in Chechnya frankly admit.

Naturally, they are speaking 'off the record' and don't give their names. The overwhelming majority hate the Chechens and are ready to repel their attacks any time of the day or night. Even when they see their colleagues, the newly re-established Chechen

OMON, they mutter insults through gritted teeth. The life of the military in Chechnya is riddled with such ambiguities. But what happens next?

'International relations officer. The name's Zobov, Anatoly Borisovich. Deputy commander of the Chelyabinsk police combined unit,' says the young man, by way of introduction.

'An international relations officer?' At first the phrase comes as a shock. You think to yourself, that's going a bit far. 'What "international relations" exactly are you monitoring here? With whom? The Chelyabinsk policemen with the Arab mercenaries on the other side?'

'No, with the Chechens, the civilian population. Our relations now are, in essence, international.'★

Calmly disregarding my irony, Major Zobov tells me what his job is. He is not overly insistent, but he is completely convinced of the necessity of his work. Day after day is spent talking to the inhabitants of Argun where his unit is based. He goes to the market place, the local administration, and simply walks about the streets, although this is hardly a safe thing for him to do.

The major is not trying to change the minds of the local people: he realises that is impossible. He's just trying to restore bridges that were dismantled long ago, make some contact no matter how shaky, get acquainted with people, to establish ties, perhaps even make friends, if possible.

In other words, this really is the Ministry of Foreign Affairs in its purest form.

In such local conditions Zobov's ultimate goal is highly original: a softening of attitudes and behaviour, even if it is only within a single small Chechen town. Let them see that we're also human beings and then we'll all find things easier, since we've been thrown together in this way.

★ Chelyabinsk is a city in the Urals; that is, a thousand miles north-west of Chechnya.

To anyone not living next to a war zone such efforts may seem something of a joke. Stupid, even. Naive and a little crazy.

Don't rush to conclusions. The introduction of an international relations officer is above all an honest response. It is a recognition of life as it actually is, not as the General Staff want it to be, and without any of Manilov's window-dressing. It is something our army desperately needs today. People have pushed aside their ideological blinkers and have realised that this is not Moscow, where you can chatter without fear of retribution. In order to survive down here you must not only dig deeper trenches, but also reach agreement with the people on the other side of the barbed wire.

Major Zobov's new job is one example of how the military, driven to the brink by fear, have themselves begun to seek ways out of the Chechen impasse. Paradoxically, and in spite of all the martial rhetoric, the path they have been tracing is unmistakably political.

Never say never, indeed.

The place where we meet the major deserves to be described. Recently the temporary police department in Argun, to which the Chelyabinsk policemen are seconded, suffered the heaviest losses of any in the combined forces group in the North Caucasus. It was here this June that a suicide-bomber drove a truck crammed with explosive into the building at full speed. That's why the major is so convinced of the necessity of his work: it has been paid for by the blood of his comrades and he must do all he can to prevent a recurrence of that tragedy.

Unfortunately this local Ministry of Foreign Affairs is the only one of its kind in Chechnya. Zobov is unique. So it's too early to speak of achievements or results. But it represents a breakthrough. The officers have taken stock and realised that even if they pile up concrete blocks to the sky itself, that will not protect them if someone is determined to kill them. All it requires is enough explosive. So there is only one way out. You must look people in the eye, listen to what they say, and persuade them to try and revoke that death sentence.

Alas, the overwhelming majority of units are still very far from so thoughtful a response. A harsh and vengeful atmosphere predominates. An armoured train was blown up outside Gudermes and that very night the military carried out an operation to pacify and intimidate the population. Stupid and incompetent as always, because those it 'pacified' did not cause the explosion. Others suffered merely because they happened to be nearby and, the soldiers argue, it doesn't matter, they're all bandits. Such a war will be endless. The victims of pacification will inevitably thirst for revenge and the next armoured train will fly skywards.

Meanwhile there is some chance, at least, for the men from Chelyabinsk and the people of Argun. I'm sure that Major Zobov finds his job a hundred times more difficult than those who take refuge in uninhibited vengefulness. For he is trying to change the course of a river, while Sidorov from the Petersburg OMON is merely riding with the current and heightening the fear all round.

School

We didn't just bump into Sidorov, by the way. We were sent to talk to him by the women living in the courtyard opposite his post in Grozny. They themselves were afraid to go. The Petersburg men are billeted in School No. 18 and the mothers asked us to find out if they would leave the building before term begins on 1 September. The OMON men had no intention of going anywhere, but their commander was quite ready to 'live' alongside the educational process in the school.

As proof of this, Sidorov invited us to tour the entire three-storey building. Whereupon it became clear that no co-existence of this kind would be possible. The former classroom walls were now a mural of soldiers' comments. The kindest of these read: ALL WOLVES DESERVE A DOG'S DEATH. The rest were obscenities from floor to ceiling, outlining in graphic terms what should be done to finish off the Chechens. It was a vivid textbook of ethnic hatred, past which Sidorov had marched as proudly as if they were tapestries on display at the Hermitage Museum.

The section of this textbook the pupils would pass in the school corridor as they went to their classrooms was especially elaborate and vicious. So children from Lenin Street in Grozny will not go back to their desks this autumn.

We discussed all this with Sidorov. He shrugged his shoulders and tried to persuade us that he was only a minor figure in the war and not himself to blame. But it's a matter of choice, isn't it? If we choose, we may find ourselves in an ambiguous position. It's up to us. We can also choose to find a way out.

CHECHNYA

Bread and Bullets

24 August 2000

Everything donated by our readers has now reached its destination. Several tons of clothes, food and medicine are today in Grozny in the almost completely devastated district where the old people's home stands.

'Now we'll survive the winter,' says Sister Zinaida Tavgireyeva. 'We'll have the best dinners in Grozny.'

'Could I take this coat right now?' asks Leonarda Zemchonok, her eyes twinkling. A tiny old woman in a threadbare dress, she has deftly plucked a gay red-patterned dressing-gown from one of the bags. What can I say? Yes you may? No you can't?

Most of the old people simply cannot believe their eyes as the soldiers carefully unload these unheard-of treasures from the army truck and APC. Ordinary people, just like them, had put together tons of donations – not the State which was directly responsible for their well-being and would have demanded several formal applications before sending a single dress.

On 18 August, about to leave Grozny for Gudermes, I call to say goodbye. Looking better and happier, the old women come out in their new clothes to meet me: they are about to enjoy their first lavish dinner: 'Your rice and raisins, cooked in your oil.' We embrace.

But I must mention some strange things as well.

The military base at Khankala is only half an hour away from Grozny. The trip from Moscow to Khankala takes time and required several hours of loading and unloading. Yet thanks to local attitudes it was much harder to transport our cargo on this last leg of the journey.

From our very first appeal to help the old people in Grozny we were supported by Anatoly Kvashnin, head of the General Staff, his deputy Valery Manilov, and the deputy minister of defence Vitaly Azarov. Thanks to their efforts our humanitarian cargo reached a military aerodrome in an air-force plane and helicopter. Major Gennady Dzyuba of the Ministry of Defence's press service was ordered to accompany our cargo to its destination.

Alas, the further we got from Moscow and from senior officials the more the emphasis shifted. Major Dzyuba did not have the faintest desire to go to Grozny. Every half-hour he did not fail to remind us, 'Soldiers shouldn't risk their lives for your rice, let alone for you.' Mockingly, he gave us a lecture on the 'tasks of the counterterrorist operation' which, he said, had nothing to do with the old people's home.

Finally he declared that my newspaper had only undertaken this operation, thereby burdening an officer 'from the central apparatus' such as himself with our 'foolishness', in order to boost its sales. It was a cheap and outrageous accusation and there was nothing to do but publicly call Major Dzyuba a 'swine'.

He hastily began preparations to fly back to Moscow and denounce us. He left for the capital without even entering the old people's home, thereby disobeying a direct order. 'You won't forget me! I'll see you lose your accreditation here!'

Are we afraid of losing the right to work in Chechnya? Most certainly, because we know there are too many people there who need our help and can place no trust in the likes of Major Dzyuba.

So who did deliver our consignment? Officers and soldiers who had not received any orders to do so. They were moved by the plight of these lonely old people and saw that the inaction and insolence of the major threatened to wreck the efforts of hundreds of normal people. Many officers in Khankala and Grozny came up and offered their help. They had had no instructions from the

General Staff, but simply learned what the problem was. While Dzyuba intrigued against us, they got on with the job. 'What are your names?' I asked. 'Tell me, and I'll publicly thank you in our newspaper.' 'We don't need any thanks,' they replied.

In particular we have to thank Nikolai Ivanovich, military commandant of the district where the home is located, who became the guardian angel of our operation. He uttered no grand phrases about the 'tasks of the counterterrorist operation', but quietly and steadily worked beyond the call of duty. His military trucks and APC went to Khankala and brought back the supplies for the old people. His soldiers put their weapons aside and, under the command of Captain Dmitry Kharin, shifted tons of humanitarian aid without breaking for a cigarette or needing any encouragement.

As we left, the home's deputy director, Satsit Alieva, said with tears in her eyes: 'Tell everyone who did this to help us that they will certainly go to heaven.'

You think she's exaggerating? Not at all. It's just that no one brings anything to this home – apart from promises. Hunger, sickness and impoverishment reign here. The readers of *Novaya gazeta* are the only ones to provide these old people, abandoned by the State, with the bare minimum essential for their survival. If not me, then who? That's exactly the situation here.

GROZNY—MOSCOW

Postscript

What brilliant mind decided to shift these lonely old people back to Grozny, you may ask, when even army officers avoid going there? Well, it was the idea of Nikolai Koshman, the former deputy premier and plenipotentiary representative of the Russian Federation government in Chechnya.

When his own position as Moscow's chief deputy in the republic was weakening he decided to engage in some PR. To show the decision-makers in the capital that, under his wise leadership, civilian life in Grozny was 'getting back to normal' he sent an emissary to Ingushetia: Magomed Vakhayev, the head of his administration's social welfare department. Vakhayev assured the elderly that ideal conditions had now been created for them in Grozny, and deceived them into returning. They fell victims to a cheap trick in Koshman's struggle to retain power. Koshman was replaced nevertheless and everyone completely forgot about these starving old men and women.

Murder or Execution?
One Year On and Still No Investigation

22 January 2001

For the civilian population the tragedy in Novye Aldy was the most terrible incident of the second Chechen war. Yet there has never been a court case or even an investigation. The prosecutor-general's office is doing everything it can to make sure that no one is charged with the war crimes committed there.

Malika Labazanova comes from Novye Aldy on the outskirts of Grozny. She has worked at a bakery all her life and early each and every morning, with no break for holidays or weekends, she journeys into the city centre to work. That is the only joy she now has in life.

Only once has she ever had to stop work for a time and that interval split her life in two – before and after 5 February 2000. For during the taking of Grozny by federal forces that winter, Malika stayed at home and witnessed the brutal massacre the soldiers carried out in Novye Aldy on 5 February.

From 6 February onwards Malika herself was laying out the corpses in the basement. It was she who protected them from the hungry dogs and crows, and she who then buried the bodies. After which, she washed down the basement tiles.

That was not the end of the nightmare, however. A tragedy that claimed more than 100 victims was followed by another that drags on to this day. As a result Malika, who has never been involved in any kind of public activity, is today chairwoman of the Aldy committee, set up last autumn by the relatives of the victims. The committee's main goal is to make the authorities reply to one question, and one alone: who was responsible for the terrible deaths of their loved ones?

October 1999 to February 2000

In September and October 1999, after military operations began and Grozny came under fire, many inhabitants of Novye Aldy left for Ingushetia. Others remained behind and families were separated. The old people and those who looked after them decided to guard their homes from looters of every description, whether the newly arrived federal forces or their fellow citizens.

Those who stayed protected their houses and their village from the Chechen fighters. When the federal forces first moved into Grozny in early December the nearest positions held by Chechen armed groups were only two kilometres away (in the 20th precinct, another district of Grozny). There were no fighters in the village itself. Nevertheless throughout December 1999 and January 2000 Novye Aldy was mercilessly bombed and shelled every day.

People hid in their basements and only once in a while did they come out to draw water from the spring. As a result of these trips, 75 of the basement-dwellers died in two months. They were shot dead, or, lacking medical aid, they died from their wounds. Some were old people who simply could not take the stress, or withstand the hunger and the cold.

On 30 January, as we all know, a special military operation began to lure Chechen fighters out of Grozny – Shamanov's little trick. The Chechen field commanders were deliberately misinformed that, if they were prepared to pay, then the Feds were ready to create a corridor for their organised retreat from the city. The money was handed over, but the fighters soon found they had been led into a minefield. Meanwhile, federal artillery and aviation mercilessly struck at the surrounding villages through which lay the corridor that the General Staff had designated. Novye Aldy took its full share of the punishment.

On 3 February, when it became clear that federal troops were gradually taking over the positions of the Chechen fighters in the 20th precinct, a delegation from Novye Aldy, for the most part old men, set out under a white flag to talk to the commanding officers of the 15th motorised infantry regiment. The soldiers opened fire on the delegation and one of the Russians living in Novye Aldy was killed outright. Nevertheless the old men managed to persuade the soldiers to stop shelling the village and on the afternoon of 4 February it became quiet again in Novye Aldy.

Soon the first checks on people's ID documents and residence permits were carried out. The soldiers thumbed through the passports of those who had now emerged from the basements and said something strange to them: 'Get out now. Those coming after us are animals. Their order is to kill.' The old men did not believe this, however, and even decided that it was a trick to get them out of their houses so they could be looted.

On 5 February, from early morning, a second 'cleansing' operation began in the village. It proved to be an irrational and bloody settling of scores with anyone who got in the way.

The Cleansing

Aza Bisultanova is a young schoolteacher. It's hard to understand what she's teaching the children today. How can she give any lessons now? She is still in a state of shock following what happened, though eleven months have passed. On 5 February her 68-year-old father, Akhmet Abulkhanov, died. 'If only they'd just shot him . . .' she mutters.

It was Abulkhanov, a respected figure in Novye Aldy, who walked through the village on the morning of that Day of Judgement and persuaded people to leave their basements. It was he who chivvied the doubters: 'Why do we need to hide any longer? Things will only get better from now on. If we stay in the basement the soldiers will think we're guilty of something. But we've done nothing wrong.' It was Abulkhanov who took the hand of the smiling soldier who entered their courtyard and said, 'Thank you, my boy. We were waiting for you. I'm glad to see you come at last.'

'Take out your teeth, old man,' said the soldier, 'and bring some money as well, or I'll kill you.'

Abulkhanov did not understand and continued to stroke the soldier's hand. But Malika Labazanova, who was standing nearby and would witness the reprisal that followed, quickly took off her earrings, handed over her wedding ring, and explained that the fillings in her teeth were not pure gold but simply plated. They allowed her to go to the neighbours and get some money. Malika came back and held out all that could be found: 300 roubles. The soldier took the notes and roared with laughter: 'You call that money . . .?'

They shot the old man, turning his execution into target practice that took off the top of his head. Next they killed three others. One had been disabled since childhood and tried desperately to make them listen: he was disabled, he had papers to prove it.

For some reason Malika was spared. She was ordered to drag the bodies into the basement and she obeyed. The soldiers decided to burn the cow alive in the barn. And also all of the sheep. The cow was already locked in when one of the young privates suddenly took pity on the beast and tried to help it escape the fire. His senior officer warned him to stop or he would kill him too. The blazing, terrified sheep ran from the fold, their mouths gaping, gasping for air, and dropped dead.

People too were burnt alive. Zina Abdulmejidova, Husein Abdulmejidov, Gula Khaidayev, Kaipa Yusupova, Yelena Kuznetsova and Victor Cheptura were so disfigured that one could no longer tell their age.

The only term for what happened is *hell on earth*.

To begin with, those villagers who by some miracle survived were convinced the soldiers were simply out of their minds. Perhaps insanity had led them to carry out this massacre or perhaps they'd been taking drugs. Someone in his right mind would never permit himself to do such a thing. All subsequent events, however, demonstrated that the motives behind the 5 February events were quite different.

For several weeks, contrary to all their traditions, the families did not bury their dead. They were waiting for staff from the prosecutor's office to take statements, begin an official inquiry, and carry out the necessary investigative procedures. When they could wait no longer, they buried their loved ones. Then they waited for death certificates to be issued. Only a few received them. However, soon the man from the Grozny prosecutor's office who had issued these documents specifying that knife wounds, bullet wounds and so on had been the cause of death was hurriedly transferred somewhere else. All to whom he had given such certificates were called in to the Zavodskoy district administration and ordered to hand them back in exchange for 'death certificates on the new forms' (that was the explanation offered). These, it turned out, did not even contain an entry for the cause of death.

January 2001: One Year On

Soon a year will have passed since the atrocity in Novye Aldy, the Khatyn massacre of modern-day Russia.* There has been no investigation. During the entire eleven months since it happened, the witnesses have not once been questioned. No one has presumed to create photofit pictures of the criminals, though many of the killers did not hide their faces.

Photofit descriptions, indeed! The majority of the affected families have not even received death certificates. They have almost nothing to present in court, in order to assert their constitutional right to justice.

Today it is quite obvious that the investigation by the Prosecutor-General's office has been successfully halted. Officially the office fobs off any interested parties from Novye Aldy with the assertion that they are monitoring the situation. To everyone

---

* All the inhabitants of the Belorussian village of Khatyn, several hundred people, were massacred or burned alive by German soldiers in 1942.

else involved they offer the shameless lie that the Chechens, faithful to their customs, refuse to allow the bodies to be exhumed and therefore the investigation is prevented from going ahead.

This lie is logical and understandable if, of course, you look at things from the point of view of those shielding the killers. Hardly any civilians have the chance to check anything since Grozny is almost constantly closed to outside visitors. *Novaya gazeta* has managed to discover a little, however.

The inhabitants of Novye Aldy, it turns out, no matter how terrible they may find it, are begging, pleading and demanding that all the necessary exhumation procedures be completed. They insist that the chief material evidence in this investigation, the bullets that were fired, finally be removed from the bodies and then it will be possible to establish who were the monsters in military uniform that carried out the massacre. The response to all these persistent demands was an outrageous insult. A brigade of forensic experts from the military roared into the village and demanded that people add their signatures to already completed forms stating that the relatives refused to permit exhumation.

The Prosecutor-General's office – which has proved so responsive when the oligarchs are under discussion* – begins to wriggle and make excuses in this case. Lower-ranking staff at the office who have had something to do with the Novye Aldy case will agree to 'speak out' only if they are given complete anonymity. It is as though they were being asked to reveal the State's most highly guarded nuclear secrets. They say there is pressure from the very highest authority and orders have been given to halt the investigation, codenamed '5 February'. Under no circumstances does Putin want to quarrel with the country's leading military figures.

Our sources in the Prosecutor-General's office tell us that if the Novye Aldy nightmare were exhaustively investigated and led to

---

* Since Putin's election as President the two most prominent media magnates in Russia Boris Berezovsky and Vladimir Gusinsky have been pursued by the prosecutor's office on a variety of charges and have both taken refuge abroad.

charges against individual officers, then other similar cases would follow. The staff we talked to also referred to their own fears, since the officers who risk being prosecuted for these atrocities have supposedly been threatening them as well.

That's a little hard to believe, of course. Only time will tell. Meanwhile we must accept the fact that among the majors, colonels and generals that the country is praising, defending and decorating with awards there are also war criminals. Among the heroes are a percentage of unspeakable scum. And we all live together, side by side.

Not long ago, on 23 November, Hasan Musayev was buried in Novye Aldy. On 5 February 2000 this old man had watched as four of his relatives were shot dead. He fell to the ground and a soldier held a gun to his head when he heard a voice say: 'You can live. And suffer because we didn't shoot you.'

Old Hasan certainly suffered and he died from his third heart attack. Surely no one in Russia feels any relief at that?

CHECHNYA—MOSCOW

Chronology
Russia and Chechnya

1991 *January*: Soviet tanks in Lithuania met by strong local resistance and international outcry. *February*: Yeltsin visits Estonia and condemns attacks on the Baltic States. *June*: Yeltsin defeats Communist Ryzhkov in elections to become first President of RSFSR (Soviet Russia). *August*: Attempted *coup d'état* against USSR President Gorbachev. Three die in Moscow. *6 September*: In Chechnya, Dudayev's supporters storm parliament building in Grozny. Later this date became Independence Day. *December*: End of Soviet Union. All 15 of its constituent republics become sovereign and independent states; eight join to form the new Commonwealth of Independent States.

1992 *January*: Beginning of economic shock therapy in Russia. Prices freed and rise 8–20 times. Free street trading allowed. Gamsakhurdia, President of Georgia, overthrown. Dudayev gives him refuge. *July*: Russia joins International Monetary Fund (IMF) and gets $1 billion loan. *October*: Privatisation of the economy begins.

1993 *January*: Fears of hyperinflation in Russia as monthly inflation runs at 30 per cent. Moscow supports Abkhazians in their struggle against the Georgian government. Basayev gains battle experience at head of Abkhaz battalion. *June*: Abulfaz Elchibei, President of Azerbaijan, overthrown in coup. *4 October*: Storm of Supreme Soviet building in Moscow. Hardcore supporters of parliament refuse to accept dissolution. 100–200 defenders die. *December*: Voters approve new Russian Constitution but in elections to new parliament, the Duma, choose a majority of Communist and nationalist deputies.

1994   *15 February*: Tatarstan reaches separate agreement on its status with Moscow leaving Chechnya isolated as the only non-signatory of the new Federation Treaty. *11 December*: Federal forces enter Chechnya to 'restore constitutional order'.

1995   By *March* rouble begins to stabilise, monthly inflation 10 per cent. *17 December*: New Duma elections give Communists strong showing and make their leader prime contender in coming presidential elections.

1996   With single-figure ratings in polls, Yeltsin says he will run for President. IMF conditionally agrees $10.2 billion loan. *21 April*: Dudayev killed by Russian rocket. *July*: Yeltsin wins second round in presidential elections, gaining 54 per cent to Communist Zyuganov's 40 per cent. *August*: Peace brokered with Chechnya at Khasavyurt by Alexander Lebed.

1997   *January*: Maskhadov elected President of Chechnya in election monitored by the Organisation for Security and Cooperation in Europe (OSCE). *July*: Yeltsin announces that industrial depression has ended.

1998   *January*: Symbolic end to inflation. 1,000 rouble note becomes a rouble, kopecks reappear. *17 August*: Russia defaults on $40 billion in short-term debts and devalues the rouble by 200 per cent. *December*: Four Western engineers beheaded in Chechnya.

1999   Early in year Maskhadov reluctantly establishes Sharia law in Chechnya. *March*: Bombing of Kosovo. *May*: Russian forces dash to Pristina. Oil prices reach 30-year high. *August*: Third successive Russian Prime Minister with a background in the security services appointed. Vladimir Putin succeeds Sergey Stepashin.

Second Chechen War

1999

August

- 7 Self-styled Wahhabites from Chechnya, led by Shamil Basayev and the Saudi warrior Khattab, stage an armed rebellion in neighbouring Daghestan. They take over seven villages near the border.
- 9 Vladimir Putin, Head of the Federal Security Service (FSB), is nominated Prime Minister by Yeltsin. (The Duma later confirms the appointment in the first vote.)
- 13 Moscow warns that Islamist bases will be attacked, 'even in Chechnya'.
- 15 Chechen President Aslan Maskhadov declares a state of emergency.
- 25 Federal forces take back the Daghestan villages of Tando and Rakhata.
- 31 Bomb explodes in Moscow's Manegezh shopping centre: five seriously injured. Two separatist Islamic villages in northern Daghestan (Karamakhi and Chabanmakhi) are captured by federal forces.

September

- 4 Federal planes bomb Chechen villages next to the Daghestan border. 62 Russian soldiers and members of their families die in an explosion in Buinaksk (Daghestan).
- 8 93 die in Moscow apartment block bombing.
- 13 116 die in second Moscow apartment block bombing. Yeltsin announces a nationwide 'antiterrorist campaign'.
- 14–20 15,000 are expelled from Moscow and 69,200 made to re-register in 'Operation Foreigner'. 'Unity' Party backing Putin formed to contest parliamentary elections in two months' time.

	Federal armed forces (20,000–30,000 strong) mass along the frontiers of Chechnya.
16	17 die in Volgodonsk bombing in southern Russia.
23	Grozny is bombarded by the Russian air force for first time since 1994–5. Police in Ryazan find and defuse explosives in an apartment block.

October

1	Russian troops enter Chechnya. Prime Minister Putin announces that he no longer recognises the legitimacy of Maskhadov's government.
5	Maskhadov imposes martial law in Chechnya.
6–10	Chechen forces withdraw from the north of the republic, retreating behind the Terek River.
18	Russian army enters the suburbs of Grozny.
21	Ground-to-ground missiles hit Grozny. Chechen side announces 137 dead.
27	Second missile attack, leaving reported 112 dead (Chechen sources).
29	Refugee column fleeing towards Ingushetia is bombed by federal forces.

November

12	Russian army enters Gudermes, second largest town in republic.
17	Capture of Bamut. Missile bombardment of Grozny and Urus-Martan.
18	OSCE (Organisation for Security and Cooperation in Europe) summit meeting in Istanbul demands that Russia seek a 'political solution' to the conflict.
end Nov.	As a result of two months fighting around a quarter of a million refugees from Chechnya flee to neighbouring Ingushetia.

December

- 2 Federal forces enter Argun.
- 6 Russians take Urus-Martan. Civilians in Grozny are given an ultimatum: they must leave Grozny by 11 December.
- 10 European Union threatens Moscow with sanctions. Moscow repeats its ultimatum.
- 12–20 Federal troops penetrate several areas of Grozny and announce the capture of the city's civilian and military airports.
- 19 Elections to Duma, the lower house of parliament. The new Unity Party, built around the figure of Putin, gets almost as many votes as the Communists.
- 20–21 Violent battles near Serzhen-Yurt, 25 miles south-east of Grozny.
- 25 Attack on Grozny. About 2,000 Chechen fighters prepare for house-to-house fighting.
- 27 Maskhadov declares that Grozny will be defended to the last.
- 31 President Yeltsin resigns and Putin takes over as acting president.

2000

January

- 3–6 Chechen fighters recapture Alkhan-Kala and Alkhan-Yurt, but are forced to withdraw after three days.
- 7 Moscow announces the suspension of operations in Grozny, in order to protect civilians and avoid an ecological catastrophe. Shamanov and Troshev are replaced by new military commanders.
- 10 Moscow revokes the truce in response to Chechen attacks in different localities.
- 12 Federal troops retake Argun, Shali and Gudermes following their temporary occupation by Chechen fighters.
- 16 Federal troops launch a new offensive to capture Grozny.

18 Committees of Soldiers' Mothers dispute official figures: they claim that 3,000 have already been killed and 5,000 wounded in the present campaign.
29 The defenders of Grozny begin to surrender. By 1 February, 216 have laid down their arms.
31 Minutka Square captured in centre of Grozny.

February

1 Chechen fighters withdraw from the capital.
3–4 Russian army proceeds to 'cleanse' Grozny. Chechens confirm that most of their armed men have left the city.
Main army spokesman Manilov says there are 93,000 federal troops in Chechnya.
6 Putin announces on television that 'the operation to liberate Grozny is over'.
Fighting continues in mountainous south of country where the Chechen fighters have regrouped, notably in and around the encircled settlements of Shatoy and Komsomolskoe.
29 Released Radio Liberty journalist Andrey Babitsky describes abuse of detainees at the Chernokozovo filtration centre near Grozny.

March

3 During the capture of Shatoi, federal troops free two Polish scientists being held as hostages by a Chechen band.
5 Heavy fighting around Komsomolskoe where the fighters have regrouped (according to Russians, there are 2,000 of them).
Putin visits Grozny and announces there will be a reduction to 23,000 of a permanent garrison stationed in the country.
21–22 Komsomolskoe taken by federal forces.
26 Russian presidential elections: Putin wins in first round, taking 52.9 per cent of the vote.

29 Chechen ambush of a Russian armoured column near Argun (fighters claim 60 dead). Despite assertion of Russian General Staff, Chechen fighters continue to move freely.

April

1–4 Mary Robinson, high commissioner for UN, visits Chechnya. She denounces human rights infringements by Russian troops.

6 Parliamentary Assembly of the Council of Europe suspends the voting rights of the Russian delegation and demands that the Council of Ministers begins procedure to expel Russia.

10 In interview with biggest circulation Russian daily newspaper, Chechen president Maskhadov declares himself ready to enter a dialogue without prior conditions.

13 Kremlin indicates it is ready to enter discussion with Chechen representatives.

May

7 Putin inaugurated as Russian president.

11 11 soldiers die in Chechnya after rocket-propelled grenade attack.

13 Seven presidential plenipotentiaries appointed to rein in the Russian regions; General Kazantsev is put in charge of the Southern Area, administered from Rostov.

17 2,500 Chechen 'policemen' (led by Gantamirov) disbanded. Sergey Zverev, deputy to Koshman, the Russian-appointed administrator of Chechnya, is killed in an ambush.

30 Koshman dismisses Gantamirov for absenteeism.

June

8 'Temporary' presidential rule established. The Mufti of Chechnya Kadyrov replaces Koshman.

25 Troshev, now military commander for the North Caucasus Military District, claims that the war is over.

July

- 2–3 Five suicide-bombing attacks. Total of 42 soldiers die at Argun, Gudermes, Urus-Martan and two other localities.
- 9 Bombs in Vladikavkaz and Rostov kill eight.
- 13 Gantamirov is appointed Kadyrov's deputy and mayor of Grozny, but almost immediately has armed confrontation with Gudermes leader.

August

- 8 Bomb in central Moscow underpass kills 12 and injures 97.
- 12 *Kursk* submarine sinks.
- 18 In defiance of the authorities, newspapers publish a list of servicemen onboard the *Kursk*.
- 20 By-election for Duma seat in Chechnya. Retired Interior Ministry general Aslanbek Aslakhanov beats 11 other candidates, gets 31 per cent of the votes.

September

- 9 *Moscow Times* claims up to 1.3 million 'dead souls' voted for Putin in presidential elections. Half a million votes cast for him in Daghestan were doubtful.

October

- 6 Largest oil discovery in world for last 30 years claimed after preliminary exploration of Kashagan deposit in Caspian Sea.
  Three explosions in Stavropol Region; two in Nevinnomysk and one at Pyatigorsk rail station.
- 12 Seven killed in explosion outside police station in Grozny.
- 26 Report by Human Rights Watch denounces 'indiscriminate and disproportionate' federal bombing, and documents widespread arbitrary detention, torture and extortion.

29　Seven federal soldiers and two local waitresses killed in café blast. Trial begins of three former paratroopers accused of murdering journalist Dmitry Kholodov in October 1994.

November

9　Russia's Security Council declares intention to reduce the armed forces by 600,000 (or 20 per cent of total) by the year 2005.

13–15　Media magnates Berezovsky and Gusinsky fail to appear at the prosecutor's office, on charges of fraud and embezzlement. Arrest warrants are subsequently issued.

22　IMF mission leaves Moscow without reaching new agreement. Almost certain that Russia cannot now restructure its debt of $3.9 billion to the Paris Club.

December

3　Federal aviation bombs suspected concentrations of Chechen armed groups in Shali district and Vedeno Gorge.

9　A Moskvich automobile packed with explosive blows up next to the mosque in Alkhan-Yurt, killing 22.

12　Two Russian army privates kidnapped in Vladikavkaz on 4 December freed in Sernovodsk.

20　Five students of the Grozny teacher-training college were killed, and four others wounded, in a mortar attack.

28　Residential buildings belonging to the Akhmadov brothers in the centre of Urus Martan blown up by the security services.

2001

January

22　Putin announces cuts in armed presence in Chechnya and transfer of antiterrorist operation to FSB.

25　PACE restores voting rights of Russian delegation, claiming a change in heart by the federal administration.

Biographical Notes

Aushev, Ruslan
(b.1954) Major-General, in Soviet Army since 1971, veteran of Afghan campaign (1980–7). President of Ingushetia since March 1993.

Basayev, Shamil
(b.1965) Most famous Chechen field commander, anathematised by Russian authorities as a terrorist. Studied in Moscow in 1980s and lived by trading computers. In November 1991 hijacked plane to Turkey; in 1992–3 led Chechen battalion fighting for Abkhazian separatists against Georgians; a leader of the defence of Grozny, 1994–5; led June 1995 raid on Budyonnovsk; in 1997 lost presidential elections to Maskhadov and briefly entered his government.

Berezovsky, Boris
(b.1946) Media magnate and politician. Research associate at Academy of Sciences institute who moved from car dealership into finance and gained influence over various media outlets, above all Channel One TV (ORT). Out of favour following Yeltsin's resignation.

Dudayev, Dzhokhar
(1944–96) First President of Chechnya (1991–6). In Soviet air force and away from Chechnya after 1962 (with Russian wife Alla). Service in Afghanistan, based in Estonia 1987–90; in 1990 returned home, and led Chechen revolution. Killed in April 1996 when rocket tracked his satellite phone signal.

Gantamirov, Beslan	(b. 1963) Policeman turned businessman. Organiser of National Guard that helped Dudayev to power. Mayor of Grozny 1991–3, then went into opposition. Arrested and imprisoned in Moscow on fraud charges, May 1996. Returned to Chechnya in support of federal forces, October 1999. Again Mayor of Grozny from June 2000.
Kadyrov, Ahmad-Hadji	(b. 1951) Chief Mufti of Chechnya 1995–9; from June 2000 head of provisional administration appointed by Moscow.
Kazantsev, Victor	General. Overall commander of combined forces in Chechnya. Head of North Caucasus Military District; in May 2000 appointed presidential 'super-governor' for the Southern Area.
Khattab	Alias of Saudi-born citizen fighting in Chechnya since February 1995. Veteran of Afghanistan, he brought with him mujahedin, self-professed Wahhabis, of Saudi and North African origin.
Kovalyov, Sergey	(b. 1930) Veteran human rights activist. In prison camps and internal exile from 1974 to 1984; member of every Russian parliament from 1990. He stood down in 1999. Presidential human rights commissioner 1993–6 and most prominent critic of first war; spent winter of 1994–5 in Grozny as federal aviation bombed the Chechen capital.
Lebed, Alexander	(b. 1950) Lieutenant-General turned politician. Served in Afghanistan and 'hot spots' of former Soviet Union, especially Moldova (1992–5). Ran for president in June 1996; in Yeltsin's administration until his dismissal in October 1996; signed peace accords with Chechnya. In May 1998 elected governor of Krasnoyarsk Region, Siberia.

Maskhadov, Aslan	(b.1951) Colonel. Soviet army officer, 1969–91. Served in Baltic States and took part in January 1991 action by Soviet forces against Lithuanian independence activists. Chief of Staff of Chechen forces 1993–7; elected president of Chechnya in 1997.
Putin, Vladimir	(b.1952) President of Russia, elected March 2000. KGB officer for 15 years (7 spent in Dresden), moved to Petersburg city administration, 1990–6 becoming deputy mayor; 1996 joined presidential staff, 1998 headed FSB (KGB successor), August 1999 appointed prime minister. Acting president in January 2000.
Shamanov, Anatoly	(b.1957) Major-General, served in both Chechen wars. Elected governor of Ulyanovsk Region in December 2000.
Shoigu, Sergey	(b.1955) Builder. RF Minister for Emergency Situations, 1991–9, led column of humanitarian aid to Serbia in spring 1999; made leader of Unity Party backing Putin.
Starovoitova, Galina	(1946–98) Ethnographer who became Russia's most prominent woman politician. Yeltsin's adviser on nationalities and ethnic policy 1990–2; from 1989 deputy of each successive Soviet and Russian legislative body. Led rump of 'Democratic Russia' movement that supported Yeltsin in 1989–92. Shot dead in Petersburg.
Yeltsin, Boris	(b.1931) Communist Party leader in Urals from 1968, transferred to Moscow in 1985, became a figurehead of radical opposition in Soviet Union, 1987–91. Elected President of Russia in June 1991; re-elected in July 1996. Started both wars in Chechnya. Resigned on New Year's Eve 2000.

Putin's Russia

My Country's Army, and its Mothers

The Army in Russia is a closed system no different from a prison. Nobody gets into the Army or into prison unless the authorities want them there. Once you are in, you live the life of a slave.

Armies everywhere try to keep what they do quiet, and perhaps this is why we talk about generals as if they were members of an international tribe whose personality profile is the same all over the planet, irrespective of which particular president or state they are serving.

There are, however, some peculiarities specific to the Army in Russia, or rather to relations between the Army and the civilian population. The civilian authorities have no control over what the Army gets up to. A private belongs to the lowest caste in the hierarchy. He is nobody. He is nothing. Behind the concrete walls of military barracks, an officer can do anything he wants to a soldier. Similarly, a senior officer can do anything he fancies to a junior colleague.

You are probably thinking that things surely cannot be that bad.

Well, they aren't always. Sometimes they are better, but only because a particular humane individual has called his subordinates to order. That is the only time there is a ray of hope.

'But what about the country's leaders?' you may wonder. 'The President is the Army's ex-officio Commander-in-Chief and hence personally responsible for what goes on, isn't he?'

Unfortunately, when they make it to the Kremlin, our leaders make no attempt to rein in the Army's lawlessness but are more likely to give senior officers ever greater power. Depending on whether or not a leader indulges the Army, it either supports him or undermines him. The only attempts to humanise the Army were made under Yeltsin as part of a programme of promoting democratic freedoms. They didn't last long. In Russia, holding on to power is more important than saving soldiers' lives, and under a barrage of indignation from General Headquarters Yeltsin ran up the white flag and surrendered to the generals.

Putin hasn't even made any attempts. He is an officer himself. End of story. When he first appeared on Russia's political radar screen as a possible head of state rather than as an unpopular Director of the universally detested Federal Security Bureau (FSB), he began making pronouncements to the effect that the Army, which had been diminished under Yeltsin, was henceforth to be reborn, and that all it lacked for its renaissance was a second Chechen war. Everything that has happened in the northern Caucasus since then can be traced back to this premise. When the Second Chechen War began, the Army was given free rein, and in the presidential elections of 2000 it voted as one for Putin. The Army has found the present war highly profitable, a source of accelerated promotion, more and more medals, and the rapid forging of careers. Generals on active service lay the foundation for careers in politics and are catapulted straight into the political elite. For Putin rebirth of the Army is a done deed after its humiliations under Yeltsin and defeat in the First Chechen War.

How exactly Putin has helped the Army we shall see in the story that follows.

No. U-729343. Forgotten on the Battlefield

It is November 18, 2002. Nina Levurda, retired after 25 years as a schoolteacher, is a heavy, slow-moving woman, old and tired and with a string of serious ailments. She has been waiting for hours, as she has many times over the past year, in the unwelcoming waiting room of the Krasnaya Presnya Intermunicipal Court in Moscow.

Nina has nowhere else to turn. She is a mother without a son: even worse, without the truth about her son. Lieutenant Pavel

Levurda was born in 1975. To the Army he is No. U−729343. He was killed in Chechnya at the start of the Second Chechen War, the war that, according to Putin, saw the Army reborn. How it was reborn we shall see from the tale of the last months of No. U−729343. It is not the fact that he was killed but the circumstances of his death and the events that followed it which have compelled Nina to do the rounds of legal institutions for the past eleven months. She has had just one aim: to get a precise legal answer from the State as to why her son was left behind on the battlefield. And, coincidentally, to ask why, since his death, she has been treated so abominably by the Ministry of Defence.

As a child, Pavel Levurda dreamed of a career in the Army. Not a common state of affairs nowadays. Boys from poor families do apply for places at the military academies, but their aim is to get degrees and then get discharged. The endless self-congratulatory reports from the President's office about increasing competition for admission to military institutes are entirely true. But this has less to do with any increase in the Army's prestige than with the abject poverty of those seeking an education. The same situation explains the catastrophic shortage of junior officers in military units. When junior officers graduate from military college, they simply fail to appear at the garrisons to which they have been posted. They suddenly become 'seriously ill' and send in certificates testifying to all manner of unexpected disabilities. This is not difficult to arrange in a country as corrupt as Russia.

Pavel was different. He really wanted to be an officer. His parents tried to talk him out of it because they knew what a hard life it was. Petr Levurda, his father, was himself an officer, and the family had spent their lives being shifted around remote garrisons.

Quite apart from that, in the early 1990s everything was falling apart in the wake of the Soviet Empire's collapse. A school-leaver would have had to have been mad, everyone agreed, to choose to go to a military academy that couldn't even feed its students.

Pavel insisted on his dream career and went away to study at the Far East College for Officers of the Armed Forces. In 1996 he was commissioned as an officer and sent to serve near St Petersburg. Then, in 1998, he was thrown into the frying pan: 58 Army.

Fifty-eight Army has a bad reputation in Russia. It is synonymous with the degeneration of the armed forces. Of course this began before Putin. He does, however, bear a heavy responsibility, in the first place for the fact that the total anarchy among officers goes unchecked, and in the second for effectively placing officers above the law. To all intents and purposes, they are not prosecuted no matter what crimes they commit.

Fifty-eight Army was, in addition, the Army of General Vladimir Shamanov. A Hero of Russia who fought in both Chechen wars, he became notorious for his exceptional brutality towards the civilian population. General Shamanov is retired now. He resigned and became Governor of Ulyanovsk Province, benefiting from his role in the Second Chechen War when he was never off the television screen. Each day he would inform the country that 'all Chechens are bandits' who thoroughly deserved to be eliminated. In this he enjoyed Putin's full support.

The staff headquarters of 58 Army is in Vladikavkaz, the capital of the Republic of North Ossetia-Alaniya which borders Chechnya and Ingushetia. Its troops fought in the First Chechen War and they are still fighting there now. The officers' corps of 58 Army, following the example of their general, were also renowned for their exceptional brutality towards both the people of Chechnya and their own soldiers and junior officers. Rostov-on-Don is the location of the General Headquarters of the North Caucasus Military District, to which 58 Army is subordinate. The greater part of the archive of the Rostov Committee of Soldiers' Mothers consists of files relating to desertion by privates as the result of beatings by officers of 58 Army, which is also well known for the blatant theft of supplies from their warehouses and for wholesale treason. They sell weapons stolen from their own stores to field commanders of the Chechen resistance. That is, they aid the enemy.

I personally know many junior officers who have gone to

extraordinary lengths to avoid serving in 58 Army. Levurda, however, decided otherwise. He didn't break ranks, he wrote letters which made heavy reading, he came home on leave, and his parents saw their son becoming more and more morose. No matter how often they urged him to resign, however, he would reply, 'What must be done must be done.' Pavel Levurda clearly was someone the authorities would have been justified in describing as a young Russian with a special sense of duty towards his Motherland and a profound patriotism. In fact, he was hoping for a genuine, rather than a Putinesque, rebirth of the Russian Army.

In 2000, Pavel Levurda had another opportunity to refuse to go to war in the northern Caucasus. Few would have blamed him. Many junior officers found ways to obtain instant exemption. But, as Pavel explained to his parents, he felt he couldn't desert his soldiers.

On 13 January 2000 Pavel went off to war, first reporting to 15 Motorised Infantry Guards Regiment of the 2 (Taman) Guards Division (Army Unit 73881), in Moscow Province. On January 14 Nina heard her son's voice on the telephone for the last time. He had signed a special contract to go to Chechnya, and . . .

It was clear enough what that dreadful 'and' portended.

'I cried. I did my best to change his mind,' Nina remembers. 'But Pavel said there was no going back. I asked my cousin who lives in Moscow to go straight to the Taman Division, to try to talk him out of it. When she got to the unit she found she had missed him by just a few hours. He had already flown out to Mozdok.' This small town in North Ossetia is on the border with Chechnya. When the war began, it was the main base of the Unified Command of Forces and Troops mobilised for Putin's 'antiterrorist operation'.

And so, on 18 January 2000. No. U-729343 found himself in Chechnya.

'At present I am on the south-western outskirts of Grozny . . .' wrote Pavel in his first and only letter to his parents from the war. It is dated 24 January 2000.

The city is blockaded from all directions, and there is serious fighting going on there. The gunfire does not stop for a minute. The city is burning, the sky is completely black. Sometimes a mortar shell falls nearby, or a fighter plane launches a missile right by your ear. The artillery never lets up. The losses in the battalion have been appalling. All the officers in my company have been put out of action. The officer who commanded this unit before me was blown up by one of our own booby traps. When I went to see my company commander he carelessly grabbed his rifle, sending a round into the ground a few centimetres away from me. It was sheer luck I wasn't hit. Everyone laughed. They said, 'Pasha, there have been five commanding officers of the unit before you, and you almost didn't last five minutes!' The men here are all right but not strong-willed. The officers are on contract, and the soldiers, with a few exceptions, though very young, are holding out. We all sleep together in a tent, on the ground. There is an ocean of lice. We're given shit to eat. No change there. What lies ahead we don't know. Either we'll attack who knows where, or we'll just sit around until we turn into idiots, or they'll pull us out and pack us off back to Moscow. Or God knows what. I am not ill, but I feel so low. That's all for now. Love, kisses. Pasha

This might not seem a good letter for reassuring one's parents. In war you lose the ability to be reassuring and forget what might shock someone far away when you have been shocked a hundred times more yourself.

It later became clear that Pavel's letter really was intended to reassure his parents. When he wrote it, he wasn't in fact lying in a tent wondering what lay ahead. From at least 21 January he was actively involved in the 'serious fighting', having first taken command of a mortar unit and, shortly afterwards, of an entire company. The other officers were indeed 'out of action' and there was no one else to take command.

Neither was he 'on the outskirts' of Grozny.

On 19 February, assisting the battalion's intelligence groups to break out of an encirclement and 'covering the retreat of his comrades' (according to the citation nominating him for the Order of Valour) from the village of Ushkaloy, Itum-Kalin District, Lieutenant Levurda was severely wounded and died of 'massive haemorrhaging following multiple bullet wounds'.

So he died in Ushkaloy. In the winter of 2000 the fighting was at its fiercest there – a desperate partisan war in highland forests, on narrow paths. But where was Pavel's body?

No coffin containing Nina Levurda's son's remains came home to the family to be buried. His remains, she discovered, had been lost by the very State he had tried with such desperate loyalty to serve.

Having taken on the roles of military prosecutor and investigating officer, Nina found out that on 19 February, the official date of her son's death, the 'comrades' whose retreat he was covering did indeed get away. They simply abandoned Pavel, along with six other soldiers who had saved them, by breaking through the encirclement, at the scene of heavy fighting. Most of those left behind were wounded but still alive. They shouted for help, begged not to be abandoned, as the inhabitants of the remote mountain village later testified. The villagers bandaged some of the wounded themselves, but could do no more. There is no hospital in Ushkaloy, no doctor, not even a nurse.

Pavel Levurda was left behind on the battlefield and then forgotten. It was forgotten that his body was lying there. It was forgotten that he had a family that would be waiting for his return. The survivors simply stopped thinking about those who had died so that they might live.

What happened to Pavel Levurda after his death is typical of our Army. This disgraceful episode encapsulates its thinking. For the Army, a human being is nothing. No one keeps track of the troops. There is no feeling of responsibility towards the families.

They only remembered about Pavel Levurda on 24 February, when, according to information provided by General Headquarters in Chechnya, Ushkaloy was completely cleared of Chechen fighters and 'came under the control' of Federal forces. (This explanation was in fact concocted later to prove that 'there was no objective possibility' of recovering Pavel's body.)

On 24 February, in fact, the Army collected from Ushkaloy the bodies of only six of the seven soldiers who had broken through the encirclement. They couldn't find Pavel Levurda, so they forgot about him again.

Back home, Pavel's mother was hysterical. The only communication she had had was that official letter of 7 February. The Ministry of Defence's 'hotline' wasn't much help. Talking to the duty officers there was like talking to a computer about the grief that was relentlessly grinding her down. 'Lieutenant Pavel Petrovich Levurda is not on the list of those dead or missing.' Such was the invariable reply.

Nina listened to the 'fully informative' hotline for several months. Unbelievably, even after she had located Pavel's remains by her own efforts, even when she had been officially notified of his death, the commanding officers had not got round to updating the information on their database.

But to return to our story... On 20 May, three months after the fighting in Ushkaloy, local police discovered 'a burial site containing the body of a man showing signs of violent death'. However, it was only on 6 July, after another one and a half months of Nina's daily telephone calls to the hotline and the local Army commissariat, that the police filled in the relevant form, 'Orientation/Task No. 464', in response to a missing-person inquiry.

On 19 July the form finally reached the CID in Bryansk, where Pavel's family were living. Nina, rushing round every conceivable office, had lodged a missing-person inquiry at the police station there. So it was that on 2 August, Detective Constable Abramochkin, an ordinary policeman, came round to see Pavel's parents.

The only person at home was another Nina, Pavel's 14-year-old niece. DC Abramochkin asked her some questions about Pavel, discovered what belongings he had had with him, and was greatly surprised to find he was talking to the family of a soldier. Having been assigned this routine investigation, it was DC Abramochkin and not an official from the Ministry of Defence who informed the mother of a hero that her son had officially been classified as missing without trace, and that from 20 February his entitlement to all forms of provision and allowances had been cancelled. The Itum-Kalin police asked Abramochkin to go round to the parents in Bryansk to find out 'the postal address of the permanent deployment of Army Unit 73881 in which Levurda, P. P. had been serving' so they could contact its commanding officer in order to establish the circumstances relating to the death of a person who, from his mother's description, appeared to resemble one of their officers!

The quote is from the official correspondence. It tells us a lot both about the realities of the Army and about the nature of the war Putin is waging in the Caucasus. In this Army the right hand has no idea what the left hand is doing, so it is easier to post a letter to parents far away than to telephone through to General Headquarters in Khankala (the military base near Grozny).

DC Abramochkin, seeing the state the family was in, strongly advised Nina Levurda to go to Rostov-on-Don as soon as she could. He had heard that the remains of the unknown soldier from Ushkaloy had been taken to the main military mortuary there for identification by Colonel Vladimir Shcherbakov, Director of 124 Military Forensic Medical Laboratory, a man well known and respected in Russia. It should be noted that Shcherbakov does this work not at the behest of commanding officers, generals or General Headquarters, but because his heart tells him it is the right thing to do.

Abramochkin also advised Nina Levurda not to expect too much, because, as we say, 'anything can happen in Russia', where mix-ups involving dead bodies are only too common. The Bryansk Committee of Soldiers' Mothers was in the meantime helping with the Levurda saga, and it was only through their good offices and the efforts of DC Abramochkin that the elite 15 Guards Regiment and the even more elite Taman Guards Division finally twigged that the seventh body, left behind by his 'comrades', just might be that of Pavel Levurda.

'We arrived in Rostov on 20 August,' Nina tells me. 'I went straight to the laboratory. There is no security on the entrance. I walked in and went into the first inspection room I came to. I saw the inspector had a head separated from its body on a stand on his examination table. More precisely, it was a skull. I knew immediately that it was Pavel's head, even though there were other skulls next to it.'

Is there any way of assessing or compensating the distress caused to this mother?

Of course there isn't. In any case who can argue against forensic inspectors needing to have skulls on their tables?

And yet . . . What an artless lot we are becoming, thoughtless, crass and, because of it, amoral.

Nina was given sedatives after the encounter with her son's skull, which she had indeed correctly recognised. At this precise moment a representative of Pavel's unit came rushing in to see her. DC Abramochkin, having learned the unit's address from the bereaved parents, had sent a telegram, and the commanding officer had sent a representative to Rostov to take care of the formalities.

The representative showed Nina a notice. She looked at it and fainted. In the notice Guards Lieutenant-Colonel A. Dragunov, acting commanding officer of Army Unit 73881, and Guards Lieutenant-Colonel A. Pochatenko, chief of staff of the same unit, requested that 'Citizens Levurda' be informed that 'their son, while on a military mission, true to his military oath, manifesting steadfastness and courage, has died in battle'. The unit was trying to cover the tracks of its wretched 'forgetfulness'.

When Nina had recovered, she read the notice more carefully. There was no indication of when her son had died.

'Well, what about the date?' Nina asked the representative.

'Just write it in yourself, whatever you like,' he replied.

'What do you mean, write it in?' Nina shouted. 'The day Pasha was born is his date of birth. Surely I have a right to know the date of his death!'

The representative shrugged, as if to say, 'Don't ask me,' and handed her a further extract from an order to the operational forces to 'remove Lieutenant Levurda from the list of members of the Regiment'. This too bore no date and indicated no reason but did have various stamps and signatures at the bottom. Again, with the artless gaze of a child, the representative asked Nina to fill in the blanks herself and hand it in, when she got home, to the local Army Commissariat so that Pavel could be removed from the register.

Nina said nothing. What is the point of talking to a person who has no heart, no brain and no soul?

'But surely that's easiest, isn't it? Rather than me having to go all the way to Bryansk?' the representative continued uncertainly.

Of course it was easier. There is no denying that being artless, being crass, can make life easier. Take our Minister of Defence, Sergey Ivanov, a crony of the President since Putin worked for the FSB in St Petersburg. Every week Ivanov appears on television to deliver the President's war bulletins. With the inflections of Goebbels on Second World War newsreels, he tell us that nobody will make us 'kneel down before terrorists', that he intends to pursue the war in Chechnya to some supposed 'victorious conclusion'. We never hear a word from Minister Ivanov about the fate of the soldiers and officers who enable him and the President not to seem to be kneeling down before terrorists. This political line is wholly neo-Soviet: human beings do not have independent existences, they are cogs in the machine whose function is to implement unquestioningly whatever political escapades those in power dream up. Cogs have no rights. Not even to dignity in death.

It is so much more bother not to be crass. For me that would mean being able to see beyond the 'General Line of the Party and Government' to the details of how it is implemented. In the present instance, these details are that, on 31 August 2000, No. U-729343 was finally buried in the city of Ivanovo, to which Pavel's parents had moved in order to escape the dark associations of Bryansk. The forensic inspectors in Rostov returned Pavel's head to Nina. Unfortunately, that seemed to be all the remains they had.

Many people in Russia have heard of Nina Levurda because, having committed what remained of her son to the earth, on the ninth day after the funeral she set off to the headquarters of 15 Regiment in Moscow Province. When she started out from Ivanovo, her intention was only to look Pavel's commanding officers in the eye and to read in them, when confronted by their officer's mother, at least some remorse for all the things they had 'forgotten' to do.

'Of course, I didn't expect them to apologise,' Nina says, 'but I did think I might at least see some sympathy in their faces.'

When she arrived at the Taman Division, however, nobody wanted to see this mother. The commanding officer was simply unavailable. Nina sat for three days waiting to meet him, without food, tea, sleep or anyone paying attention to her. Senior officers scurried to and fro like cockroaches, pretending not to notice she was there. It was then that Nina Levurda vowed to sue the State, to bring an action against the Ministry of Defence and Minister Ivanov for the moral suffering they had caused her. Not in connection with her son's death: he did after all die in the performance of his duty. But in respect of what happened subsequently. Translated from convoluted legal jargon into plain speech, she wanted to know who was responsible.

What happened next? First, the Order of Valour awarded posthumously to Nina's son was presented to the family in the Army Commissariat in Ivanovo. Second, the Army took its revenge. The Ministry of Defence and the Taman Division went on the warpath against this mother who had dared to express her outrage at their behaviour.

This is how they went about it. In just under a year there were eight court hearings, the first on 26 December 2001, the last on 18 November 2002, none of which came to any conclusions whatsoever. The court did not even get round to considering the substance of Nina's writ, because in their impunity the representatives of the Ministry of Defence ignored the hearings completely. And they were right to do so. The case of 'Nina Levurda against the State' first came before Judge Tyulenev (Krasnaya Presnya Intermunicipal Court, Moscow). He decided that a mother 'has no right to information' about the body of her own son, and the Ministry of Defence was accordingly under no obligation to supply her with such information. Nina went to the Moscow City Court, where, in view of the manifest absurdity of the previous verdict, the case was referred back to the Krasnaya Presnya Court for a new hearing. The State machine's technique against the bereaved mother was a systematic boycott of the court sessions by Minister Ivanov's official representatives and by Land Forces Command, of which the Taman Division and 15 Regiment are part. They simply failed to appear, brazenly and systematically. So Nina Levurda had to keep going back to Moscow from Ivanovo, only to find herself confronted with an empty dock, her journey wasted. A simple woman dependent on her State pension, which aims only to keep you from starving, and with a husband who had taken to the bottle after Pavel's funeral as a way to escape from their suffering.

In the end, Judge Bolonina of the Krasnaya Presnya District Court, to whom the case had been referred from the Moscow City Court, became exasperated. At the fifth hearing missed by the defendants, she fined the Ministry of Defence 8,000 roubles. Paid for by the taxpayer, of course. It is a pity this fine was not paid by Minister Ivanov to Nina Levurda. There is no provision for anything of that sort. Russian legislation protects the interests not of the weak but of the all-powerful authorities.

On 18 November 2002, after the imposition of the fine, representatives from the Ministry finally turned up in the courtroom, but they were strange representatives. They knew nothing about the case and declined to identify themselves, complaining that chaos at the Ministry of Defence was the cause of all the problems. The upshot was that the court was again adjourned, this time to 2 December.

Nina was in tears as she stood in the grim corridor of the court building.

'Why are they doing this?' she asked. 'You would think they had done nothing wrong.'

How enviable to be Sergey Ivanov, head of our Ministry of Defence, which is so pitiless towards our people! Life is straightforward for him. He doesn't have to bother himself with details, with mothers whose sons have died in that 'war on international terrorism' about which he waxes so lyrical. He does not have to hear their voices or feel their pain. He knows nothing of the lives he has destroyed, nothing of the thousands of mothers and fathers abandoned by the system after their children have given their lives for it.

'Putin can't do everything!' the President's Russian admirers protest.

Indeed he can't. As President it is his job to think about methods, about approach. He is the person who shapes them. In Russia, people imitate the man at the top.

Well, we have described his approach to the Army. He is entirely to blame for the brutality and extremism instilled in both the Army and the State. Brutality is a serious infection that can easily become a pandemic. First perpetrated against people living in Chechnya, now it is used against 'our people', as the patriotically inclined like to describe Russian citizens. Including those Russians who fought patriotically against those who experienced it first.

'Well, he made his choice and followed his destiny,' says Nina, wiping the tears from her face. Judge Bolonina stalks past in her robes, inscrutable. 'But for heaven's sake, these are human beings!'

Are they? I sometimes wonder whether Putin really is human, not just an icy, metallic effigy. If he is human, it doesn't show.

Tanya, Misha, Lena and Rinat:
Where Are They Now?

So, where are we now? We who lived in the USSR, where most of us had a stable job and a salary we could rely on, who had unbounded and unshakeable confidence in what tomorrow would bring. We who knew there were doctors who could cure us of all ailments and teachers who would teach us. And who also knew that we would not pay a kopek for all this. What kind of existence are we eking out now? What new roles have we been allocated?

The changes since the end of the Soviet era have been threefold. First, we underwent a personal revolution (in parallel, of course, with the social revolution) at the time of the demise of the USSR and during the reign of Boris Yeltsin. Everything vanished in an instant: Soviet ideology, cheap sausage, money and the certainty that there was a Big Daddy in the Kremlin, and even if he was a despot, at least he was responsible for us.

The second change came with the 1998 debt default. Many of us had managed to earn a bit in the years after 1991, when the market economy was effectively introduced, and there were signs that a middle class was being formed. A Russian middle class, admittedly, not like what you might find in the West, but a middle class nonetheless to support democracy and the free market. Overnight all this disappeared. By then many people were so tired of the daily struggle for survival that they could not rise to a new challenge and simply sank without trace.

The third change came under Putin, as we embarked upon a new stage of Russian capitalism with obvious neo-Soviet features. The economy in the era of our third President is a curious hybrid of the free market, ideological dogma and various odds and ends. It is a model that puts Soviet ideology at the service of big-time private capital. There are an awful lot of poor, indeed destitute, people. In addition, an old phenomenon is flourishing again: the *nomenklatura*, a ruling elite, the great bureaucratic class that existed under the Soviet system. The economic system may have changed, but members of this elite have adapted to it. The *nomenklatura* would like to live the high life like the 'New Russian' business elite, only their official salaries are tiny. They have no desire to return to the old Soviet system, but neither does the new system suit them ideally. The problem is that it requires law and order, something Russian society is demanding ever more insistently, and accordingly the *nomenklatura* has to spend most of its time trying to obviate law and order to promote its own enrichment.

The result has been that Putin's new-old *nomenklatura* has taken corruption to heights undreamt of under the Communists or Yeltsin. It is now devouring small and middle-sized businesses, and with them the middle class. It is giving big and super-big business, the monopolies and quasi-State businesses, the opportunity to develop. (In Russia this means these are the *nomenklatura*'s preferred source of bribes.) This is the kind of business which in Russia produces the highest and most stable returns not only for its owners and managers but also for their patrons in the State administration. In Russia, big business without patrons, or 'curators', in the State administration does not exist. All this misconduct has nothing to do with market forces. Putin is trying to gain the support of the so-called *byvshie*, the *ci-devants*, who occupied leadership positions under the Soviet regime. Their hankering after old times is so strong that the ideology underpinning Putin-style capitalism is increasingly reminiscent of the thinking in the USSR during the height of the Period of Stagnation in the late Brezhnev years – the late 1970s and early '80s.

Tanya, Misha, Lena and Rinat are real people, not fictional characters, ordinary people who, together with the rest of the country, have been struggling to survive. They were all my friends. This is what has happened to them since 1991.

Tanya

It is early winter, 2002. The *Nord-Ost* saga has just ended. Russian society, particularly in Moscow, is in a state of shock. I appeared on television, playing a small part in these events, and as a result old friends reappeared in my life.

The late-night call was from Tanya. Actually she had always rung in the small hours, or so late at night that everyone was already asleep.

I hadn't seen Tanya, my sometime neighbour, for ten years or so. In those days she had been downtrodden, but now she was a queen. She looked triumphant and very chic, not because she was expensively dressed, which she was, but because she was self-possessed and poised. This was something new.

In the Soviet period, Tanya's life had been one long torment. Almost every evening she would come down to see me (I lived on the ground floor of an old block of flats, and she lived at the top). She would weep over how her life was completely ruined.

In those years Tanya was an engineer in a research institute and accordingly was regarded as belonging to the 'Soviet scientific and technical intelligentsia', a substantial social category that no longer exists.

How did one come to belong to that stratum? At the time, a girl from a good family – Tanya was the only daughter of well-established parents – was expected to enter higher education, and if when she finished secondary school she showed no particular inclinations or aptitudes, she went to study at a technical institute, of which there were any number, and became an engineer. After graduating she was required to work for three years at the speciality the State had trained her in at its own expense. Accordingly, there was a whole army of people in the country who were deeply dissatisfied with life, young specialists who had never wanted to be engineers and who now sat out their working days in research institutes producing nothing useful whatsoever.

Tanya was a fully paid-up member of this army, with the profession of engineer of communal facilities in nuclear power stations. For days at a time and without the least enthusiasm, she would sit in her institute designing projects for drainage and water-supply systems which nobody ever built, receiving a minuscule salary in return. She was always unhappy because of a chronic shortage of money. She tried to feed and clothe her family decently, frantically ministering to her two small, perpetually sick children and her husband, a rather odd man called Andrey, a young lecturer at a prestigious technical university in Moscow.

As a result Tanya was a typical neurasthenic, endlessly tormenting herself, Andrey and the children with her bad moods, her hysteria, her depressions and her constant dissatisfaction.

To make matters worse, Tanya was from Rostov-on-Don. She had managed to move to Moscow by marrying Andrey, whom she had met on a Black Sea beach. She was regarded as little better than one of the *limitchiki*, menial 'quota workers' who, in the mid-1970s, were granted temporary residence permits in Moscow in return for working in unpopular or undersupplied occupations. At that time there were no end of female 'engineers' in the capital, girls from the provinces who had married Muscovites. No one wanted to remain outside Moscow and girls from good families did their best to move there.

Tanya did not know what she wanted, but she did know very clearly what she did not want: to be an engineer and to be living in penury with the impoverished Andrey. We talked about it a lot. Tanya was angry because she saw no way out.

There were often ructions at home. In accordance with Soviet tradition, Tanya, not having a place of her own in Moscow, should have lived with Andrey in his flat, but he did not have a flat either. So they ended up sharing one large flat with Andrey's parents and his two elder brothers, each of whom also had a family and a couple of children.

All in all, it was a typical Soviet beehive, but with no option to swarm and achieve independence. Andrey, to make things worse, came from a genteel old Moscow family consisting of exceptional people. One, for example, was a famous professor who had taught the violin at the Moscow State Conservatory. He was the second husband of Andrey's grandmother, who had also been a professor of violin there. His grandmother had died long ago, but her husband was still in the beehive. Like Tanya, he had nowhere else to go.

Andrey's parents were professors of physics and mathematics. The elder brother was a professor of chemistry at Moscow University who made one discovery after another, although this had little material impact on his life.

The situation made Tanya more and more exasperated. She considered Andrey's family to be a bunch of incompetent failures despite the dozens of academic qualifications they possessed, and Andrey's family reciprocated wholeheartedly, disliking and constantly finding fault with her. Tanya, we have to remember, was from Rostov-on-Don, where even in Soviet times anyone who could trade did trade in anything they could. Illegal underground workshops flourished there. Many rich men divided their time between prison and the outside world, and no one considered it a disgrace. The newspapers called them speculators and spivs, but the young women of Rostov were happy enough to marry them.

When we first met in the early 1980s, Tanya already thought she had made a bad mistake in marrying Andrey. Love hadn't come into it. She admitted she had simply swallowed the bait of residence in Moscow. She only came out of herself when she could produce pretty things she had picked up who knows where and was inviting you to buy them. She undoubtedly had a special gift of commercial persuasiveness. She could sell you a blouse of appalling quality at thrice the price while assuring you, 'It's what people are wearing in Europe.' When the fraud came to light, she would not be embarrassed in the least. This talent for speculative trade was something that Andrey's traditionalist, highly educated family despised.

Now, in 2002, Tanya invited me to her home, which turned out to be that same spacious flat in the heart of Moscow.

The flat had been magnificently refurbished. The place was crammed with the latest technology, excellent copies of famous paintings, high-quality reproduction antique furniture. Tanya was almost 50, but her skin was youthful and healthy, her clothes bright. She talked in a loud, confident voice, very openly, and although she laughed a lot her face remained unwrinkled. This could only mean she had had plastic surgery, which in turn could only mean she had made the big time.

'Has Andrey struck it rich?' I wondered to myself. Tanya strode through the rooms. Ten years ago she had preferred to whisper in this flat, to sit in the corner of one of the rooms, avoiding her in-laws.

'Well, where are the family?'

'I'll tell you, only don't faint. All this belongs to me now.'

'It's yours? Congratulations! But where do they live?'

'In a minute, in a minute. Everything in good time.'

A handsome young man about the age Tanya's sons must be now, I supposed, slipped quietly into the room. The last time I'd seen her boys they'd been children, so I blurted out, 'Can this really be . . . Igor?'

Igor was Tanya's and Andrey's elder son and must by then have been 24 or 25.

Tanya burst out laughing. Peals of merriment, mischievous, echoing, youthful. Not at all like Tanya.

'My name is David,' the handsome, ox-eyed young man with dark curly hair murmured. He kissed Tanya's manicured hand. I remembered a time when her hands hadn't looked like that, as they had been worn by many hours of washing clothes for a large family. David drifted off into the depths of the flat. 'Well, don't let me spoil things for you, girls.'

Oh, dear. We really were not girls.

'All right, tell me. Reveal the secrets of your youthfulness and prosperity,' I begged my old friend. 'Where are your family?'

'They aren't my family any more.'

'What about Andrey?'

'We split up. My sentence of hard labour came to an end.'

'Have you remarried? This boy? David?'

'David is my boyfriend, short-term, just for the sake of my health, really. He's my toy boy. I'll keep him for as long as I feel like it.'

'Good heavens! Who are you working for?'

'I don't work for anyone. I work for myself,' Tanya answered firmly and with a metallic edge to her voice that didn't seem to go with the image of the slightly indolent, manicured lady with a young lover who was sitting opposite me.

Tanya is a happy product of the new life. In the summer of 1992, when there was nothing to eat in the majority of homes in Moscow (this was called 'economic shock treatment', part of the market reforms of the then Prime Minister Yegor Gaidar), Tanya, together with her children and the rest of the professor's family, were living in the country at their old dacha.

In that terrible, hungry summer, all Muscovites, if they had a dacha, were sitting it out in their wooden shacks in the country and growing vegetables for the winter so as to have at least something to eat. The research institute where Tanya worked had closed for the summer. They had no work at all and hadn't in any case paid anybody's salaries for ages. The employees, town dwellers all, had gone off to hoe their vegetable patches or to trade in the markets which had sprung up in large numbers on the streets of starving Moscow. Tanya was busy growing vegetables of her own and looking after the children. Andrey often stayed in the city and didn't come back to sleep at the dacha because, unlike the majority of research institutes, his technological university had not closed.

One morning for some reason Tanya turned up in Moscow unexpectedly, unlocked the door of their flat, and found Andrey and a girl student in her matrimonial bed. A loud-mouthed woman from the south of Russia, Tanya bawled at Andrey so the whole apartment block could hear her.

Andrey made no excuses. He said he loved the student. The student herself said nothing, got dressed and went through to the kitchen, where she began boiling the kettle for tea as if nothing had happened.

For Tanya her rival's silence and her manifest familiarity with the layout of the flat was the last straw. She decided there and then that she hadn't been putting up with Andrey's pathetic family all her married life only to let a rival invade their space. She told Andrey not to imagine he could get away with it. He got his things together and left with the student.

That, in effect, was the day Tanya's new, completely independent life began. Andrey behaved abominably, giving her not a kopek to support herself or the children. Three years later, when Tanya had made a little money, she would in fact occasionally feed him and even buy him clothes. But not from any feeling of sympathy. Tanya fed Andrey because revenge is sweet. She gave him red caviar, a symbol of luxury in Soviet times which she could now afford. Andrey gobbled it up until it was coming out of his ears, not even blushing at the humiliation because he was so hungry. At times he even ate at the soup kitchens set up at churches, pretending for good measure to be a believer. He even learned how to cross himself.

In 1992, the summer of the free-market breakthrough, this was all still in the future. After a week, when there was nothing left to feed the children, and with her mother-in-law insisting that she must forgive Andrey and take him back, Tanya went off to trade at a nearby market.

Her mother-in-law shrieked, 'The disgrace of it! The disgrace!' and took to her bed. She soon came round, however, when Tanya began buying her medicine with the disgraceful money she was making at the market. Not one of the old lady's sons, her husband or her other daughters-in-law had been able to do anything like this for her. Matters had taken on a tragi-comic aspect when it was resolved at a family council that they would never, come what may, sell off the family heirlooms, the antique furniture inherited from their forebears, the rare antique music albums, the pictures by famous nineteenth-century Russian painters. Tanya's mother-in-law, lying obstinately in her bed and readying herself for death rather than disgrace, was the first to vote against the idea. In the early 1990s, other long-established families who had held on to their heirlooms through the Stalin years were selling them off on the cheap or, as people said at the time, 'for a meal'.

Tanya meanwhile was out at the market from 6.00 in the morning until 11.00 at night. It was not work but hard labour. It was the purest purgatory, but it had one redeeming feature: this was slavery with a price tag. Tanya stood in the market and earned real roubles which rustled in her pocket. What was more, you got your cash on the day. You stood there and you got the money, not later but right then, and that was what mattered. Tanya always came home with money. She also came home with swollen legs, barely able to put one foot in front of the other, and with enormous swollen 'crab-claw' hands, incapable even of washing herself or making herself look half human. But – she was almost happy!

'You may not believe it, but I was happy not to be dependent on anyone else any more. Not on the Director of the institute who didn't pay me, not on Andrey who was giving me nothing, not on my mother-in-law with her family heirlooms and traditions. I depended solely on myself.' Tanya, now rich and beautiful, told me the story of how it had all changed ten years ago. 'My mother-in-law? Well, one fine day I just told her where to get off. "Go **** yourself!" And what do you think? For the first time she didn't preach back at me. It was a revelation. A revolution took place before my eyes. The seemingly incorruptible old Moscow intelligentsia was being broken. It was being broken by the money I was giving my mother-in-law. She stopped lecturing me because I started feeding her. Me, the one who was always in the wrong. Gradually all of them, that whole family which had looked down on me for so many years because I didn't come from the same sort of background and because, as they always said, I had inveigled Andrey into marrying me because I wanted to move to Moscow, the whole bunch learned to smile at me and even to listen attentively to what I had to tell them.

'And it was just because I was feeding them all by trading at that market. I gloried in it. I was prepared to continue doing it for just one reason: to get more and more money, more and more, and to humiliate them by rubbing their noses in it.'

When Tanya returned home towards midnight she would collapse on the bed. She no longer had any time for her sons. She did not check their homework. She would collapse and then she was out like a light. Early the next morning everything started again.

Her mother-in-law began looking after Tanya's children – for the first time, it has to be said, since they had been living under the same roof. Tanya was amazed yet again.

In the market Tanya found herself working for an adroit young man who was a 'shuttle', as people said then. Nikita's 'shuttling' consisted of importing cheap clothes from Turkey, cheap watermelons from Uzbekistan, cheap mandarins from Georgia; in fact, anything cheap from anywhere at all. Tanya and the other women working for him sold his goods. There were no taxes, no State levies. In the market the rules were the same as inside a prison. Disagreements were resolved at knifepoint, extortion was rife, people got beaten up. The women traders were mostly in the same situation as Tanya, single women with children abandoned at home, former members of the scientific and technical intelligentsia whose institutes, publishing houses and editorial offices had closed. They were little better than whores for their bosses.

Soon Tanya was sleeping with Nikita. He picked her out from the others, despite the difference in their ages, and took her with him to Turkey on a buying trip. He took her once, a second and a third time, and within two months Tanya, a woman with a commercial streak, had become a shuttle herself, having seen that it really wasn't rocket science.

Then Nikita was murdered, shot by no one knew whom. One morning they found him at the market with a bullet-hole in his head, and that was that. Nikita's saleswomen migrated across to

Tanya and were glad to do so. Tanya proved much more efficient than Nikita, and business began to boom. As a bonus, Tanya was less of a shit than the deceased.

After another six months Tanya stopped travelling to Turkey. Not because she was tired, although life as a shuttle was hard. At that time you had to carry the goods yourself, in enormous bundles which you dragged round airports and railway stations, skimping at every turn, even on luggage trolleys, which had to be paid for. She stopped travelling herself because she had discovered her niche: she was exceptionally good at business.

Tanya flourished and her business soon grew to the extent that she hired at first five and then another five shuttles and became the proprietress of what, in the context of a local market, was a large business. The shuttles travelled, her women traded, and Tanya managed them all. She was already going around, as people put it, 'not dressed like a Turk', which meant, like a European. She was a habituée of all the restaurants, where she ate, got drunk, threw her money about and relaxed after work. She had plenty of money left over for herself, her family and her workers. Takings in those years were astronomical. She had lovers befitting her income and years: virtuosos. Tanya got rid of them when she felt like it. Andrey, to be frank, had not been up to much in that department . . .

Another year passed and Tanya decided to refurbish the flat, having first taken over ownership of it. She bought some rather poky flats for Andrey, his brothers and her father-in-law, which made all of them happy. Tanya kept her elderly mother-in-law with her. Pity aside, she needed someone to look after her sons. The elder, Igor, had reached puberty and was causing problems, while the younger boy was sickly.

Tanya did, however, carry through the refurbishment as a kind of retaliation.

'I just really wanted to show them who owned the place!'

She threw everything out, absolutely everything. She sold off all the heirlooms and expunged all traces of her in-laws' dusty gentry past.

Nobody protested. Her mother-in-law went off to the dacha and kept out of the way.

The result was a modern European flat equipped with cutting-edge technology.

After the renovation Tanya decided to move on: she abandoned the shuttle business and went into commerce proper, buying a number of shops in Moscow.

'What? Those shops belong to you?' I couldn't believe my ears. Tanya was the owner of two excellent supermarkets I would drive to after work. 'Congratulations! But your prices . . .!'

'I know, but Russia is a rich country!' Tanya parried, laughing.

'Not that rich. You've become an imperialist. A bit hard-nosed.'

'Of course. Yeltsin's gone, and with him the easy money and the romance. The people in power now are insatiable pragmatists, and I am one of them. You are against Putin, but I am for him. He almost seems like a brother to me, downtrodden in the past and getting his own back now.'

'What do you mean by "insatiable"?'

'The bribes. The endless bribes you have to give everyone. Just to keep hold of my shops, I pay up. Who don't I give bribes to?! The pen-pushers at the police station, the firemen, the hygiene inspectors, the municipal government. And the gangsters whose patch my shops are on. Actually, I bought them from gangsters.'

'Aren't you afraid to do business with them?'

'No. I have a dream: I want to be rich. In today's Russia that means I have to pay them all off. Without that "tax" I would be shot tomorrow and replaced by someone else.'

'You aren't exaggerating?'

'If anything, I am understating things.'

'What about the bureaucrats?'

'Some of the bureaucrats I pay myself, and the rest are paid by the gangsters. I give the gangsters money and they keep those other gangsters, our bureaucrats, sweet. Actually, it's quite convenient.'

'Where is Andrey now?'

'He died. In the end he couldn't take the fact that I had moved up in the world and he was eating my caviar. He asked me to take him back, but I wanted none of it. I told him to find himself another student. Anyway, I don't want to live with an ugly man. I've decided I like handsome men. I go to male strip shows and choose my partners there.'

'You're kidding! Don't you miss family life? Domestic bliss?'

'No. I don't. I've just started living. There is a downside, of course there is. You may think it is all sordid, but what was so pure about the way I used to live?'

'What about the children?'

'Igor, unfortunately, has turned out a weakling, like Andrey. He's on drugs. I've sent him to a clinic. This is the fifth time already ... I am having Stasik educated in London. I'm very pleased with him. Very. He's first in everything there. My mother-in-law looks after him. I rent a small flat for her. Stasik lives in a student hostel during the week, and at the weekends in this flat with my mother-in-law. I paid for her to have a hip replacement. They did it in Switzerland. She's come back to life, running around like a young woman, and she absolutely worships me. I think she really does. It's a great thing, is money.'

David swirled into the room bearing a tray. 'Time for tea, girls,' he crooned. 'Just the three of us. All right, Tanechka?'

Tanya nodded and said she'd be right back. She wanted to change for tea. David exuded degeneracy and languor. It was all rather sick-making. A couple of minutes later Tanya returned. She was covered in diamonds, her ears ablaze, her décolletage ashimmer. Even her hair was glittering.

The show was for my benefit. I politely registered appreciation. Tanya was really pleased, as radiant as her diamonds from the pleasure of presenting herself, the new Tanya, to an old friend.

We quickly drank our tea and said our goodbyes.

'Only not for ten years this time!' Tanya proposed as we parted.

'Let's make an effort,' I replied, and thought as I went down the stairs that in the Putin era people really did meet up more often. Old friends, I mean. There was a time in Russia, the late

Yeltsin period, when everybody was terribly busy just surviving, when people didn't phone each other for years, some embarrassed because they were poor, some because they were rich. It was a time when many emigrated for ever; when many put a bullet in their brains because nobody seemed to need them any more; when people snorted cocaine out of disgust with themselves. Now, however, it was as if everybody who had survived was meeting up again. Society had become noticeably more orderly, and people even had free time.

When the new times had arrived, women were the driving force, going into business, divorcing their husbands. The husbands became gangsters, and many died in shoot-outs in the first years of the Yeltsin period. These things happened because, on the eve of perestroika, many Russian women had felt, like Tanya, that they would never be able to change their lives. Suddenly here was their big chance.

A week later I had to be at a press conference in connection with a by-election to the municipal Duma, I think. And there, quite unexpectedly, I met Tanya again. In our already rather structured and, as under the Soviets, cliquish society, owners of supermarkets just don't go to political press conferences.

Tanya manifested herself to the world of journalists with never a hair out of place, in a classic black business suit and without a single diamond to be seen. David was there as well, and he too was top notch, faultlessly performing the role of Tanya's business secretary, modest but not ingratiating. No 'girls' on this occasion.

I sat with the journalists. Tanya was on the other side of the barricades. Handed a microphone, she was the last to speak. She was one of the candidates standing for a seat in the municipal Duma. She told the journalists, including me, how she saw the problems of the homeless in Moscow, and promised to fight for their rights if the voters did her the honour of electing her a member of the legislative assembly.

'What on earth do you need this for? You're rich already,' I asked Tanya when the press conference was over.

'I told you, I want to be even richer. It's very simple: I don't want to pay bribes to our councillor.'

'Is that all?'

'You have no idea of the level of corruption nowadays. Gangsters in Yeltsin's time didn't even dream of this. If I become a councillor that will be one "tax" less.'

'But why have you taken to defending the homeless in particular?' We wandered into a French café nearby. Tanya had chosen it; it was too expensive for me.

'I think that backdrop will make me look good. Anyway, I really can help them pull themselves up by their bootstraps. I've done it myself.'

'And why at the press conference, at the end of your speech, did you talk about Putin? About how much you love and respect and trust him. Did your image makers tell you to say that? It's in terrible taste.'

'No, it isn't. It's what you have to do nowadays. I know that without any help from "image makers".' Tanya stumbled over these difficult English words which have immigrated into Russia along with the new life. 'If I didn't mention Putin, our local FSB man would be round to see me in the shop tomorrow to complain I wasn't saying what everybody says. That's the kind of life we business people lead now.'

'So what if he came round and said that?'

'So nothing. He would just demand a bribe.'

'What for?'

'To "forget" what I hadn't said.'

'Listen, aren't you tired of all this?'

'No. If I need to kiss Putin's backside to get another couple of shops I'll do it.'

'But what do you mean by "get"? You just buy them, don't you? Pay for them, and that's it?'

'No, things are different now. To "get" something you have to earn the right from the bureaucrats to buy the shop with your own money. Russian capitalism, it's called. Personally I like it.

When I tire of it I'll buy myself citizenship somewhere and move on.'

We parted. Of course Tanya got elected. She's said not to be bad. She puts her heart into battling for the poor of Moscow. She's organised another canteen for the homeless and refugees, she's bought another three supermarkets, and she often speaks on television in praise of our modern times. She rang recently and asked me to write an article about her. I did. The one you are reading right now. She asked to read it before it was published, was horrified and said, 'It's all true.' She made me promise not to publish it in Russia before her death.

'How about abroad?'

'Go ahead. Let them know what our money smells of.'

So now you do.

Misha and Lena

Misha was married to Lena, my schoolfriend from early childhood. She had married him when they were at college in the late 1970s. At that time Misha was a very clever, talented boy who translated from German, who dubbed films while still a student at the Institute of Foreign Languages and whose future seemed very bright. When he graduated he was inundated with attractive offers of employment, not something that happened at all often.

Misha landed a job in the Ministry of Foreign Affairs, which was very prestigious, especially towards the end of the Soviet period. It was unusual for a boy without family connections to get into such a closed corporation as our MFA. Misha had none. He had been brought up by his grandmother, a humble cleaning woman. His mother had died suddenly, from a brain tumour, when Misha was only 14. His father had promptly abandoned his orphaned family and run off with another woman.

So there was Misha in the MFA. We were great friends. We would go on picnics together, grill kebabs in the forest over a campfire and enjoy ourselves thoroughly. Lena and I were very close, and Misha was keen to be friends too.

Underpinning our relationship were my two small children. When Misha came visiting he simply couldn't take his eyes off them. He would watch them with delight no matter what nonsense they got up to, talk to them and play with them for hours at a time.

All our friends knew that Misha very much wanted to have children. He was obsessed with it, but Lena was a talented linguist. She was writing her dissertation and kept postponing having a baby until after she had graduated in philological sciences.

Misha was very jumpy as a result. He gradually developed a complex about the fact that they did not have any children. He began to suffer himself and to torment all those around him, most of all Lena. However, Lena was made of stern stuff, and once she had made her mind up nothing was going to change it. She would defend her dissertation and get her degree, and after that she would get pregnant. That was all there was to it.

Misha reacted by taking to the bottle. He put up with his disappointment for as long as he could but then just went off the rails. At first he didn't drink a lot, and people laughed at it and teased him, but then his bouts began to last for several days at a time. He would disappear, and goodness knows where he was spending his nights. Later still he would drink for weeks at a time. Lena thought perhaps she should give in and not finish her dissertation, but how do you make a baby with a man who is permanently inebriated?

Then the new times came: Gorbachev, Yeltsin, and the only reason Misha wasn't fired for his chronic drinking (he would have been sacked instantly under the Communists) was that there was no one to replace him. MFA staff who knew languages and had experience of working on the other side of the Iron Curtain were suddenly worth their weight in gold. They abandoned the cash-strapped MFA to work for the commercial firms and branches of foreign companies that were springing up. Misha got no offers, even though the Germans were the first to dash into the Russian market and translators from German were the most sought after of all.

Even at the MFA Misha's days were numbered, and he was eventually fired. Late one night at the very end of 1996, in December when there was about 30 degrees of frost, someone rang my doorbell. It was Lena, wearing only her nightdress under a coat. You just don't walk around Moscow dressed like that in winter, and certainly not if you are Lena, who was always immaculately turned out. She was an equable, well brought-up and intelligent young woman. Now, however, one foot was bare as if she were some totally destitute person without a home to go to, while on the other foot the top of a half-laced boot was flapping like a flag. My friend was shivering as if she had fallen through ice and just been pulled out of the freezing water. Something had frightened her half to death, and the shock had made her incoherent.

'Misha, Misha,' she repeated over and over again, sobbing loudly, quite unlike her usual self and seemingly unaware of where she was or of the people around her.

The children had woken up by now and came quietly out of their room. They stood by Lena, spellbound by an anguish they could not understand. Lena finally noticed them, pulled herself together, took a tranquilliser with a glass of water and began to explain what had happened.

Misha had been away from home for three nights in a row. Lena wasn't really expecting him back. She had got used to his drinking bouts and his absences, and so she went to bed. She had to go to the institute early in the morning. Shortly after midnight, however, Misha suddenly turned up. This was unusual.

This time he came straight in through the door and, just as he was, in his winter coat and dirty shoes, unwashed and stinking, walked into the bedroom and stood over Lena in menacing silence, staring at her in the semi-darkness. He seemed completely out of his mind. His black eyes were shining unnaturally, and there was a silvery gleam on his cheeks. His once handsome face was contorted in a grimace. Lena pulled the covers up and said nothing.

She knew from bitter experience of living with an incipient alcoholic that it was pointless to say anything. Despite appearances, you were talking to someone who could not hear. You just had to wait for him to fall asleep.

Misha, however, moved closer to the bed and said, 'That's it . . . It's all your fault . . . that I drink . . . and now I am going to kill you.'

Lena heard a note of quiet determination in Misha's voice that left no room for doubt. She jumped up and rushed round the room. At first Misha cornered her on the balcony, and she thought she'd had it, but drunks are clumsy and she was able to slip past him, grab some things by the front door and run out across the snow to the nearest refuge, my block of flats.

After that they got divorced, and although neither was at all maudlin by nature, they would both come to sob in my kitchen and tell me how much they loved each other but how they could never live together again.

I continued to see Misha, although increasingly rarely. He would drop by occasionally, mainly to ask for money, because he was continuing to drink and very hard up. He had only the occasional translation to make ends meet.

On his rare sober visits, he told me he was trying to stop drinking and start a new life. He had developed an interest in Orthodox Christianity, was reading religious books, had been baptised, had found a confessor whom he trusted, was going to confession and communion and finding solace in that. He was convinced that redemption was possible. Misha's outward appearance was not, however, that of someone on the road to salvation. He was in a bad way, his hair greasy and unkempt. He wore a threadbare and obviously second-hand black coat which was much too short for him, and when I asked where he was living, blurted out some nonsense to the effect that nobody understood him and it was so difficult to live anywhere when nobody understands you.

Under Yeltsin this was not a particularly unusual or surprising sight. A lot of penniless people were wandering the streets, people who had been well-educated, respectable citizens but who had lost their jobs and taken to drink when they could find no place for themselves in the new reality. It was precisely on this fertile ground of general dissatisfaction, unemployment and the redundancy of many who had been members of the professions in the Soviet period that Orthodoxy became fashionable, and all the failures who had lost their work, their spouses or their reasons for being ran to the Church, although not all of them by any means were genuine believers.

Accordingly Misha was seen as one of many people on that path. He came to see me one time, sober and yet joyful, and invited me to congratulate him. He had become a father the day before, he had a son. We hastened to say how pleased we were: at last his dream had come true. For some reason, however, Misha was not in the seventh heaven we expected.

The boy was called Nikita. A long time before, when Misha was still married to Lena, he had often mused that if he had a son he would call him Nikita.

'Who is Nikita's mother?' I asked cautiously.

'A young girl.'

'Do you live with her? Are you married . . . or going to get married?'

'No. Her parents don't like me.'

'Then rent a flat and live with your son. That is so important.'

'I haven't got any money.'

'Start earning some.'

'I don't want to and I can't. I just can't – it's simply not possible.'

He cut off any further attempts at conversation.

More than a year passed. Yeltsin abdicated power, nominating Putin as his successor. The Second Chechen War started. Putin was constantly on television. One moment he was flying a military aircraft, the next issuing instructions in Chechnya. The election, a foregone conclusion, was approaching.

Late one night Lena rang. 'Do you know what,' she said in a barely recognisable voice, completely hoarse, like the voice of a singer after a concert. 'I have just had a phone call. Misha has killed the woman he was living with. She has left a 14-year-old son from her first marriage. The boy was in the flat when it happened. Misha got drunk. Apparently the woman was older than him, felt sorry for him and drank with him so he wouldn't feel so lonely. Anyway, they were drinking together yesterday when Misha took a knife and said what he said to me: "I am going to kill you."'

Lena burst into tears. 'It could have been me,' she said. 'Do you remember? You were all trying to persuade me not to get divorced. You said he would sort himself out, that he needed treatment. But he would just have killed me.'

The court was lenient on Misha, especially after the story of his life was related. He was sentenced to four and a half years. Not much for a murder. The court held that he was not mentally ill or suffering from diminished responsibility, despite his alcoholism.

Misha was sent to a labour camp in Mordovia, in the depths of the forests. Six months later, the commandant of the camp came to see Lena in her Moscow flat, where by now she was living with a new husband and the son she had finally had. The commandant was not the brightest of men but evidently had a kind heart. The decision to visit Lena was his own. He considered it his duty, as he was in the capital on business, to find her, despite the fact that she was divorced from Misha, and tell her that 'her Michael' (as the commandant described him, to the horror of her new husband) was the best prisoner he had ever met, the most literate and hard-working person in the camp. The commandant, who evidently had a pedagogical bent, had appointed him to look after the prisoners' library, and Misha had completely reorganised it. He was reading a lot himself and working with the other criminals in the role of psychologist. Misha had single-handedly constructed a wooden church inside the camp's barbed wire and was preparing to become a monk. He was corresponding with a monastery to find guidance on his chosen path. The commandant also informed Lena that he supported Misha's monastic inclinations, since he could see only good coming from them for his contingent of murderers, rapists and old lags. At Misha's request he was going to buy church plate in the shop of the Moscow Patriarchate and take it back to the camp.

The jailer ended by promising he would intercede to have Misha's sentence reduced on the grounds of exemplary conduct.

'Lena, are you not glad?' he asked the divorced wife, noticing that she was practically in tears.

'I am frightened,' she replied.

'There's no need for that,' Misha's commandant replied. 'He has changed a lot, he isn't dangerous. He doesn't drink any more, and he won't kill anyone else. At least, I don't think he will.'

The commandant smoothed his hair, drank his tea, rubbed his hands together as if intending to produce fire from his palms, and added, 'To tell the truth, I am a bit sorry he will be leaving.'

We started readying ourselves for whatever might transpire. Misha might resurface in Moscow at any moment. In the event it was 2001 before he reappeared. For a few weeks he bobbed around, again with nowhere to stay, his German forgotten, by now completely incapable of adapting to the new life.

I had known he was in Moscow for a long time, but we met by chance on Tverskoy Boulevard. When our paths crossed I barely recognised the features which had once been so familiar. We sat down on a bench and spoke for three hours or so without a break. He didn't ask about my children, and I didn't ask about his son. Misha simply needed someone to talk to, someone to hear him out.

He talked the whole time about choosing the right monastery. I looked closely at the man in front of me. Of the earlier Misha, or what he had been in his youth, almost nothing remained. He looked grey, old and flabby. Of the talent you once could have felt in him, nothing could be seen. There was only a grudge against fate, and a lot of prison slang. In addition, Misha treated me to a lot of banal nonsense about the meaning of life, in the way it is written about in crude brochures for the barely literate. I realised the kind of library they must have in the camp in Mordovia.

'Have you found a job?'

'Where? The pay is low everywhere and they expect a lot.'

'Well, we're all in that situation now. We just have to put up with it . . .' I began.

Misha interrupted me. 'Well, I don't want to be like everybody else.'

He certainly had that in spades.

'How are you getting on with the monastery?'

'They can't take me for the time being. There's a queue and you have to pull strings even for that. You have to know people. Having been in prison doesn't help.'

'I suppose it's understandable. You really haven't been out of prison for long.'

'Well, I don't understand it.' Misha became aggressive.

'What are you planning to do?'

'I shall go into that little church.' Misha gestured behind him, and there indeed stood one of the oldest churches in Moscow, solidly rooted in the years. 'I'll ask them to take me on as a watchman. They told me you need the right number of points on your CV to get into a monastery.'

We both laughed. Only someone born in the USSR and who had spent a fair part of his conscious life there knew how typically Soviet that approach was to getting a good job when you couldn't do it through string-pulling. And here we were, talking about a monastery, faith, religion, the rules of the Church, which couldn't be further removed from the everyday reality of the Soviet way of life. We fell about laughing at the idea.

'It's weird,' Misha said, 'how in the new Russia the ways of Orthodoxy and of Soviet life have suddenly come together.'

From beneath the dropsical eyelids of a man with kidney or heart trouble the old Misha suddenly glanced at me, merry, on the ball, playful, gallant.

'Of course they have. Aren't you afraid the Church you are so keen to sign up to has turned into that local committee of the Young Communist League you once fled from? That everything has just been repainted in new colours, and when you finally get into the monastery you'll be bitterly disappointed and . . .'

I bit my tongue. No glib words came to mind.

'You were going to say I would kill someone again, blaming my problems on them?'

'No, of course not,' I stammered, although that was exactly what I had been about to say. Misha and I seemed to be back on the same wavelength.

'That is exactly what you were going to say. I can only reply that I am afraid myself, of course, but I have nowhere else to go. If I stay here I shall certainly end up in prison again. I felt better in prison, in a confined space; the monastery is like a labour camp, only with different guards. I need to live under guard. I can't control myself, seeing the kind of life we have around us.'

'And what kind of life is that?'

'Cynical. I can't bear cynicism. That is why I started drinking.'

'But why did you kill your woman friend? Was she cynical?'

'No, she was a very good person, and I can't remember why I killed her. I was drunk.'

'So, at all events you won't stay in the world.'

'Under no circumstances. I couldn't stand it.'

I didn't meet Misha again, but I do know that he didn't manage to get into a monastery. The paperwork dragged on. The Orthodox bureaucracy in Russia is much like the State bureaucracy, indifferent to anything that doesn't affect it directly. Misha went along to the Patriarchate, taking them forms, working as a church watchman, actually living in a church. He gradually started to drink again. He turned up at Lena's a couple of times asking for money. The first time she gave him 100 roubles, the second time she refused. She was quite right. She and her husband were not working to enable Misha to get drunk when he felt like it. Of course she was right.

Except that Misha threw himself under a Metro train. We heard about it much later, and only by chance. And we discovered that Misha, one of the most talented Russians I ever met, had been buried as homeless and 'unclaimed'. More exactly, they buried his ashes, because in such cases the remains are cremated. Nobody knows where his grave is.

Rinat

You can mount a frontal attack or you can make a detour. The compound of the Special Intelligence Regiment of the Ministry of Defence, its most elite subdivision, is not, of course, a place for civilians like me to be strolling around. Sometimes, however, it has to be done. I have been brought here by Rinat, one of the regimental officers. Rinat is a major. Nobody knows who his parents were. He was brought up in an orphanage. His face is oriental, with slanting eyes, and he speaks several Central Asian languages. His speciality was intelligence gathering. Rinat fought clandestinely in the Afghan War for years. He then infiltrated Tadjik armed bands in the mountains and on the Afghan–Tadjik border, catching drug smugglers red-handed. On behalf of the Russian government he also secretly helped some of the current presidents of former Soviet republics to come to power. Naturally, he spent a lot of time in Chechnya during both the first and the second Chechen wars. His chest is covered with medals.

Rinat and I are looking for a hole in the fence. He wants to show me the squalor in which, for all his medals, he lives in the officers' barracks; he wants to show me too the house in the military village which he had hoped to move into but found himself out of luck. Although this regiment is highly trained and very famous, we find the hole we are looking for. An impressive hole it is too, not just big enough for the two of us to squeeze through: you could drive a tank through it.

We walk on for five minutes, and there it is, the village where the spies live. It is morning. Around us we see the unsmiling faces of officers on their day off. The weather is far from cheering.

Churned-up clay squelches underfoot. We are not walking but slithering, looking down at the ground in order to maintain our footing.

I look up and, wondrous vision, see before me like a mirage among the other dismal five-storey buildings a fine new grey-green multi-storey block of flats.

'That's how it all started,' Rinat says. 'Of course, I wanted a flat. I've had enough of wandering the world. My son is growing up, and I am constantly away in wars.'

The major falls silent in mid-sentence and suddenly embarks on a manoeuvre that puzzles me. He hides his face and doubles over as if we are being shot at and need to find a trench to shelter in. Rinat whispers quietly that we should pretend not to know each other: he also asks me not to look ahead and not to wave my arms or attract attention.

'But what's wrong?' I ask. 'Is it an ambush?'

I'm joking, of course.

'We mustn't make him angry,' Rinat says softly, continuing his distracting manoeuvre. Like well-trained spies we quickly, deftly, but without fuss, change direction.

'Whom mustn't we annoy?' I enquire when Rinat raises his head with a sigh of relief, indicating that the danger has passed.

'Petrov, the deputy commanding officer.'

Our manoeuvring is explained by the fact that Petrov had been driving towards us. His car had pulled up to the fine new block of flats because that is where Petrov lives. Only after he had disappeared inside did Rinat relax and continue our stroll around the compound. We kept ending up back at the fine building, which Rinat gazed upon with longing and envy.

To tell the truth, I am perplexed. I know a little about Rinat's combat record, his fearlessness, and I am amazed. What is it, I wonder, that he fears most? Death?

'No, I have learned to live with death. I don't mean to boast.'

'Being captured?'

'Yes, I am afraid of that of course, because I know I would be tortured. I have seen it happen. But I am not all that afraid of being captured.'

'What then?'

'Probably peace, civilian life. It's something I know nothing about. I am not prepared for it.'

Rinat is 37. All he has done in his life is take part in wars. His body is covered in scars. He has peptic and duodenal ulcers, and his nerves are in tatters. He has constant agonising pain in his joints and cerebral spasms after several wounds to the head.

Recently, the major decided it was time to settle down, to come back from the wars to our ordinary world. He found he knew absolutely nothing about it. For example, who would give him a place to live? Surely he deserved a flat for all he had been through defending the interests of the State. Or some money?

As soon as Rinat started asking Petrov about such things, it became apparent that he could expect nothing. Rinat concluded that while he had been carrying out special government missions across mountains, countries and continents, his State had needed him and had rewarded him with medals and orders. As soon, however, as the major's health gave out and he decided to try to settle down, he found there was nothing waiting for him, and the military hierarchy were simply going to turn him out on the street. They were even going to expel him from the squalid nook in the officers' barracks where he and his son were presently sleeping.

Rinat has a son, Edik, whom he is bringing up on his own. The boy's mother died several years ago, and for a long time Edik lived alone in the officers' barracks, waiting for his father to come back from his numerous wars and important combat missions.

'I know how to kill an enemy so he doesn't make a sound,' Rinat tells me. 'I can climb a mountain swiftly and silently and take out those who are occupying it. I am an excellent rock climber and mountaineer. I can "read" mountains from twigs and bushes and tell who is there and where they are hiding. I have a feel for mountains, they say it is a natural gift, but I am incapable of getting a flat. I am incapable of getting anything at all in civilian life.'

Before me is a helpless professional killer trained by the State. There are many like him now. The State sends people off to yet another war, they live in the midst of war for years, return and do not know what peaceful life is with its law and order. They take to drinking, join gangs, become hitmen, and their new masters pay them big money to take out those they say need to be murdered in the interests of the State.

And the State? It doesn't give a damn. Under Putin it has effectively ceased to interest itself in officers who have returned from the wars. It seems as if the State is actively engaged in ensuring that there are as many highly trained professional killers in criminal gangs as possible.

'Is that what you are thinking of going into, Rinat?'

'No, I don't want to, but if Edik and I find ourselves on the street, I can't rule it out. I can only do what I am trained to do.'

Rinat and I finally squelch through the mud and slush to a dismal shack. Called 'the three-storey building', it is the officers' barracks. We go up to the second floor, and behind a peeling door is a squalid, spartan room.

In the whole of his life the major has never had a home to call his own. First there was the orphanage in the Urals. Then there was the barracks of the military college he enrolled at from the orphanage. Later still, garrison hostels alternating with tents when he was on active service. He has been 16 years in the Army, a rolling stone under military oath. For the last eleven years Rinat has moved on constantly from one combat mission to the next. It is not a life that has led him to acquire possessions.

'But I was happy,' the major says. 'I never wanted to stop fighting. I thought it would last for ever.'

All that Rinat has acquired is now stored in one parachute bag. The major opens his standard-issue cupboard with an inventory number on its pathetic battered side and shows me the bag.

'Sling it over your shoulder and go off on your next mission,' he succinctly summarises his values.

A boy is sitting on the divan and looking at us sorrowfully: this is Edik.

I interrupt the major. 'You were married, though, so you must have had a household of some kind.'

'No, we had nothing. We didn't have time.'

While Rinat was fighting in Tadjikistan, helping the present President, Rakhmonov, to take power, he slipped away and got married in Kirghizia. The newlyweds had met during Rinat's previous combat mission in the city of Osh, where the girl lived and where Rinat had been sent because a bloody conflict had broken out there between ethnic groups.

They got married right there, their passion and love flaring up amid the butchery and the pain. Rinat then presented his young wife to his commanding officer. The commanding officer shrugged and asked him to leave his wife in Osh, because for a spy a sweetheart was an Achilles heel. Rinat left his wife behind and went back to Tadjikistan to join an armed group on the frontier.

One day his commanding officer told him that he had a son and that his wife had called him Edik. Later still, in June 1995, Rinat's young wife, a student at the local conservatory, was killed by people who had discovered whom she was married to. She had just turned 21 and that day had been on her way to sit her second-year exams.

At first Edik lived with his grandmother in Kirghizia. The boy was too little to live in officers' hostels, and in any case Rinat rarely spent the night even in the grim, unswept rooms the State provided for him. He was still engaged in secret operations and at large in the mountains of our country. He was severely wounded twice more and spent periods in various hospitals.

'Even so I did not want a different life,' Rinat says, 'but Edik was growing up.'

The time finally came when he decided to collect his son, and after that Edik stayed with his grandmother only when Rinat was away on six-month military missions.

We are sitting in their cold, dismal little room. Edik is a quiet boy with bright eyes which see everything. He is very grown up. He talks only when his father goes out and only when he is asked a question: the son of a spy, in a word. He understands that his father is going through a difficult period now, and that this is why in the next school year he wants to send Edik to the Cadet Officers' College. But the boy does not like this idea.

'I want to live at home,' he says calmly and in a very manly way, without any suggestion of whining. Nevertheless he repeats it several times: 'I want to live at home, at home.'

'And is this your home? Do you feel at home here?'

Edik is an honest boy. He knows that when you cannot tell the truth it is better to say nothing, and that is what he does.

Indeed, who could call this pen for combat officers, with the drunken bawling of contract soldiers on the other side of the thin walls, with its inventory of regulation furniture, 'home'? Edik knows, however, that they are trying to drive his father out even of here, so let this be home.

Relations between the regiment's commanders and the major began to sour when Rinat asked to be allocated a flat in that fine new building we had been walking around while hiding from the deputy commanding officer. The major supposed he was within his rights, since for many years he had been at the top of the waiting list for accommodation.

'When I asked Petrov he was indignant: "You haven't done enough for the regiment,"' Rinat relates. 'Can you believe it, that is exactly how he put it. I was very surprised and told him, "I have been fighting the whole time. I rescued pilots from a mountain when nobody else could find them. The State needs me."'

The major had, indeed, been put forward for the country's highest award of Hero of Russia for his actions when a military fighter aircraft crashed in the mountains of Chechnya near the village of Itum-Kale in June 2001. Several search-and-rescue teams went into the mountains to find the crew but without success. The commanders remembered Rinat with his unique experience of combat, his feel for the mountains and his ability to find men by reading twigs, sticks and leaves.

He found the dead airmen in just 24 hours. One body had been booby-trapped by the Chechen fighters, and Rinat made it safe. So the families have graves to tend.

The active service officers have a saying that commanders who lose their head in combat and in the mountains are best in civilian occupations. Rinat told Petrov, 'I know what kind of a hero you were in Chechnya, always skulking in staff headquarters.' The deputy commanding officer responded, 'Now you're really in the shit, Major. For that little remark I'll make you a down-and-out. I'll discharge you without accommodation. You'll be out on the street with that son of yours.'

Petrov set about implementing his threat with a vengeance. First he humiliated the major by setting him to decorate the parade ground and also to manage the regimental club, organising film shows for the soldiers.

Petrov next ordered Rinat to design posters for the parade ground (he is an excellent artist), which was the job of Petrov's wife. She simply ceased to turn up for work, and all the officers knew that Rinat was doing it instead while she took her ease in that fine new block of flats.

Then Edik was taken ill and had to go to hospital. The doctors told Rinat he should stay at his son's bedside. Rinat was constantly asking for time off, and Petrov, ignoring the medical certificate provided by the doctors and backdating the record, took to recording him absent without leave. Petrov convened an officers' court, manipulated the minutes and used them to remove the major from the waiting list for an apartment. He was agitating to have Rinat summarily dismissed from the Army without any privileges. In short, Rinat is in deep trouble.

'What have I done?' Rinat bows his head, aware that he is being outmanoeuvred.

The wars our country takes part in continue afterwards, wherever those who were involved in them find themselves. This means, primarily, within the subdivisions to which they return after completing their missions. The staff officers there are pitted in a fight to the death against the field officers. The latter find themselves discharged for disobedience, their past records ignored, with a barrage of insults hurled after them. Rinat is not the only one. The officers in the Army now divide into two unequal categories. The first are those who have genuinely taken part in combat operations, who have risked their lives, who have crawled their way through the mountains, burrowed into the snow and earth for days at a time. Many have been wounded on numerous occasions. You feel desperately sorry for them. It is difficult for them to find a place for themselves in the civilian life which seems so normal to us. They can't find a common language with the staff officers, who have also been in Chechnya, so they rebel and get drunk and feel terrible. The staff officers, as a rule, outmanoeuvre them at every opportunity: they bear false witness against them, they run to their superiors, they tell tales, they plot. Before you know it, the awkward squad are being lined up for discharge. What have they done? They have been themselves, of course. By the mere fact of their presence in the units, the field officers daily remind the staff officers who is who in this world.

And the staff officers? They rise through the ranks faster than a speeding bullet. They fix themselves up very nicely, get all the flats and dachas.

In the end Rinat gave up. He gave up the Army which he loved so much and went off to who knows where with Edik, a homeless, penniless field officer. I fear for him, because I can guess where he has gone. I fear for all of us.

More Stories from the Provinces

The Old Man from Irkutsk

The winter of Putin's third year in office, 2002–3, was very cold. We are a northern country, of course: Siberia, bears, furs, all that sort of thing. So you might expect we would be ready for it.

Unfortunately everything always takes us by surprise, like snow falling off a roof onto your head. This includes our frosts, which is why the following terrible events came to pass.

In Irkutsk, in the depths of Siberia, an old man was found frozen to the floor of his flat. He was past 80, an ordinary pensioner, one of those the emergency services refuse to turn out for because they are just too old. Their response to a telephone call is a straightforward and unreflecting: 'Well, what do you expect? Of course he's feeling ill. It's his age.' This elderly citizen lived alone, a veteran of the Second World War, one of those who freed the world from Nazism, with medals and a State pension. He was one of those to whom President Putin sends greetings on 9 May, Victory Day, wishing him happiness and good health. Our old men, our war veterans unspoiled by too much attention from the State, weep over these form letters with their facsimile signature. Anyway, in January 2003, this old man died of hypothermia. He froze to the floor where he fell. His name was Ivanov, the most common Russian surname. There are hundreds of thousands of Ivanovs in Russia.

War veteran Ivanov froze to the floor because his flat was unheated. It should have been heated, of course, like all the flats in the block where he lived; like all the blocks of flats in Irkutsk in the third year of Putin's stewardship.

Why did this happen? The explanation is simple. The heating

pipes wore out throughout Russia, because they had been in service since Soviet times, and those times have been gone for more than a decade, and thank God for that. For a long time the pipes leaked and leaked, and Communal Services, whose responsibility they are, did nothing about it. Communal Services is a centralised, State-run monopoly. Every month we have to pay them quite a substantial sum for their non-existent technical support, but they virtually ignore us, carry on not doing their job and periodically demand a rate increase. The government gives way, but those employed by Communal Services are so used to doing nothing that that is what they continue to do.

The day finally came when the monopolised pipes which had been leaking for so long, and which had not been repaired for so long, burst. At that moment, in the middle of winter, in severe frosts, it was discovered that there was no way of replacing them. Communal Services had no money to pay for this. Nobody knew what the money we had been paying them had been spent on. All the communal facilities which had been in service since the Soviet period had finally deteriorated. The fact that there was nothing to replace them with was not to be expected because we produce thousands of kilometres of all sorts of pipes every year. 'The country has no funds available for this purpose,' the agents of Putin's government announced with a shrug, as if it was nothing to do with them. 'What do you mean there is no money?' the opposition politicians parried feebly, making their customary show of standing up for the rights of the people. The President publicly ticked off the Prime Minister. And that was the end of it. The politicians agreed to differ. There was no scandal. The government did not resign. Even the appropriate minister did not resign. So what if people had to keep pacing around their flats to keep warm, sleeping and eating in their winter coats and felt boots? The pipes would be repaired come the summer.

The old man who died was hacked with crowbars off the icy floor by the other people living in his communal flat and quietly buried in the frozen Siberian earth. No period of mourning was declared.

The President pretended that this had not happened in his country or to a member of his electorate. He remained totally aloof during the funeral and the country swallowed his silence. In order to consolidate his position, Putin even changed tack. He gave a grim speech to the effect that terrorists were responsible for everything wrong in Russia and that the State's main priority was the destruction of international terrorism in Chechnya. Apart from that, national life was back on the rails. The public could not be allowed to reflect on the imperfection of the world developing before their eyes.

Soon it was spring. Putin began preparing for his re-election in 2004. There could be no place for regret at defeats suffered, only joy at victories. Accordingly, a whole lot of new holidays were announced; in fact, an unheard-of quantity of them. Including the observance of Lent.

The nearer summer came, the less people talked about the complete collapse of Russia's heating infrastructure the previous winter. Citizens were called upon to rejoice in great numbers at the preparations for celebrating the tercentenary of St Petersburg, and to take pride in the sumptuousness of refurbished Tsarist palaces fit to dazzle the world's elite with their splendour. And that is exactly what happened.

Putin invited all the world's leaders to St Petersburg, and the city was subjected to an insensitive repainting of façades. The old man in Irkutsk, and indeed all the old men in St Petersburg, were forgotten by everyone, including Putin.

'Mind you, if he had died in Moscow . . .' the metropolitan pundits would say, suggesting that then there would have been a scandal and a half, and that the authorities would have replaced the pipes before next winter.

Schroeder, Bush, Chirac, Blair and many other VIPs proceeded to our northern capital and effectively crowned Putin as their equal. They were received with pomp and ceremony. They pretended to regard Putin with respect, and old Mr Ivanov and the millions of Russian pensioners who can barely make ends meet weren't given a thought. Putin's reign reached its high point, and almost nobody noticed. He decided to base his power solely on the oligarchs, the billionaires who own Russia's oil and gas reserves. Putin is friends with some oligarchs and at war with others, and this is called statecraft. There is no place for the people in this scheme of things. Moscow is life-giving warmth and light, while the provinces are its pale reflection, and those who inhabit them might as well be living on the moon.

Kamchatka: The Struggle to Survive

Kamchatka is at the furthest reach of Russia. The flight from Moscow takes more than ten hours. The planes on the Petropavlovsk–Kamchatsky route are pretty basic and predispose you to muse on the immensity of our complicated Motherland and about the fact that only a tiny proportion of our people live in Moscow, playing their big political games, setting up their idols and knocking them down, and believing that they control this enormous country.

Kamchatka is a good place to recognise how remote the Russian provinces are from the capital. In fact, distance has nothing to do with it. The provinces live differently, they breathe a different air, and this is where the real Russia is to be found.

There are as many sailors living in Kamchatka as there are fishermen, indeed even more. Despite the massive cutbacks in the armed forces, the power base here remains the same: whoever the Kamchatka Flotilla of the Pacific Fleet votes for wins the elections.

As you might expect in a coastal town, there is a predominance of black and navy-blue everywhere: reefer jackets, sailors' vests, peakless caps. The only thing missing is the fleet's legendary smartness. The jackets you see are worn, the vests much laundered, the caps faded.

Alexey Dikiy is the commander of a nuclear hunter-killer submarine, the *Vilyuchinsk*. He is the elite of our fleet, and so is his vessel, part of the armament of the Kamchatka Flotilla.

Dikiy received an outstanding education in Leningrad – today's St Petersburg – and then made brilliant progress up the career ladder as a highly talented officer. By the time he was 34 he was a uniquely qualified submariner. In terms of the international military labour market, every month of service raised his value by thousands of dollars. Today, however, Alexey Dikiy, Captain First Class, is eking out a wretched existence, there is no other way of putting it. His home is a dreadful officers' hostel with peeling stairwells, half derelict and eery. Everybody who could has left this place for 'the mainland', throwing their military careers to the winds. The windows of many now uninhabited flats are dark. This is cold, hungry, inhospitable terrain. People have fled mainly from the poverty. Captain Dikiy tells me that in good weather he and other senior naval officers go fishing in order to put a decent meal on their tables.

On the table in his kitchen he has placed what our Motherland pays in return for irreproachable loyal service. Dikiy has just brought a captain's monthly rations home from his submarine in one of the fleet's bed sheets. The rations consist of two packets of shelled peas, two kilograms of buckwheat and rice in paper bags, two tins of the very cheapest tinned peas, two tins of Pacific herring and a bottle of vegetable oil.

'Is that all?'

'Yes. That's it.' Dikiy is not complaining, just confirming a fact. He is a strong and genuine man. More precisely, he is very Russian. He is used to privation. His loyalty is to the Motherland rather than to whoever happens to be her leader at any given time. If he allowed himself to think any other way, he would have been out of here long ago. The captain accepts that anything can happen, including famine, which is precisely what his rations evoke.

These tins and paper bags contain the month's supplies for the three members of Captain Dikiy's family. He has a wife, Larisa, who qualified as a radio-chemist. She has a degree from the prestigious Moscow Institute of Engineering and Physics, whose graduates are headhunted straight from their benches in the lecture room by the computer firms of Silicon Valley in California.

Larisa, however, living with her husband in a closed military township of the Pacific Fleet, is unemployed. This is a detail of no interest to naval headquarters or to the faraway Ministry of Defence. The recruitment policies of staff headquarters mean they stubbornly refuse to see the gold lying at their feet. Larisa cannot even get a teaching job in the school for submariners' children. All the posts are filled, and there is a waiting list. Unemployment among the non-military personnel here runs at 90 per cent.

The third member of Captain Dikiy's family is his daughter, Alisa, a schoolgirl in second grade. Her situation is also unenviable. There is nothing in this military township to bring out the abilities of Alisa or the other children. No sports centre, no dance floors, no computers. All the garrison's children can lay claim to is a dismal, dirty courtyard and a building with a video recorder and a selection of cartoons.

Truly, Kamchatka is at the outer reach of our land and at the extremity of State heartlessness. On the one hand we find here cutting-edge technology for the taking of human life, and on the other a troglodytic existence for those who supervise it. Everything relies entirely on personal enthusiasm and patriotism. There is no money, no glory and no future.

The place where Dikiy lives is called Rybachie. It is an hour's drive from Petropavlovsk-Kamchatsky, the capital of the Kamchatka Peninsula. Rybachie is perhaps the world's most famous closed military township, with a population of 20,000. It is the symbol and the vanguard of the Russian nuclear fleet. The township is packed with the most modern types of weaponry. This is where Russia's east-facing nuclear shield is situated, and where those who keep it intact and in working order live.

Captain Dikiy's submarine is one of the most important constituents of this nuclear shield, from which it follows that Dikiy himself is a vital component. His submarine is a technologically perfect piece of weaponry the like of which is to be found nowhere else in the world. It has the capability to destroy entire surface flotillas and the best submarines of the world's powers, including the US. Under Dikiy's command is a unique weapon armed with nuclear missiles and an impressive array of torpedoes. While we have such a defence capability, Russia is not seriously vulnerable, at least not from the direction of the Pacific Ocean.

Captain Dikiy himself, however, is highly vulnerable, and primarily from the direction of the State he serves. But he rarely thinks along those lines. Like many other officers, he is skilled at surviving without any money at all. His salary is low and paid irregularly, often as much as six months late.

When there is no money, Dikiy declines to eat on board his submarine (though officers are entitled to meals there). He takes home his entitlement in the form of a packed meal and shares it with his family. He has no other way of feeding them. As a result, Dikiy is a pale shadow of a man. He is unconscionably thin. His face has an unhealthy pallor, and it is clear why: the captain of the main constituent of Russia's nuclear shield is undernourished.

Of course, constantly being in a radiation zone also takes its toll. In the past this had its compensations, because submariners were highly eligible as bachelors, but everything has changed. Nowadays the girls look away when naval officers walk past.

'Actually, the poverty is not the real problem,' Dikiy says. He is an ascetic, a penniless romantic, an officer to the marrow of his bones, almost a saint in our times when all values are assessed in the cynical language of the dollar. 'You can live with poverty as long as you have a clear goal and understandable operational tasks. Our real misfortune is the parlous state of the country's nuclear fleet, the sense of hopelessness. They don't seem to understand in Moscow that these armaments have to be taken seriously. In ten years' time, if the present level of financing is maintained, there will either be nothing here in Rybachie, or NATO will be refuelling at our piers.'

In order to escape from the hopelessness of what is occurring in front of his eyes, Dikiy has decided to continue his studies at the General Headquarters Academy. He wants to write a dissertation about the state of Russia's national security at the end of the twentieth and beginning of the twenty-first centuries. He hopes when he has concluded his research to be able to give an academically grounded answer to the question that troubles him: In whose interests was it to undermine Russia's national security?

His interim conclusions are not favourable to Moscow, but the captain is not antagonistic or offended at what has been going on. He thinks it is appalling that Moscow behaves as it does, but there is nothing to be done about it. Except to tough it out, because we are stronger and more intelligent than our superiors.

Dikiy's job means his life is not his own. His cannot do things which everybody else can. In order to be on five-minute standby for his submarine, he can never go off anywhere. He must always be contactable. He can't just go into the countryside berrying, picking mushrooms or walking with friends. He has to live at the post he has accepted and cannot pass it over to anyone else. He has to be with his officers to make sure they do not become demoralised in these difficult times. He has to find time to look in at the barracks to keep a fatherly eye on what the ratings are getting up to. He is a busy man.

Many a military officer, living like a beggar much as Captain Dikiy does, can at least go out to earn a bit on the side after a day's work, feed his family and afford to buy clothes and even his uniform (a majority of officers actually have to do this). Captain Dikiy has neither the time nor the opportunity to do so. In the short hours that remain after work he is literally *required* to relax, to catch up on his sleep, to restore his equanimity. When he boards his submarine he must be relaxed. It is a requirement of the job. The consequences of nervous debility could be catastrophic.

'I have to be as calm and balanced at work,' Dikiy explains, 'as if I had just come back from holiday, as if everything was sorted and I didn't have to worry about how I am going to feed my wife and daughter tomorrow.'

'You say you have to. It seems to me that this is viewing the situation the wrong way round. You are serving the State, and so surely it is up to the State to create the right conditions for you to come to work in a calm frame of mind.'

Dikiy smiles a rather patronising smile, and I am not sure who this strange, tough, special man is feeling more condescending towards: me for asking such questions, or the State which spurns those who serve it best. It turns out that it is towards me.

'The State is not able to do that at present,' the captain says finally. 'It isn't, and there's an end to the matter. What point is there in demanding something that isn't there? I am a realist and not quick to anger. All the sentimentalists and the bad-tempered people left here long ago. They resigned from the Navy.'

'I still do not understand, though, why you yourself have not resigned. You are a nuclear specialist with an engineering qualification. I am quite sure you could find yourself a decent job.'

'I can't resign because I cannot abandon my ship. I am a commander, not one of the ratings. There is no one to replace me. If I left, I would feel a traitor.'

'A traitor to whom? The State, surely, has betrayed you?'

'In time the State will come to its senses. For now we just have to be patient and preserve our nuclear fleet. That is what I am doing. Even if the Ministry of Defence pursues a policy of betrayal, my duty is to Russia. I am defending the people of Russia, not the State bureaucracy.'

There you have the portrait of a Russian submarine officer in our times. He is stuck out there at the furthest reach of our land, and, true to his military oath, he daily covers the embrasure with his own body because there is nothing else to cover it with.

In order to fulfil his obligations in the midst of the profound financial malaise which has befallen the armed forces, complete dedication is demanded of the commander. Every day he leaves home at precisely 7.20 in the morning and returns at 10.40 at night.

He is on board his submarine for ten hours and more. There is no other way. The Navy is falling apart before our eyes, and with technology which is not being serviced and properly maintained, incidents are possible at any moment, including a major disaster. The only thing that hasn't changed at all is the raising of the flag. This ritual is observed every day at 8 a.m., come hurricane, blizzard, accident or change of government.

Incidentally, Dikiy walks from his home to where the *Vilyuchinsk* is moored. It takes him precisely 40 minutes. He walks not because the exercise is good for him but because, of course, he doesn't have the money for a car of his own, and because no other transport is provided by the Navy. Actually, it is laid up. The Second Flotilla, to which the *Vilyuchinsk* belongs, is in the throes of a fuel crisis, as indeed is the rest of Kamchatka. No cars or buses run to the jetties. The Navy does not have enough petrol. No petrol in a country selling oil to all and sundry! But that is the least of it. What if they run out of bread? The garrison is constantly in debt to the local bread factory, which goes on supplying the ships on tick.

Can you believe it? The service personnel who maintain the nuclear shield of an international superpower are being fed on charity!

I wonder how the President feels when he attends the G8 summit meetings.

Well, okay. All the officers in Rybachie walk to work in the mornings. On the road the officers' corps is usually buzzing like an angry beehive. They are discussing the questions on all their minds: How long can they put up with this situation? What kind of an abyss are we rushing towards?

Their heated political discussions are fuelled by the view in front of them. As you walk towards No. 5 Pier, for example, where the *Vilyuchinsk* is moored, you can contemplate Khlebalkin Island, where there is a derelict ship-repair yard. Two or three years ago, 15 or 16 submarines would be in the Khlebalkin yard for servicing. Today the surface of the water is calm and mirror-like, and not a single ailing vessel is to be seen. The officers were informed that even the servicing of submarines was now subject to a regime of rigorous economy.

'It's an appalling sight,' Dikiy says. 'We know exactly what it signifies. Our equipment must be properly maintained. You can't just go on expecting miracles. Submarines are not like spry old men who never need to see a doctor. Accidents are inevitable.'

This disintegration has demoralised some of the Rybachie officers completely. It has turned others to debauchery. They have seen it all in the garrison of late: wholly bizarre behaviour and suicides.

'The present situation makes the officers bitter,' Dikiy tells me. 'That is why I am so insistent that everybody should be there for the raising of the flag on the dot of 8.00. The men should see the eyes of their commander, and read in them that everything is in order, everything is being held steady, we are continuing to fulfil our duty no matter what. In spite of everything.'

'Officers' bullshit! Fine words for soft heads!' Many reading these lines may dismiss Dikiy's sentiments in that way. To some extent they will be right. These really are lofty sentiments, but the situation of those officers who have not yet resigned from the disintegrating Pacific Fleet is that today they continue to perform their demanding duties solely because those fine words are their anchor. They are men with ideals and principles. That's why they are in the Navy. They volunteered for the submarines because of the prestige and in the expectation of dazzling military careers with high salaries. They have known different times and expect them to continue.

As real life does not have the consistency of a film or a novel, the sublime coexists very happily in Rybachie with the ridiculous and the routine.

'It's impossible to live the way your husband does! Sometimes at least a man needs time to himself!'

Larisa Dikiy is a chortling beauty born in Zhitomir in Ukraine, a woman who has sacrificed her own life to live on the verge of starvation so that her husband can fulfil his duty. She laughs mischievously in reply: 'Well, actually I rather like things the way they are. At least I always know where my husband is! He has nowhere to hide from me, so I'm saved all those pangs of jealousy!'

Dikiy is standing beside us. He smiles an awkward smile, like a schoolboy who has just received a declaration of love from the prettiest girl in his class. I discover that the captain is a shy man. He blushes. I could almost weep. I see clearly that the enormous burden of responsibility the commander of a nuclear submarine bears is completely incompatible not just with his standard of living and way of life but also with his age and appearance.

At home, without his uniform, Alexey Dikiy, Captain First Class, looks just like the boy who comes top of the class, thin and melancholy. By Moscow criteria, where young people still mature rather late, that is precisely the situation. Dikiy, remember, is only 34.

'But you have already clocked up 32 years of service in the Navy. It's time you retired!' says Larisa.

'Actually, I could,' the captain says, again embarrassed.

'What do you mean? You joined the fleet when you were two? Like the son of a noble family who was registered in a regiment when he was born and by the time he came of age already had a good service record and epaulettes?' I press him for an answer.

The captain smiles. I can see he is looking forward to what he is going to tell me. His father was indeed a naval officer, now, of course, retired. Dikiy grew up in Sevastopol, at the Black Sea naval base. 'As regards my 32-year service record at 34 years of age . . .' he begins, but is promptly interrupted by his vivacious wife.

'It means that he has spent his entire service life in the most difficult sector of all, the submarine fleet, in the immediate vicinity of reactors and nuclear weapons. One year's service there is counted as three.'

'You don't feel that on those grounds alone the State should long ago have showered you with gold?' I persist. 'Are you not insulted that you have to share your dinner between three people as if you were a student?'

'No. I am not insulted,' he replies calmly and confidently. 'It would be quite senseless for us submariners to come out on strike. In our closed city everybody lives just the same way I do. We survive because we help each other to survive. We are constantly borrowing and reborrowing food and money from each other.'

'If somebody's relatives send them a food parcel, that family will immediately organise a feast,' Larisa tells me. 'We have a visiting circle. We get fattened up. That's how we live.'

'Do your parents send you parcels from Ukraine?'

'Yes, of course. And then we feed all our equally hungry friends.'

She laughs loudly.

As one of our writers put it, you could make nails out of these people.

It is a curious fact that the years are passing — a great deal of time already separates us from the fall of the Communist Party — yet certain habits from the past remain untouched. Foremost among them is a pathological lack of respect for people, especially those who, in spite of everything, work devotedly and selflessly, who truly love the cause they are serving. The government has never learned how to say thank you to people who are dedicated to serving our country. You are working hard? Well, great, carry right on until you snuff it or we break your heart. The authorities become more brazen by the day, crushing the will of the very best of our citizens.

With the single-mindedness of a maniac, they stake their money on the worst.

There is no doubt that Communism was a dead loss for Russia, but what we have today is even worse.

I continue my discussion of lofty matters with Captain Dikiy at the central control point of the *Vilyuchinsk*. Rybachie is completely closed to outsiders and the inquisitive, and even officers' wives are not allowed access to the classified piers. For me, however, Military Intelligence has unexpectedly made an exception.

The predatory, combative ethos of the *Vilyuchinsk* is evident already from the shore. On the bow, on a black background, is a daunting piece of artwork: a grinning killer whale's head. The naval artist in his desire to make the monster as intimidating as possible has given it a good many more teeth than are likely to be encountered in nature. The whale's depiction there is not random. From the day it was built, the submarine was called *Kasatka*, 'Killer Whale', and it was renamed only recently. Quite why is a puzzle to the officers, but they have no problem with it.

My introductory tour provides me with an extremely important insight, which is probably why I was allowed onto the submarine in the first place. I wander past the mouth of a terrifying volcano – God forbid it should ever be stoked up the wrong way. An atomic reactor plus nuclear missiles is an explosive mixture. The submarine is packed with nuclear weapons, the economy is in crisis, and the armed forces are in a state of disarray. What could be more scary than that?

As we continue the tour, Dikiy hammers his views home, and in ideological matters he is really quite pedantic. There can be no compromises in the armed forces, no matter what changes are taking place in society. He categorically rejects the notion of a right to disobey a 'criminal order', an idea that has been circulating stubbornly through Army units since 1991. His view is that giving an inch, allowing a subordinate to fail to carry out even a single instruction or order because he considers it foolish or inappropriate, will cause the whole system to fall apart in a domino effect. The Army is a pyramidal structure, and you cannot take that risk.

I see that both Captain Dikiy and the others who join in our conversation, all of them serving officers whose uniforms are decorated with ribbons for heroic submarine campaigns lasting many months, discriminate between two concepts. There is the Motherland, which they serve, and there is Moscow, with which they are in a state of conflict. There are, they say, two separate states: Russia and her capital city.

The officers are frank. Viewed from Kamchatka, nothing of what goes on in the Department of the Armed Forces makes any sense. Why does the Ministry of Defence obstinately refuse to pay for the maintenance of the nuclear submarine fleet, when it knows full well that it is not only impossible but indeed categorically forbidden for them to undertake such work locally using their own resources? Why do they mercilessly write off ten- to fourteen-year-old vessels which still have many years of life in them? Why, in fact, are they systematically turning their nuclear shield, created by the efforts of the entire nation, into a leaky old sieve? And at a time when a real threat exists, primarily in the form of large numbers of Chinese nuclear submarines constantly lurking adjacent to Russia's territory?

Also present on my exploration of the *Vilyuchinsk* is the most important person in the region, Valery Dorogin, Vice Admiral of Kamchatka and commander of the North-East Group of Troops and Forces. Shortly afterwards Dorogin is to end his military career to become a Deputy of the State Duma. The officers speak frankly in his presence, in no way inhibited by his seniority. One feels none of the hierarchical pressure or barriers of rank which are usual in a military setting.

In large measure this is because Dorogin is flesh of the flesh of Rybachie. There is nothing the officers and commander are going to conceal from each other. Dorogin has served here, in this closed naval township, for almost 20 years. For a long time he was, like Dikiy, commander of a nuclear submarine. Now his elder son, Denis Dorogin, is serving in Rybachie. Just like everyone else, the commander walks to the pier in the morning. Like everyone else he observes the disintegration. Like everyone else he is here without any means of subsistence, waiting for friends to 'fatten him up'.

The North-East Group, the agglomeration to which Kamchatka belongs together with Chukotka and Magadan Provinces, has been set up again as a result of the swingeing cutbacks. A similar grouping existed before the 1917 Revolution and under the Bolsheviks in the 1930s.

In any grouping one category of troops inevitably dominates.

In Kamchatka, home of the nuclear shield, it is predictably the submarines, and this is why a vice admiral is in command. Accordingly, he has under him infantry and coastal troops, aviation and anti-aircraft defence forces. At first there was a certain amount of contention and dissent, but then everything settled down. To a large extent this was due to Dorogin's influence. He is a legend on Kamchatka.

The vice admiral has spent 33 years in the Navy. His total service record is 48 years because of his time in the submarines. However, the legend of Dorogin is based not on his military past but on the present. He lives in Petropavlovsk-Kamchatsky. Until recently his monthly salary as the military man responsible for an enormous territory and second in rank only to the governors of three major Russian provinces was 3,600 roubles, or just over 100 dollars.

In reality, as we say in Russia, along with his pension, which he paid up long ago, he receives just under 5,000 roubles a month. By way of a comparison, a city bus driver in Petropavlovsk-Kamchatsky earns 6,000 roubles a month.

Dorogin lives in a military apartment on Morskaya Street, in exactly the same conditions as the other officers. There is no hot water, and it is cold, draughty and uncomfortable.

'Why don't you just buy a basic boiler?'

'We don't have the money. If we get some we'll buy one.'

The thing Dorogin values most is his reputation. His life is ascetic. The apartment is not bare, but there is no way it befits an admiral. His most precious possessions are concentrated in his study. These are nautical knick-knacks from decommissioned ships which once served in the Russian Far East. His great love is naval history.

'What about your house in the country? You must have a dacha. Every admiral in Russia has one.'

'I do, certainly,' Dorogin replies. 'And what a dacha. Oh, dear! We'll go and take a look at it tomorrow, otherwise you won't believe it.'

Tomorrow arrives and I see a patch of land planted with

potatoes and cucumbers on the outskirts of Petropavlovsk-Kamchatsky. These vegetables will feed the vice admiral's family over the winter. A decommissioned iron railway carriage stands on bricks in the midst of the vegetable garden: a place to work. If we compare it with Moscow expectations about the living standards of a military commander, it is a complete disgrace.

Kamchatka, as we have seen, is not Moscow. Everything here is more straightforward and more good-hearted. Some fishermen present me with a sack of red fish they have just caught, silversides. I give the fish to Galina, the vice admiral's wife, feeling a bit awkward because I am sure the wife of the Commander-in-Chief of Kamchatka must have tons of such fish brought to her door, but I simply have no way of cooking them myself.

To my great surprise, Galina thanks me effusively and bursts into tears. In her poverty she sees these fish as great good fortune. She cooks dinner and is able to invite guests, even to pickle fish for the future. To crown it all, by luck some of the fish have gold inside them: red caviar.

Galina Dorogina tells me that although the wives of the senior officers have lived all their lives on the peninsula, they have seen very little of exotic Kamchatka. 'Our lives have passed in training courses and campaigns, brief reunions and long partings,' she says.

For all that, Galina has no regret, not even for what have in effect been wasted years. 'The truth of the matter is that nothing has changed much for the officers' wives. If 20 years ago we were cold and hungry and I had to queue all day for a dozen eggs and they wrote my number in the queue on my hand, the only difference now is that we have absolutely no money. There are eggs in the shops, but the officers have no money to buy them with.'

Vice Admiral Dorogin's thinking is an ideological mishmash, an amalgam of Communist and capitalist notions. This probably is to be expected from a man who spent almost all his life under the Soviet regime, was a member of the Young Communist League and the Communist Party, and now has to live with the realities of the free market. From my point of view, his ideas are outmoded;

they are stale ideology which lost its validity with the demise of the USSR. Against that, the vice admiral fully understands democratic aspirations and why they are needed.

Towards which of these ideological poles is his heart really drawn, and in which of these dimensions does he really feel at home? It is not easy to tell, but I decide to try.

Dorogin is answerable for everything in Kamchatka, from the submarines to the state of the military museum. Here is just one episode from his life.

Among the units of the North-East Group is 22 Chapayev Motorised Division. It bears that name because it is the same division as was formed in the Volga region in 1918 by Vasily Chapaev, a legendary hero of the Civil War. It was here that his girlfriend, Bolshevik Anka, who figures in hundreds of questionable Soviet jokes, was a fighter.

After the Second World War, the Chapayev division was redeployed to the Far East, and today it is famous in Kamchatka for the fact that its first company retains a soldier's bed for Vladimir Ilyich Lenin, leader of the world proletariat. In 1922 Lenin was made an honorary Red Army soldier in the division and the bed was accordingly allocated. Since 1922, wherever the division has been sent, it has been a tradition to transport Lenin's bed along with the other equipment. Even today the bed enjoys a prominent position in the barracks. It is neatly made up, and the walls around comprise a Lenin Corner with drawings on the topic of 'Volodya was a good student!' All these items are registered in a logbook kept in a secret location in the division.

The commander of the First Lenin Company, Captain Igor Shapoval, 26, considers that the spirit of Lenin keeps his soldiers up to scratch.

'Are you serious?'

'Yes. They see this neatly made bed and try to emulate it.'

I find this laughable, but then I find that Vice Admiral Dorogin believes no less than Captain Shapoval in the lofty ideological role of Lenin's bed.

'New recruits find it a bit odd at first, but they come to respect it,' Dorogin says. 'When democracy triumphed in Moscow, there were attempts to get rid of Lenin's bed in Kamchatka, but we managed to save it. It's hardly in the same category as your monument to Dzerzhinsky at the Lubyanka.'

Dorogin does not believe in change for its own sake. History is what it is, and you didn't need to be all that clever to demolish a monument to the founder of the Bolsheviks' secret police. He also considers that since the Lenin Corner was established in the Chapaev division by a special resolution of the Council of People's Commissars, at the very least it would require a directive from the government of Russia, signed by the Prime Minister, for the bed to be dispatched to the scrap heap.

We talk about which example soldiers in Kamchatka should now be invited to follow. The present commander of the division, Lieutenant-Colonel Valery Oleynikov, says unambiguously, 'The example of those who fought in Chechnya and Afghanistan.'

The previous commander of the First Lenin Company had indeed fought in Chechnya. Lieutenant Yury Buchnev received the award of Hero of Russia for fighting in Grozny. We continue this discussion about example, and I suggest that educating soldiers on the example of what is going on in Chechnya can hardly be a good idea. Dorogin keeps out of the discussion, which, as a senior officer, he should. He is serving his country, and as a matter of principle his political views should be of no concern to anyone. But about the future he is entirely willing to speculate. Ideology is one thing, the Army cutbacks are quite another. The officers feel they are sitting on a powder keg.

'We are half expecting that at any moment the State will give a very raw deal to those who have served it loyally,' comments Alexander Shevchenko, the division's chief of staff. The other officers, including Dorogin, agree. None of those likely to be retired have civilian qualifications commensurate with their rank and status in the services, and of course they will have nowhere to live. If they have to leave the armed forces, they will lose their homes, because at present all of them are living in military flats. Igor Shapoval is an engineer who maintains military vehicles. He is skilled in the cold working of metals, so when he ceases to be an officer he can look forward to a career repairing tractors, or serving the civilian population in a key-cutting kiosk. Shevchenko already has experience of civilian employment. For two of the three years he studied in Moscow at the Artillery Academy, he earned money on the side as a watchman in a florist's basement, covering the 24 hours jointly with three other student officers.

The view in Kamchatka is that the Ministry of Defence does not agree that in principle an officer should dedicate himself only to his military duties and not fritter away his time by working on the side.

'With things the way they are, it is only too easy to draw a man into illegal activity,' says the vice admiral. 'I myself have been offered 2,000 dollars in an envelope. This was by someone who was directed to me by a friend. He offered the bribe in a very respectable way: "You need money for medical treatment for your wife." At that moment he was absolutely right. The condition was that I should approve a contract for the sale of scrap brass on terms unfavourable to the Army, not at 700 dollars a ton but at 450. Actually, my signature was the last in a series of signatures of senior military figures. I could simply have thrown the man with the envelope out, but I called in the prosecutor. I thought it might be an example to others.'

Of course, Dorogin is in many ways a saintly man. Like many other officers he is serving his country not for money but from a sense of duty. Only here, at the furthest reach of our land, are such spiritually healthy people to be found.

How long the patience of Dikiy, Dorogin and others will hold out nobody knows, not even they themselves. Today's Navy is dependent on the older and middle generations of naval officers. There are almost no young ones. They don't come out here. The few who do are not willing to resign themselves to the idea that they should devote all their strength to the Navy and receive nothing in return. What kind of officers will the Navy have left in a few more years?

'Patriotism?' A young captain second class from Rybachie smiles wryly. He is an officer on the submarine *Omsk*. 'Patriotism is something you have to pay for. It is time to put an end to this nonsense, this playing at being paupers. We need to get back on our feet, not limp through life like Dikiy. He is a commander, yet he always has cheap trainers on his feet and drinks cheap brandy. The way the fleet is being treated is out of order, and the only way to respond is by making up your own rules.'

'What do you mean by that?'

By 'making up your own rules' the young officer means making a living by fair means or foul. He says that all the officers of his age are quietly trading whatever they can get their hands on from under the counter.

'I get fish and caviar brought to my home now,' he says proudly. 'Two years ago I was bartering spirits I'd stolen from the ship, and people had no respect for me then.'

'For the young officers a good standard of living is beginning to be the main reason for being in the Navy,' mourns Vice Admiral Dorogin. In his opinion any thought of responding to State neglect by 'making up your own rules' is just as fatal for anybody in the service as questioning a commanding officer's orders.

Old Ladies and New Russians

Two old ladies, Maria Savina, a former champion milkmaid, and Zinaida Fenoshina, a former equally champion cowherd, stand in the middle of the forest, angrily shaking upraised sticks in the direction of a bulldozer. It is roaring away at full throttle, and they are shouting as loudly as they can for all to hear: 'Be off! Away with you! How much longer must we put up with this sort of thing?'

From behind ancient trees, surly security guards appear and

surround them as if to say, 'Leave now while you still can, or we shoot.'

Nikolai Abramov – a retired vet, the village elder and the organiser of the demonstration – spreads his arms. 'They want to drive us off our own land. We shall defend it to the death. What else is left?'

The theatre of operations is on the outskirts of the village of Pervomaiskoe in the Narofomin District of Moscow Province. The epicentre is the grounds of an old estate formerly owned by the Berg family. It dates from 1904 and is today protected by the State as a natural and cultural heritage site.

When they have calmed down a little, the old people shake their heads sadly. 'There, in our old age we've joined the Greens. What else can we do? There's only us to defend our park from this scum. Nobody else is going to.'

The scum are New Russians who have hired soulless barbarian developers to erect 34 houses right in the middle of the century-old Berg Park. Maria and Zinaida are members of a special ecological group created by the village assembly of Pervomaiskoe to organise direct action against the despoilers of the environment.

Paying little attention to the Green activists, the trucks continue to drive and the tractors to roar among the precious ancient trees. After an hour's work they have cut a swath through the woodlands. This is to be the central 'avenue' of the future cottage settlement. Pipes, reinforcement wire and concrete slabs lie all over the place. The building work is in full swing and really is being carried out as if to maximise damage to the natural environment. Already 130 cubic metres of timber have been taken as rare species were felled. Wherever you look there are notches on cedars and firs, marking them for slaughter. The machinery brazenly wrecks the environment, churning up layers of clay from the depths and pitilessly burying deep beneath it the ecosystem of the forest floor which has formed over the years.

'Have you heard of the Weymouth Pine?' Tatyana Dudenus asks. She is head of the ecological group and a research associate at one of the region's medical institutes. 'We had five specimens growing in the grounds of our heritage park. They were the only ones in the whole of Moscow Province. The Bergs made a hobby of propagating rare tree species. Three of these Weymouth Pines have now been sawn down for no better reason than that the developers wanted to run a street for their new estate just where they were growing. Other precious species are under threat: the Siberian Silver Fir and Larch, the White Poplar, a White Cedar, *Thuja occidentalis*, the only specimen in Moscow Province. In just the last three days we have lost more than 60 trees. It wouldn't be so bad if they were destroying the less outstanding or sickly specimens, but they have quite a different approach. They decide where they want to construct a road and cut down anything that's in the way. They decide where they want to put up a cottage and clear the site, taking no account of the rarity of the trees they are destroying. The forest here is legally classified as Grade One, which means it is against the law to touch these trees. In order to obtain permission to fell them you have to demonstrate "exceptional circumstances" and support your application with a recommendation from the State Ecological Inspectorate. For every such hectare you need the express permission of the Federal government.'

When the fate of Berg Park was being decided, none of this was done. The Pervomaiskoe Greens lodged writs with the Narofomin court to bring the brazen nouveaux riches into line. They petitioned Judge Yelena Golubeva, who had been assigned the case, for an injunction to halt the building work until the hearing, since otherwise, after the trees had been felled, a verdict in their favour would be of little use.

However, as we have seen, this is the age of the oligarchs in Russia. Every branch of government understands only the language of their rustling banknotes. Judge Golubeva did not even consider granting an injunction to halt the construction work and, when it was already in progress, deliberately failed to conduct a hearing.

Nearly all those unique trees were felled.

Valery Kulakovsky emerges from the posse of guards. He is the deputy director of the Promzhilstroy Company, which calls itself a cooperative of home builders. Kulakovsky advises me to stay out of this. He says some extremely influential people in Moscow have an interest in the estate: they are going to live here. This is soon confirmed. I discover that the 'cooperative' has managed to acquire property rights over the Berg hectares, which according to the law are the property of the nation. This is totally illegal.

Kulakovsky just shrugs and tries to explain his own position. 'We are very tired of these endless demonstrations by the villagers. What do you expect me to do now, when I have put so much money into this, bought the land, started building? Who do you think is going to give it all back to me?'

He also says they have no plans to back down.

They did not back down. Berg Park ceased to exist. The felling of our finest forests in the interests of the oligarchs and their companies is going on throughout the land.

Not long before the Green old ladies of Pervomaiskoe mounted the desperate defence of their ancient park, the Supreme Court of Russia considered the same matter of principle as it applied to Russia as a whole. The case was known as the 'Forest Issue'.

'Bear in mind the interests of the property owners. They have acquired the land, built the houses, and now you want to turn everything back.' The lawyer in the Supreme Court repeated what Kulakovsky had said almost word for word.

The ecologist lawyers Olga Alexeyeva and Vera Mishchenko, who were defending the interests of society as a whole against the caprices of New Russians, had a different take on the matter: 'Every citizen of this country has the right to life and enjoyment of the national heritage. If we are truly citizens of Russia, then it is our duty to ensure that future generations receive no less a national heritage than today's generations enjoy. In any case, how can we take seriously property rights which have been acquired illegally?'

The essence of the 'Forest Issue' was that Russian ecologists, under the leadership of the Moscow Institute of Ecological Legal Issues, Eco-Juris, which brought the case, demanded the repeal of twenty-two orders of the Cabinet of Ministers transferring Grade One forests to the category of non-afforested land. This permitted the felling of more than 34,000 hectares of prime forest in Russia.

Russia's forests are divided into three categories. Grade One relates to those deemed particularly important either for society or for the natural environment. These are forests containing highly valued species, habitats of rare birds and animals, reservations and parks, and urban and suburban Green Belts. The Forestry Code of the Russian Federation accordingly recognises Grade One forests as part of the national heritage. Berg Park came into this category.

The formal applicant for this change of categories and subsequent right to fell trees was, oddly enough, the Forestry Commission of the Russian Federation, Rosleskhoz. It is the body which has the right to submit documents relating to the legal status of forests for signature by the Prime Minister. The 22 orders disputed by the ecologists had been made without the statutory State ecological inspection, with the result that the national heritage became the prey of short-term interests. Where forests were cut down they were replaced by petrol stations, garages, industrial estates, local wholesale markets, domestic waste dumps and, of course, housing estates.

The ecologists consider this last option to be the least objectionable, but only providing the new house owners behave responsibly towards the magnificent forests surrounding their houses and do not destroy their roots in the course of laying drainage systems.

While the 'Forest Issue' was being considered and the judges were taking their time, almost another 950 hectares of top-quality forests were condemned to destruction under new orders signed by the Prime Minister. The greatest damage was done in the Khanty-Mansiisk and Yamalo-Nenetsk autonomous regions, where trees were destroyed for the benefit of oil and gas companies. Moscow Province also suffered: what happened to Berg Park was the result of deliberate judicial procrastination.

While the paperwork was being taken care of and nobody had the courage to dot the legal 'i's or cross the legal 't's, the struggle for the forest in Pervomaiskoe became violent. When, at the request of the prosecutor's office, the ecological group went to record the barbaric results of the developers' activities with a videocamera, police reinforcements were brought in. A fight broke out, the camera was broken and the ecologists, all of them elderly people, were beaten up.

'Of course, we do not want to wage a war, but we have been left with no option,' Nikolai Abramov, the village elder, says by way of explanation. 'The estate was the last place in the village where we could go to walk. There were usually old people and mothers with prams there. There is a school for 300 pupils and a kindergarten in the grounds. All the rest has been developed with cottages for the New Russians.'

The veteran ecologists are aware that they are at war primarily with the super-rich, people who command amounts of money the like of which they themselves have never seen. They have heard it talk, however. At a village assembly, Alexander Zakharov, chairman of the Pervomaiskoe Rural District Council, openly declared that the sums of money involved were too great for there to be any possibility of reversing the situation. Here is what Igor Kulikov, chairman of the Ecological Union of Moscow Province, wrote to the provincial prosecutor, Mikhail Avdyukov: 'The chairman of the council publicly stated to members of the ecological group elected by the assembly that he had given their names and addresses to the Mafia, which would deal with them if they did not stop their protests.'

Alexander Zakharov is undoubtedly one of the central characters in this unseemly tale. If he had stood firm, not one dacha would have encroached on the grounds of the Berg Park. At the foot of the documents which ultimately permitted the felling of the Pervomaiskoe trees, in contravention of the law and against the resolution of the village assembly, is Zakharov's signature.

The scenario is a familiar one. First application is made to the upper echelons in Moscow for the 'transfer of Grade One forests to the category of non-afforested land'. A short time later, an order is drafted for signature by the Prime Minister. The felling of the forest ensues when, implementing the Prime Minister's order, the local forestry officials and the head of the district council give the go-ahead.

There is not much wrong with our laws in Russia. It is just that not many people want to obey them.

Akaky Akakievich Putin II

I have wondered a great deal about why I have so got it in for Putin. What is it that makes me dislike him so much as to feel moved to write a book about him? I am not one of his political opponents or rivals, just a woman living in Russia. Quite simply, I am a 45-year-old Muscovite who observed the Soviet Union at its most disgraceful in the 1970s and '80s. I really don't want to find myself back there again.

I am making a point of finishing the writing of this book on 6 May 2004. There has been no miraculous challenging of the results of the 14 March presidential election. The opposition has acquiesced. Accordingly, tomorrow sees the start of Putin II, the President re-elected by an unbelievable majority of more than 70 per cent. Even if we knock off 20 per cent as 'window-dressing' (i.e. ballot-rigging), he still received enough votes to secure the presidency.

In a few hours Putin, a typical lieutenant-colonel of the Soviet KGB, a look-alike of Akaky Akakievich, downtrodden hero of Gogol's story 'The Greatcoat', will ascend the throne of Russia once again. His outlook is the narrow, provincial one his rank would suggest; he has the unprepossessing personality of a lieutenant-colonel who never made it to colonel, the manner of a Soviet secret policeman who habitually snoops on his own colleagues. And he is vindictive: not a single political opponent has been invited to the inauguration ceremony, not a single political party that is in any way out of step.

Brezhnev was a distasteful figure, Andropov bloody, although he had at least a democratic veneer. Chernenko was dumb and

Russians disliked Gorbachev. At times Yeltsin had us crossing ourselves at the thought of where his doings might be leading us.

Here is their apotheosis. Tomorrow their bodyguard from Echelon 25 – the man in the security cordon when VIP motorcades drive by – Akaky Akakievich Putin will strut down the red carpet of the Kremlin throne room as if he really were the boss there. Around him the polished Tsarist gold will gleam, the servants will smile submissively, his comrades-in-arms, a choice selection from the lower ranks of the KGB who could have risen to important posts only under Putin, will swell with self-importance.

One can imagine Lenin strutting around like a nabob when he arrived in the vanquished Kremlin in 1918 after the Revolution. The official Communist histories – we have no others – assure us that in fact his strutting was very modest, but his modesty, you can just bet, was insolent. Look at humble little me! You thought I was a nobody, but now I've made it. I've broken Russia just as I intended to. I've forced her to swear allegiance to me.

Tomorrow a KGB snoop, who even in that capacity did not make much of an impression, will strut through the Kremlin just as Lenin did. He will have had his revenge.

Let us, however, run the reel backwards a little.

Putin's victory had been widely predicted both in Russia and throughout the world, especially after the humiliation of such democratic and liberal opposition parties as the country possessed in the parliamentary elections of 7 December 2003. Accordingly, the 14 March result surprised few. We had international observers in but everything was low key. Voting day itself was a contemporary remake of the authoritarian, bureaucratic, Soviet-style pantomime of 'the people expressing its will', which many still remember only too well, myself included. In those days the procedure was that you went to the polling station and dropped your voting slip in the ballot box without bothering whose names were on it because the result was a foregone conclusion.

How did people react this time? Did the Soviet parallel rouse anybody from inertia on 14 March 2004? No. They went obediently to the polling stations, dropped their voting papers in the ballot boxes and shrugged: 'What can we do about it?' Everyone is convinced that the Soviet Union has returned, and that it no longer matters what we think.

On 14 March I stood outside the polling station on my own Dolgoruky Street in Moscow. With the advent of Yeltsin its name had been changed from Kalyayev Street. Kalyayev, a terrorist in Tsarist times, was later regarded as a revolutionary. It became Dolgoruky Street in honour of the prince who had had his estate there in Kalyayev's time, before the Bolsheviks came.

I talked to people going in to vote and coming quickly out again after participating in the charade. They were apathetic, completely indifferent to the process of electing Putin for a second term. 'It's what "they" want us to do? Well, then. Big deal.' That was the majority sentiment. A minority joked, 'Perhaps now they'll name it Kalyayev Street again.'

The return of the Soviet system with the consolidation of Putin's power is obvious.

It has to be said that this has not only been made possible by our own negligence, apathy and weariness after too much revolutionary change. It has happened to choruses of encouragement from the West, primarily from Silvio Berlusconi, who appears to have fallen in love with Putin. He is Putin's main European champion, but Putin also enjoys the support of Blair, Schroeder and Chirac, and receives no discouragement from the transatlantic junior Bush.

So nothing stood in the way of our KGB man's return to the Kremlin, neither the West nor any serious opposition within Russia. Throughout the so-called election campaign, from 7 December 2003 until 14 March 2004, Putin openly derided the electorate.

The main token of his contempt was his refusal to debate anything with anyone. He declined to expand on a single point of his own policies in the last four years. His contempt extended not only to representatives of the opposition parties but to the very concept of an opposition. He made no promises about future policy and disdained campaigning of any kind. Instead, as under the Soviet regime, he was shown on television every day, receiving top-ranking officials in his Kremlin office and dispensing his highly competent advice on how to conduct whichever ministry or department they came from.

There was, of course, a certain amount of tittering among members of the public: he was behaving just like Stalin. Putin too was simultaneously 'the friend of all children' and 'the nation's first pig-farmer', 'the best miner', the 'comrade of all athletes' and the 'leading film-maker'.

None of it went further than tittering, however. Any real emotion drained away into the sand. There was no serious protest over the rejection of debates.

Meeting no resistance, Putin naturally became bolder. It is a bad mistake to suppose he takes no notice of anything, never reacts and only, as we're encouraged to believe, forges ahead in pursuit of power.

He pays a lot of attention and takes account of what he sees. He keeps a close eye on us, this nation he controls.

In this he is behaving exactly like a member of Lenin's Cheka secret police. The approach is entirely that of a KGB officer. First there is the kite-flying of information released through a narrow circle of individuals. In today's Russia, that is the political elite of the capital. The aim is to probe likely reaction to policies. If there is none, or if it has the dynamism of a jellyfish, all is well. Putin can push his policy forward, spread his ideas or act as he sees fit without having to look over his shoulder.

A brief digression is in order here, less about Putin than about us, the Russian public. Putin has backers and helpers, people with a vested interest in his second ascent to the throne, people now concentrated in the President's office. This is the institution which today really rules the country, not the government which implements the President's decision, not the parliament which rubber-stamps whichever laws he wants passed. His people follow the reactions of society very attentively. It is completely wrong to imagine they aren't bothered. It is we who are responsible for Putin's policies, we first and foremost, not Putin. The fact that our reaction to him and his cynical manipulation of Russia has been confined to gossiping in the kitchen has enabled him to do all the things he has done in the past four years. Society has shown limitless apathy, and this is what has given Putin the indulgence he requires. We have reacted to his actions and speeches not just lethargically but fearfully. As the Chekists have become entrenched in power, we have let them see our fear, and thereby have only intensified their urge to treat us like cattle. The KGB respects only the strong. The weak it devours. We of all people ought to know that.

Let us now go back to late February 2004. At some moment the Kremlin techniques for sounding out public opinion warned that the public was beginning to tire of Putin's insolent refusal either to debate or to campaign and of the absence of any recognisable pre-election campaign.

In order to reinvigorate the languishing electorate, the Kremlin announced that Putin had decided to take 'firm measures'. These proved to be a Cabinet reshuffle three weeks before election day.

At first everyone really was taken aback. This appeared to be an act of complete lunacy. In accordance with the Constitution, the entire Cabinet does in any case resign after an election. The newly elected President announces his choice of Prime Minister, who in turn proposes ministers for the President to confirm. What sense could it possibly make to appoint everybody now, only to have to reappoint them after the inauguration? What was the point of all this crazy activity which could only further paralyse the functioning of a government riddled with corruption, which already spent a good proportion of its working week taking care of its personal commercial interests?

However, although replacing the Cabinet a month before the Constitution required was entirely daft, it did indeed serve to reinvigorate the election process. The political elite was stirred, the guessing game about whom Putin would appoint took over the television channels, the political pundits were given something to discuss and the press finally got something it could write about the election campaign.

But this reinvigoration of politics lasted one week at best. Putin's spin doctors daily intoned over the television that the President had done this purely because he wanted to be 'absolutely honest with you', he did not want to 'enter the election with a pig in a poke' (by which was evidently meant following the constitutional procedure for replacing the Cabinet). He wanted to present his future course before 14 March.

It has to be said, alas, that people believed him: probably just over half the electorate. The half which fell for and hailed this dishonest, absurd line of argument have an important distinguishing feature. These are people who love and trust Putin without reservation, irrationally, uncritically, fanatically. They believe in Putin. End of story.

In the week preceding the appointment of a new Prime Minister the media images were all of this now familiar 'love' for Putin. Those with faith in the genuineness of his proclaimed reasons for changing the Cabinet ignored the obvious non sequiturs.

You really do have to believe unreservedly, as if you have fallen in love for the first time, if you are not immediately to be struck by the obvious question: Why didn't Putin choose a less dramatic way of presenting his future course than sacking the entire government? He had plenty of other ways to do so. He could, for example, have taken part in televised debates. But no. The week after the dismissal of the Cabinet saw hitherto unprecedented levels of cynicism. The people of Russia watching their televisions were told that actually it didn't matter what happened on 14 March. Everything had been decided. Putin would be Tsar. The spin doctors got to the point of saying, 'He wants to show you his course in advance because it's the only choice you've got.'

The day when the name of the new Prime Minister was to be announced was arranged with all the ceremony traditionally preceding the emergence of the hero of an opera to sing his first aria. The President will tell us tomorrow morning. In two hours' time.

In one hour's time. Ten minutes to go. Moreover, the one whose name would be revealed might, we were assured over the television, possibly be the President's successor in 2008.

In Russia it is very important not to look ridiculous. It can end badly. People make up jokes and you turn into a Brezhnev. When Putin announced his new government, even his most diehard supporters fell about laughing. No one could fail to see that the Kremlin had been staging a very bad farce. It was no more than a petty settling of scores, although subjected, of course, to endless spin and veiled behind all manner of claptrap and rhetorical garnishing which invoked the greatness of Russia.

But the mountains truly had brought forth a mouse. Virtually all the old ministers stayed where they had been. Only the Prime Minister, Mikhail Kasianov, was sacked. He had been getting up Putin's nose for many months in a big way, and in many small ways too. He was a legacy of the Yeltsin era. When raising the second President to the throne, the first President of Russia had asked Putin not to remove Kasianov.

Prime Minister Kasianov, alone among the main actors in Russian politics, categorically opposed the arrest of the liberal oligarch Mikhail Khodorkovsky and the gradual destruction of his Yukos oil company. Yukos was the most transparent company in our corrupt country, the first to function in accordance with internationally accepted financial practice. It operated 'in the white', as people say in Russia, and what is more it donated over 5 per cent of its gross annual profit to financing a large university, children's homes and an extensive programme of charitable work.

But Kasianov was speaking out in defence of a man whom Putin had for some time counted among his personal enemies, on the grounds that Khodorkovsky was making major financial contributions to the country's democratic opposition, primarily to the Yabloko Party and the Union of Right Forces.

In Putin's understanding of political life this was a grave personal insult. He has publicly shown on many occasions that he is quite incapable of understanding the concept of discussion, especially in politics. There should be no answering back from someone Putin considers his inferior, and if an inferior does allow himself to answer back he is an enemy. Putin does not choose to behave this way. It is not because he is a born tyrant and despot; he has just been brought up to think in the categories inculcated in him by the KGB, an organisation he considers an ideal model, as he has publicly stated more than once. This is why, as soon as anyone disagrees with him, Putin categorically demands that they should 'cut out the hysterics'. This is the reason behind his refusal to take part in pre-election debates. Debate is not his element. He doesn't know how to conduct a dialogue. His genre is the military-style monologue. While you are a subordinate you keep your mouth shut. When you become the chief you talk in monologues, and it is the duty of your inferiors to pretend they agree. This is a political version of the misrule of officers in the Army which occasionally, as with Khodorkovsky, leads to all-out war.

But to return to the government reshuffle. Kasianov was out. The ministers returned to their original portfolios and Putin ceremoniously parachuted in Mikhail Fradkov as the new Prime Minister. In recent times Fradkov had been quietly enjoying a place in our bureaucratic hierarchy as the Russian Federation's representative to the European institutions in Brussels. He is a nondescript, amiable, forgettable gentleman with narrow shoulders and a big bum. Most Russians learned that our country had a Federal minister called Fradkov only when his appointment as Prime Minister was announced, which, in accordance with Russian lore, tells us that Fradkov is a low-profile representative of that same service to which Putin has dedicated the greater part of his working life.

The country laughed out loud when it heard of Fradkov's elevation, but Putin insisted, and even started explaining his 'principled' choice to the effect that he wanted to be open with the electorate and to enter the election with people knowing in advance whom he would be working with in his fight against Russia's main evils of corruption and poverty.

The Russian people, both the half which supports Putin and

the half which doesn't, didn't stop laughing. The Kremlin farce continued. If the country as a whole did not know Fradkov, the business community remembered him only too well. He is a typical Soviet *nomenklatura* bureaucrat who, throughout his career, from the Communist period onwards, has been shifted hither and thither to miscellaneous bureaucratic posts quite independently of his professional background and knowledge. He is a typical boss for whom it is not too important what he is driving, just as long as he is in the driver's seat. While he was Director of the Federal Tax Police Service it had a reputation as the most corrupt ministry in the Russian civil service. Its bureaucrats took bribes for literally everything, for every form they issued and every consultation. The service was consequently shut down, and Fradkov, in line with the undying traditions of the Soviet *nomenklatura*, was 'looked after'. He was transferred once again, this time to Brussels.

Prime Minister Fradkov hastily flew back to Moscow from Brussels, only to provoke further merriment. In his first interview in his new capacity at the airport, he confessed he didn't actually know how to be a Prime Minister. No, he had no plans, it had all come like a bolt from the blue. He was waiting to see what arrangements had been made and what his instructions would be.

Russia is a country where much goes on behind the scenes and most people have short memories. Despite his ignorance of arrangements and the lack of instructions from Putin, which never have been made public, the Duma confirmed Fradkov's appointment by a convincing majority, making reference to its duty to 'fulfil the will of our electors who trust President Putin in all matters'. This Duma, its composition the result of the elections of 7 December 2003, contains practically no opposition to Putin and is firmly under the control of the Kremlin.

14 March arrived. Everything passed off in accordance with the Kremlin's scenario. Life went on as before. The bureaucrats returned to their tireless thieving. Mass murder continued in Chechnya, having quietened down briefly during the elections to give hope to those who for five years had been hoping for peace.

The Second Chechen War had begun in mid-1999, in the run-up to Putin's first presidential election. In accordance with Asiatic traditions, just before his second presidential election two Chechen field commanders laid down their weapons at the feet of the great ruler. Their relatives had been seized and were held in captivity until the commanders stated that they now supported Putin and had given up all thought of independence. Oligarch Khodorkovsky took to writing penitential letters to Putin from prison. Yukos was rapidly becoming poorer. Berlusconi came to visit us, and his first question to his pal Vladimir was how he too could get 70 per cent of the vote in an election. Putin gave no clear advice, and indeed his friend Silvio would not have understood if he had. Berlusconi is after all a European.

They went off on a trip to provincial Lipetsk, opened a production line for washing machines and watched a military airshow. Putin continued to give a dressing-down to high-level bureaucrats on television. That is usually how we see him, either receiving reports from officials in his Kremlin office or tearing one of them apart in monologues. The filming is methodically thought through in PR terms. There is no ad-libbing, nothing is left to chance.

Putin was even revealed to the people at Easter instead of the risen Christ. A service was held at the Church of Christ the Redeemer, Moscow's cathedral re-erected in concrete on the site of an open-air Soviet-era swimming pool. Almost a month had passed since his second election. At the beginning of the Great Matins service there stood, shoulder-to-shoulder with Putin as if at a military parade, Prime Minister Fradkov and Dmitry Medvedev, the Kremlin's new *éminence grise*, head of the President's office, a man of diminutive stature with a large head. The three men clumsily and clownishly crossed themselves, Medvedev making his crosses by touching his hands to his forehead and then to his genitals. It was risible. Medvedev followed Putin in shaking the Patriarch's hand as if he were one of their comrades, rather than kissing it as prescribed by church ritual. The Patriarch overlooked the error. The spin doctors in the Kremlin are effective but, of course, pretty illiterate in these matters and had not told the politicians what to do. Alongside Putin there stood the Mayor of Moscow, Yury Luzhkov, who had been behind the rebuilding of the cathedral and who alone knew how to invoke the protection of the Cross in a competent manner. The Patriarch addressed Putin as 'Your Most High Excellency', which made even those not directly involved wince. Given the numerous ex-KGB officers occupying top government positions, the Easter Vigil has now taken over from the May Day Parade as the major obligatory national ritual.

The beginning of the Great Matins service was even more comical than the handshakes with the Patriarch. Both State television channels did a live broadcast of the procession round the cathedral that precedes the service. The Patriarch participated in this, despite being ill. The television commentator, who was a believer and theologically knowledgeable, explained to viewers that in the Orthodox tradition the doors of the church should be shut before midnight because they symbolise the entrance to the cave where Christ's body was placed. After midnight the Orthodox faithful taking part in the procession await the opening of the church doors. The Patriarch stands on the steps at their head and is the first to enter the empty temple where the Resurrection of Christ has already occurred.

When the Patriarch had recited the first prayer after midnight at the doors of the temple, they were thrown open to reveal: Putin, our modest President, shoulder to shoulder with Fradkov, Medvedev and Luzhkov.

You didn't know whether to laugh or cry. An evening of comic entertainment on Holy Night. Really, what is there to like about this individual? He profanes everything he touches.

At about this time, on 8 April, two nine-month-old twin baby girls were declared *shaheeds* – martyrs for the their faith – in Chechnya. They came from the tiny Chechen farmstead of Rigakh and were killed before they had learned to walk. It was the usual story. After the 14 March election relentless military operations were resumed in Chechnya. The Army, in the form of the Regional Operational Staff Headquarters for Coordinating the Counterterrorist Operation, announced that it was attempting to catch Basayev: 'A large-scale military operation is under way to destroy the participants of armed formations.' They failed to catch Basayev, but on 8 April at around 2.00 in the afternoon, as part of the 'military operation', the Rigakh farmstead was subjected to a missile bombardment. It killed everyone there: a mother and her five children. The scene which confronted Imar-Ali Damayev, the father of the family, would have turned the most hard-headed militant into a pacifist for life, or into a suicide bomber. His 29-year-old wife, Maidat, lay dead, holding close their four-year-old Djanati, three-year-old Jaradat, two-year-old Umar-Haji and the tiny nine-month-old Zara. Their mother's embrace saved none of them. To one side lay the little body of Zura, Zara's twin sister. Maidat had had no room and evidently no time to think of a way of covering her fifth child with her own body, and baby Zura herself had had no time to crawl the two metres. Imar-Ali gathered up the anti-personnel fragments and established the number of the killer missile: 350 F 8-90. It was not difficult, the number was easy to read. They started burying the bodies, and the *mullah*, a Moslem scholar from the neighbouring village, declared all those who had been slain to be martyrs. They were buried the same evening, their bodies unwashed, without graveclothes, in what they were wearing when death claimed them.

Why do I so dislike Putin? Because the years are passing. This summer it will be five since the Second Chechen War was instigated. It shows no sign of ending. At that time the babies who were to be declared *shaheeds* were yet unborn, but all the murders of children since 1999 in bombardments and purges remain unsolved, uninvestigated by the institutions of law and order. The people who committed infanticide have never had to stand where they belong, in the dock; Putin, that great 'friend of all children', has never demanded that they should. The Army continues to rampage in Chechnya as it was allowed to at the beginning of the war, as if its operations were being conducted on a training ground empty of people.

This massacre of the innocents did not raise a storm in Russia. Not one television station broadcast images of the five little Chechens who had been slaughtered. The Minister of Defence did not resign. He is a personal friend of Putin and is even seen as a possible successor in 2008. The head of the Air Force was not sacked. The Commander-in-Chief himself made no speech of condolence. Around us, indeed, it was business as usual in the rest of the world. Hostages were killed in Iraq. Nations and peoples demanded that their governments and international organisations withdraw troops in order to save the lives of people carrying out their duties. But in Russia all was quiet.

Why do I so dislike Putin? This is precisely why. I dislike him for a matter-of-factness worse than felony, for his cynicism, for his racism, for his lies, for the gas he used in the *Nord-Ost* siege, for the massacre of the innocents which went on throughout his first term as President.

This is how I see it. Others have different views. The killing of children has not put people off trying to have Putin's period in office extended to ten years. This is being done by creating new pro-Putin youth movements on instructions from the Kremlin. The deputy head of Putin's office is a certain Vladislav Surkov, the acknowledged doyen of PR in Russia. He spins webs consisting of pure deceit, lies in place of reality, words instead of deeds. There is a great fashion at the present for bogus political movements created by directive from the Kremlin. We don't want the West suspecting that we have a one-party system, that we lack pluralism and are relapsing into authoritarianism. There suddenly appear groups called 'Marching Together', or 'Singing Together' or 'For Stability' or some other latter-day version of the Soviet Union's Pioneer movement. A distinctive feature of these pro-Putin quasi-political movements is the amazing speed with which, without any of the usual bureaucratic prevarication, they are legally registered by the Ministry of Justice, which is usually very chary of attempts to create anything remotely political. As its first public act the new movement usually announces that it will attempt to ensure the extension of the period of office of our beloved President. Putin was given just such a present for his inauguration on 7 May. At the end of April the members of 'For Stability' set in motion procedures for prolonging his term of office. Their underlying concept is that Putin is the guarantor of stability. At the same time the members of this pocket-sized movement demanded an inquiry into the results of privatisation. This showed them to be against Khodorkovsky, hence friends of Putin. The Moscow City Electoral Commission hastened to accept the application of the young members of 'For Stability' to initiate procedures for a national referendum to extend the President's term of office.

Such was the state of play on inauguration day, 7 May 2004. Putin has, by chance, got his hands on enormous power and has used it to catastrophic effect. I dislike him because he does not like people. He despises us. He sees us as a means to his own ends, a means for the achievement and retention of personal power, no more than that. Accordingly, he believes he can do anything he likes with us, play with us as he sees fit, destroy us as he sees fit. We are nobody, while he whom chance has enabled to clamber to the top of the pile is today Tsar and God.

In Russia we have had leaders with this outlook before. It led to tragedy, to bloodshed on a huge scale, to civil wars. I want no more of that. That is why I so dislike this typical Soviet Chekist as he struts down the red carpet in the Kremlin on his way to the throne of Russia.

After Beslan

On 1 September 2004 an unprecedentedly horrible act of terrorism was perpetrated in Russia, and from now on the name of the little North Ossetian town of Beslan will be associated with a waking nightmare beyond the imaginings of Hollywood.

On the morning of 1 September a multi-national gang of thugs seized control of No. 1 School in Beslan, demanding an immediate end to the Second Chechen War. The hostage-takers struck during the annual *lineyka*, a celebration of the beginning of the school year which is observed throughout Russia. By tradition this is an occasion to which whole families come: grandmothers and grandfathers, aunts and uncles, and especially the families of the youngest children coming to school for the first time.

This is why almost 1,500 people were taken hostage: schoolchildren, their mothers and fathers, their brothers and sisters, their teachers and their teachers' children.

Everything that happened during the period of 1–3 September, and in Russia subsequently, has been a wholly predictable consequence of the Putin regime's systematic imposition of the power of a single individual to the detriment of common sense and personal initiative.

On 1 September the intelligence services, and after them the authorities, announced that actually there were not all that many people in the school: just 354 in all. The infuriated terrorists told the hostages, 'When we have finished with you there really will be only 354'. The relatives who had gathered round the school said the authorities were lying: there were more than a thousand people trapped inside.

Nobody heard what the relatives were saying, because nobody was listening. They tried to get their message through to the authorities by way of the reporters who had converged on Beslan, but the journalists merely went on echoing the official tally. At this point some of the relatives started beating up some of the journalists.

The authorities spent 1 September and the first half of 2 September in an unforgivable state of shock and disarray. No attempts were made to negotiate since this had not been sanctioned by the Kremlin. Anybody attempting to lay the groundwork for negotiations was subjected to intimidation, while those whom the bandits called upon to come forward and negotiate – President Zyazikov of Ingushetia, President Dzasokhov of North Ossetia, Putin's adviser on Chechnya, Aslanbek Aslakhanov, and Dr Leonid Roshal (who had mediated in previous sieges) – kept their heads down or fled the country, displaying cowardice at the very moment when courage was essential. Each of them subsequently had his excuses ready, but the obstinate fact remains that none of them entered the building.

Against this background of official cowardice, the hostages' relatives' great fear was that there would be a repetition of the government's tactic for ending the *Nord-Ost* siege at a Moscow theatre in 2002, when they mounted an assault which resulted in an enormous number of innocent victims.

On 2 September Ruslan Aushev, the former President of Ingushetia, entered the beleaguered school. Reviled by the Kremlin for constantly calling for peace talks and a political settlement of the Chechen crisis, Aushev had been forced to 'voluntarily' resign in favour of the Kremlin's favoured candidate, FSB General Zyazikov.

Arriving in Beslan, Aushev had found a deplorable situation, as he later recounted. He discovered that, one and a half days after the school had been seized, none of those in the headquarters of the 'Operation to Free the Hostages' was at liberty to decide who should take part in negotiations. They were waiting for instructions from the Kremlin and paralysed by the fear of losing favour with Putin, whose displeasure would signal the end of their political careers. Evidently this consideration took priority over concern for the predicament of the hundreds of hostages. The deaths of hostages could always be blamed on the terrorists, whereas falling foul of Putin would be political suicide.

Let us state unambiguously that all the Russian government representatives in Beslan at that time were more concerned to work out what Putin wanted than to work out a way of resolving the monstrous situation in the school. When Putin did speak, no one dared to contradict. Dzasokhov, for example, told Aushev that Putin had personally telephoned him and forbidden him to enter the school if he didn't want to face immediate criminal charges.

Dzasokhov stayed put. Dr Roshal fared no better. Although himself a paediatrician, he failed on this occasion to save anyone other than himself, having been warned by an unnamed intelligence source that the terrorists were only calling for him as a negotiator in order to kill him. He too stayed put.

The officials in the operational nerve centre all succeeded in saving their careers, but failed to save the children. Even before the showdown on 3 September it was obvious that Putin's 'vertical' system of authority, founded on fear of and total subservience to one individual, himself, was not working. It was incapable of saving lives when that was what was needed.

Faced with this situation, Aushev printed off the Internet a declaration by Aslan Maskhadov, the leader of the Chechen resistance in whose name the thugs claimed to be acting. Maskhadov stated categorically that he was against the taking of children as hostages. Aushev took this declaration and went in to talk to the terrorists. He was to be the only person to conduct negotiations of any sort in the course of the Beslan catastrophe.

For his pains he was roundly abused by the Kremlin and accused of collaborating with the terrorists.

'They refused to talk to me in Vainakh,' Aushev related afterwards, 'although they were Chechens and Ingushetians. They would speak only in Russian. They asked at least to have a minister sent to negotiate, for example Fursenko, the Minister for Education, but nobody was willing to go in without the sanction of the Kremlin.'

Aushev was in the school for about an hour and himself carried three babies out in his arms. A further 26 small children were allowed to leave with him. At 2.00 p.m. on 3 September an assault was launched, and fighting continued in the town until late into the night. Many of the terrorists were killed, but many others broke through all the cordons and escaped. Officialdom began counting how many hostages had died, and is still counting today. A field was ploughed up on the outskirts of Beslan and turned into an enormous cemetery with hundreds of new graves. At the time of writing, more than one hundred hostages have simply vanished: they are classified as having disappeared without trace. Some people believe they were abducted by the terrorists who escaped, others, that they were incinerated by the thermobaric warheads of the Bumblebee rocket flamethrowers with which the Special Operations Units were equipped.

In the immediate aftermath of Beslan there was a further tightening of the political screws. Putin announced that the tragedy had been an act of international terrorism, denying the Chechen connection and blaming everything on al-Qaeda. Aushev's courageous intervention was denigrated and the mass media, on instructions from the Kremlin, set about portraying him as the terrorists' principal accomplice rather than as the only hero of the hour. That role was reserved for Dr Roshal, since the masses do need heroes to admire.

In political terms, Beslan did not prompt the Kremlin to any effort to analyse and correct its own mistakes. On the contrary, the Kremlin went on a political rampage.

Putin's favourite slogan after Beslan was that 'War is war'. His top-down authoritarianism must be strengthened. He knew better than anyone else who was behind what, and only if he held the reins would Russia be safe from terrorist acts in the future. The

Kremlin introduced a bill in the Duma abolishing direct election of provincial governors which, in Putin's opinion, only led to their acting irresponsibly.

Not a word was heard about the fact that throughout the Beslan hostage-taking it was precisely Presidents Zyazikov and Dzasokhov, effectively Putin's nominees, who behaved like cowards and liars. They provided about as much leadership as one can expect milk from a billy goat.

The proposed reform of the system for selecting governors was accompanied by a campaign of ideological brainwashing which asserted that the authorities had performed irreproachably throughout the Beslan catastrophe. Nothing could have been done differently, nothing could have been more effective. As a smokescreen, a commission of enquiry of the Russian Federal Council (the upper chamber of the Russian parliament) was set up to monitor the investigation into the hostage-taking. The chairman of the commission, Alexander Torshin, was received in the Kremlin by Putin and sent off with some presidential advice: The commission has not been stepping out of line.

The people of Beslan began to get the distinct feeling that they were being disregarded. Television coverage concentrated on the good news: the help the hostages were receiving, the mountains of sweets and toys sent to them. The question of what had happened to all those who had disappeared without trace was not looked into.

The traditional 40-day period of mourning passed and official memorial services were held. No air time was given to the heartbroken grieving of families.

Then it was 26 October, the second anniversary of the *Nord-Ost* hostage-taking in Moscow, when a band of terrorists seized the audience and actors of a musical in the middle of a performance. Two and a half days into the ensuing siege, the security services mounted an assault using an unknown chemical gas which resulted in the deaths of 130 hostages.

After *Nord-Ost* the only action undertaken by the authorities was to whitewash their actions, award themselves medals and preen. Not only were no attempts made to find a settlement to the Second Chechen War, but the noose was drawn tighter. A campaign was launched to destroy or neutralise anybody who might be capable of bringing a peace settlement nearer, or of preventing the Chechen crisis from again spawning terrorism in the region. This was a predictable response to the state terrorism of Russia's 'antiterrorist operation' directed against the peoples of Chechnya and Ingushetia. 'Antiterrorist terror' was the defining characteristic of life in Russia in the period between *Nord-Ost* and the Beslan atrocity. We are ground to dust between the millstones of terror and antiterror. The number of terrorist outrages has increased exponentially, and the path leading inexorably from *Nord-Ost* to Beslan is plain to see.

On 26 October 2004 at 11.00 in the morning there was a gathering on the steps of the theatre on Dubrovka of all those whose loved ones had died or whose lives had been blighted by the *Nord-Ost* events: the hostages themselves, the relatives and friends of those who died. Earlier that morning they had been visiting the graves of those dear to them, as is the tradition in Russia, and the service of remembrance at the theatre had accordingly been scheduled for 11.00. The *Nord-Ost* Aid Association of those affected by the tragedy publicised the event through the usual channels. The arrangements for the service were broadcast over local radio. Invitations were sent to the office of the Mayor of Moscow and to the President's Office, and assurances were received that representatives would attend.

But now the priest was waiting as the clock ticked past 11.20, 11.30, 11.50. It really was time to start. People began murmuring among themselves: 'Surely they can't just not show up?'

Then it was noon. The crowd were getting edgy. Many people had children with them, orphans of those who had died. 'We want to talk to the authorities, we came to ask them questions face to face.' Finally, more angrily, 'We need help urgently, we are being ignored, our children are no longer receiving free hospital treatment.'

Still no sign of officialdom. There was no point in waiting any longer: nobody turns up that late. Were they afraid of looking their victims in the eye? The investigation of the *Nord-Ost* incident had led nowhere. The truth about the disaster and about the gas the authorities used remained deeply classified information. Or was something else going on here?

The square around the theatre had been sealed off by police, ordinary young lads who had been sent to ensure that any passions were kept under control. They could hear what people were saying, and they were not looking happy. Eventually, it was the policemen who explained to the *Nord-Ost* victims that the authorities had already been and had already left. They had come for their own cosy, official memorial service while the families were out at the cemeteries, in order not to confront the victims of their actions. At 10.00 representatives of the Mayor of Moscow and the President's Office had come to Dubrovka to act out their own memorial service for the cameras of all the main television channels. Official wreaths had been laid, a guard of honour had performed like clockwork, appropriate speeches, pre-planned and approved by higher authority, had been delivered. It had all been very respectable: no tears, no excessive displays of grief, and the whole sanitised charade was shown repeatedly on all the television channels on the evening of 26 October. Russia could rest assured that the authorities were properly mindful of this tragic happening, and that everybody agreed they were doing the right thing. The official nationalisation of Russia's memory of the events slotted neatly into just a few minutes.

Of course, nothing stopped the thousand-strong crowd of friends and relatives, former hostages and numerous foreign journalists from paying respect to the dead. Candles were lit on the steps of the theatre where those gassed had lain barely alive, and where many of them died before medical help arrived. One hundred and thirty portraits of the dead were illuminated by the flickering flames of lovingly placed candles. It was raining, just as it had been two years before, and the rain mingled with our tears, just as it had then.

The rain could not, however, wash away the bad feeling left by this ideological cynicism. It was a sorry reaction by the state to the immense grief of those who had suffered from its incompetence, at the very place where its victims had lost their lives. The authorities' apparent contempt for their own citizens stems from their fear of us. They cannot face our grief, they cannot admit their own shortcomings or acknowledge their responsibility for the many victims of so many terrorist acts, which they have no effective strategy for dealing with.

This, alas, is precisely the future which awaits those who have suffered at Beslan. There will be an official version of the tragedy very different from the unofficial one. Grief will be permitted, within bounds, but the truth will not be told. Nobody will want to hear what those who were there have to say. Higher authority will decide what is to come out. Spontaneous emotion is not wanted, any more than it was under the Soviets. The ideological stance adopted by the authorities since the tragedy of 1 September is that nothing must be allowed to show that the authorities are incompetent (which they certainly were). Tears are permissible, but only in moderation, since everything is, after all, satisfactorily under control. While the tragedy should not be forgotten, there is no call for excessive displays of emotion which might be suggestive of despair. There can be no place for that in the land of the Soviets, because Putin is watching over us and knows better than we how matters should be arranged. There is light at the end of the tunnel, we are all fighting a war on international terrorism, and are, moreover, 'united as never before'.

On 29 October the Duma voted by an overwhelming majority to pass Putin's new law under which he would nominate candidates for the post of governor and the regional parliaments could rubber-stamp the single name being put to them. If a region's MPs should be so impertinent as to reject Putin's nominations twice, the recalcitrant parliament would be 'deemed to have passed a motion of no confidence' and would be dissolved by a directive of, yes, Putin again.

This, of course, makes a mockery of the Constitution and demonstrates complete contempt for the Russian people, but the Russian people took it only too calmly. Certainly the opposition held a few meetings, but these were quiet, local affairs and nobody paid any attention to them. Putin got his way. This is post-Beslan Soviet Russia in action.

So what is the situation after Beslan? 'The Party and the People Are One', the old Soviet slogan ran. In reality the rift grows wider by the day, while the images on television convey quite the opposite impression. Soviet-style bureaucracy is growing back and growing stronger, and bringing with it an old-style political freeze. No evidence of global warming here. Russia swallowed the lies about how the *Nord-Ost* siege was ended, and now makes no demand for justice or an objective investigation of the Beslan atrocity. For two years after *Nord-Ost*, most of the population snored peacefully in their beds, or went out dancing at discos, occasionally rousing themselves for long enough to turn out and vote for Putin. It is arguably we ourselves who allowed Beslan to happen as it did. Our apathy after the *Nord-Ost* events, our lack of concern for the ordeal of its victims, was a defining moment. The authorities saw they had us back under their thumb and relapsed into the complacency which brought about Beslan.

We cannot just sit back and watch a political winter close in on Russia for another several decades. We want to go on living in freedom. We so much want our children to be free and our grandchildren to be born free. This is why we long so much for a thaw in the immediate future, but we alone can change Russia's political climate. To wait for another thaw to come our way from the Kremlin, as happened under Gorbachev, is now foolish and unrealistic, and neither is the West going to help. It barely reacts to Putin's 'antiterrorist' policies, and finds much about today's Russia entirely to its taste: the vodka, the caviar, the gas, the oil, the dancing bears, the practitioners of a particular profession.

The exotic Russian market is performing as the West has come to expect, and Europe and the rest of the globe are perfectly satisfied with the way things are going on our sixth of the world's land mass.

All we hear from the outside world is 'Al-Qaeda, al-Qaeda', a wretched mantra for shuffling off responsibility for all the bloody tragedies yet to come, a primitive chant with which to lull a society which wants nothing more than to be lulled back to sleep.

Nothing But the Truth

So What Am I Guilty Of?

[This article was found on Anna Politkovskaya's computer after her death and is addressed to readers abroad.]

'*Koverny*': a Russian clown whose job in the olden days was to keep the audience laughing while the circus arena was changed between acts. If he failed to make them laugh, the ladies and gentlemen booed him and the management sacked him.

Almost the entire present generation of Russian journalists, and those sections of the mass media which have survived to date, are clowns of this kind, a Big Top of *kovernys* whose job is to keep the public entertained and, if they do have to write about anything serious, then merely to tell everyone how wonderful the Pyramid of Power is in all its manifestations. The Pyramid of Power is something President Putin has been busy constructing for the past five years, in which every official – from top to bottom, the entire bureaucratic hierarchy – is appointed either by him personally or by his appointees. It is an arrangement of the state which ensures that anybody given to thinking independently of their immediate superior is promptly removed from office. In Russia the people thus appointed are described by Putin's Presidential Administration, which effectively runs the country, as 'on side'. Anybody not on side is an enemy. The vast majority of those working in the media support this dualism. Their reports detail how good onside people are, and deplore the despicable nature of enemies. The latter include liberally inclined politicians, human rights activists, and 'enemy' democrats, who are generally characterised as having sold out to the West. An example of an on-side democrat is, of course, President Putin himself. The newspapers and television give top priority to detailed 'exposés' of the grants enemies have received from the West for their activities.

Journalists and television presenters have taken enthusiastically to their new role in the Big Top. The battle for the right to convey impartial information, rather than act as servants of the Presidential Administration, is already a thing of the past. An atmosphere of intellectual and moral stagnation prevails in the profession to which I too belong, and it has to be said that most of my fellow journalists are not greatly troubled by this reversion from journalism to propagandising on behalf of the powers that be. They openly admit that they are fed information about enemies by members of the Presidential Administration, and are told what to cover and what to steer clear of.

What happens to journalists who don't want to perform in the Big Top? They become pariahs. I am not exaggerating.

My last assignment to the North Caucasus, to report from Chechnya, Ingushetia, and Dagestan, was in August 2006. I wanted to interview a senior Chechen official about the success or failure of an amnesty for resistance fighters which the Director of the Federal Security Bureau, the FSB, had declared.

I scribbled down an address in Grozny, a ruined private house with a broken fence on the city's outskirts, and slipped it to him without further explanation. We had talked in Moscow about the fact that I would be coming and would want to interview him. A day later he sent someone there who said cryptically, 'I have been asked to tell you everything is fine.' That meant the official would see me, or more precisely that he would come strolling in carrying a string bag and looking as if he had just gone out to buy a loaf of bread.

His information was invaluable, and completely undermined the official account of how the amnesty was going. It was conveyed to me in a room two metres square with a tiny window whose curtains were firmly drawn. Before the war it had been a shed, but when the main house was bombed its owners had to use it as kitchen, bedroom and bathroom combined. They let me use it with considerable trepidation, but they are old friends about whose misfortunes I wrote some years ago when their son was abducted.

Why did the official and I go to these lengths? Were we mad, or trying to bring a little excitement into our lives? Far from it. Open fraternisation between an opposition-inclined gatherer of information like me or another of my *Novaya gazeta* colleagues and an on-side government official would spell disaster for both of us.

That same senior official subsequently brought to the sometime shed resistance fighters who wanted to lay down their arms but not to take part in the official circus performance. They passed on a lot of interesting information about why none of the fighters wanted to surrender to the regime: they believed the Government was only interested in public relations and could not be trusted.

'Nobody wants to surrender!' The pundits will find that hard to believe. For weeks Russian television has shown dodgy-looking individuals declaring that they want to accept the amnesty terms, that they 'trust Ramzan'. Ramzan Kadyrov is President Putin's Chechen favourite, appointed Prime Minister with blithe disregard for the fact that the man is a complete idiot, bereft of education, brains, or a discernible talent for anything other than mayhem and violent robbery.

To these unholy gatherings squads of journalist-clowns are brought along (I don't get invited). They write everything down carefully in their notebooks, take their photographs, file their reports, and a totally distorted image of reality results. An image, however, which is pleasing to those who declared the amnesty.

You don't get used to this, but you learn to live with it. It is exactly the way I have had to work throughout the Second War in the North Caucasus. To begin with I was hiding from the Russian federal troops, but always able to make contact clandestinely with individuals through trusted intermediaries, so that my informants would not be denounced to the generals. When Putin's plan of Chechenisation succeeded (setting 'good' Chechens loyal to the Kremlin to killing 'bad' Chechens who opposed it), the same subterfuge applied when talking to 'good' Chechen officials. The situation is no different in Moscow, or in Kabardino-Balkaria, or Ingushetia. The virus is very widespread.

At least a circus performance does not last long, and the regime availing itself of the services of clownish journalists has the longevity of a mouldering mushroom. Purging the news has produced a blatant lie orchestrated by officials eager to promote a 'correct image of Russia under Putin'. Even now it is producing tragedies the regime cannot cope with and which can sink their aircraft carrier, no matter how invincible it may appear. The small town of Kondopoga in Karelia, on the border with Finland, was the scene of vodka-fuelled anti-Caucasian race riots which resulted in several deaths. Nationalistic parades and racially motivated attacks by 'patriots' are a direct consequence of the regime's pathological lying and the lack of any real dialogue between the state authorities and the Russian people. The state closes its eyes to the fact that the majority of our people live in abject poverty, and that the real standard of living outside of Moscow is much lower than claimed. The corruption within Putin's Pyramid of Power exceeds even the highs previously attained, and a younger generation is growing up both ill-educated, and militant because of their poverty.

I loathe the current ideology which divides people into those who are 'on side', 'not on side', or even 'on the wrong side'. If a journalist is on side he or she will receive awards and honours, and perhaps be invited to become a Deputy in the Duma. Invited, mind, not elected. We don't have parliamentary elections any more in the traditional sense of the word, with campaigning, publication of manifestos, debates. In Russia the Kremlin summons those who are irreproachably on side, who salute at the right times, and they are enlisted in the United Russia party, with all that entails.

Today a journalist who is not on side is an outcast. I have never sought my present pariah status and it makes me feel like a beached dolphin. I am no political infighter.

I will not go into the other joys of the path I have chosen: the poisoning, the arrests, the menacing by mail and over the Internet, the telephoned death threats. The main thing is to get on with my job, to describe the life I see, to receive every day in our newspaper's offices visitors who have nowhere else to bring their troubles, because the Kremlin finds their stories off-message. The only place they can be aired is in our newspaper, *Novaya gazeta*.

What am I guilty of? I have merely reported what I witnessed, nothing but the truth.

Published in a special issue of *Soyuz zhurnalistov*, 26 October 2006

Should Lives Be Sacrificed to Journalism?
A Questionnaire for the 'Territory of Glasnost' Project

Circulated to journalists, editors, and columnists of *Novaya gazeta*.

1. *Surname and first name, or pen-name* : Politkovskaya, Anna.
2. *Topic of specialisation* : Anything of interest to our readers.
3. *Your professional credo, or motto* : What matters is the information, not what you think about it.
4. *What is your first priority as a journalist?* To provide as much information as possible.
5. *What do you think about the times you live in, the people, the country?* The people are remarkable; the country is Soviet; the times are another Time of Troubles.
6. *What do you find most difficult to write about (and which story most illustrates that)?* Our times.
7. *What do you most enjoy writing about (and story)?* People.
8. *Why and for whom are you doing your work?* For people, and for the sake of people.
9. *How do you rate the work of those in power today who take decisions at the highest level and shape Russia's reputation both inside Russia and abroad (the President, government, judiciary, parliamentary deputies, and business elite)?* Management of the state is extremely inefficient.
10. *How do you rate the willingness of people to regard themselves as representatives of civil society and to engage in open dialogue with the state authorities?* Not highly. There is too much fear in society and too little idealism.

11. *How do you rate the level of democracy and independence of the press? What do you think is happening in Russia to freedom of speech, and where do you personally obtain reliable information (not as a professional, but as a user)?* Freedom of speech is on its last legs. I only trust information 100 per cent if I have obtained it myself.
12. *What recent events do you consider to have been a landmark for yourself, the country, and society (positive or negative)?* For the country, the occupation of Ingushetia; for society, the same; for myself, the same.
13. *What do you see as the main problems facing Russian society?* The fact that most people think it will never happen to them.
14. *What qualities most impress you, and which most disappoint you, in public figures and ordinary people? (Give examples if possible.)* I admire openness and sincerity. I am nauseated by lying and people who think they are cunning.
15. *Which politicians, economists, people in the arts and culture, and also private citizens could you nominate for Person of the Year, Hero of Our Times, or as iconic personalities in present-day Russia?* There are no heroes in sight. If we had one he would stop the war.
16. *How do you rate the quality of life in Russia? What factors should be taken into account?* Very low. The number of poor people is enormous and that is a disgrace.
17. *What can and should people (society), politicians, officials (the State), and journalists do to improve the quality of life in Russia?* Journalists should write; politicians should make a fuss and not wallow in luxury; and officials should not steal from poor people.

FSB Officers Carry Out Another of their Special Operations Against Novaya Gazeta

The Editorial Team of *Novaya gazeta*

28 February 2002

As special operations go, this was a pretty dismal effort. For technical competence we award the Chekists three points, but for artistic merit, alas, zero.*

A statement issued by FSB representative Ilya Shabalkin claims that *Novaya gazeta* and its special correspondent Anna Politkovskaya are trying to exploit her assignments in Chechnya to 'resolve their financial problems and disagreements with certain foundations'. Shabalkin has declared that Politkovskaya's assignments are characterised by undesirable sensationalism and are hindering the counterterrorist operation in Chechnya. He also baldly asserts that these sensations are part of an attempt to persuade the Soros Foundation to write off a grant of $14,000 which *Novaya gazeta* received for work in political hotspots.

Shabalkin claims that our newspaper has failed to provide the Foundation's Open Society Institute with an interim report, and that the Foundation has informed us in writing that it proposes to cease its financial support. Chekist Shabalkin additionally makes a particular point of claiming that Anna Politkovskaya lacked accreditation to work as a journalist in Chechnya.

All the pointers to a monstrous conspiracy are there: the link to American money, spreading disaffection among Russian troops on the orders of transatlantic fat cats, and absence of official permission to be operating in Chechnya at all.

The discovery of this plot against the Russian Federation was announced on all the main TV channels, distributed over the Interfax newswire, and gleefully published on the websites

---

* The Cheka was a state security service established in 1917. It was the forerunner of the KGB, now the FSB.

of the Effective Politics Foundation. It's a chore, but we have to respond. *Novaya gazeta*, like hundreds of other organisations, was awarded a grant, of $55,000, by the Soros Foundation for the purposes of establishing a database of individuals who have disappeared without trace in Chechnya; to facilitate the release of prisoners and hostages; and to provide support to an orphanage and old people's home. It is worth remarking that, although the grant was awarded last year, we have been doing all this work since 1994.

Our colleague Vyacheslav Izmailov succeeded in freeing more than 170 kidnap victims. Through the efforts of *Novaya gazeta*, and particularly those of our columnist Anna Politkovskaya, dozens of old people survived two winters in an old people's home in Grozny. With the aid of the Interior Ministry we moved the old people, who had completely lost hope, back to their relatives. The Soros Foundation appreciated these efforts and offered financial support, which we were glad to accept.

Of the $55,000 awarded, we have so far received only a first payment of less than $14,000. The reason is quite simply that for three months we had to hide Anna Politkovskaya outside the borders of Russia. When it was confirmed that an assassination attempt was being prepared against her, the law 'On Protection by the State' was invoked until the suspect was arrested. She was granted a special status which we are not at liberty to write about.

For these reasons our report was submitted in February this year. The Soros Foundation has no complaint against *Novaya gazeta*, and in the coming 12 months we will be receiving the remaining $41,000, and will continue our work.

In the allegations of hype surrounding Politkovskaya's assignments, Chekist Shabalkin has excelled himself. It was not we, or Politkovskaya, but the Press Office of the Joint Military Command which on 9–10 February issued a statement claiming that Politkovskaya had left the Commandant's Office in Shatoy without informing the military. Politkovskaya had good reason to leave. The facts communicated to her by the Military Prosecutors were too serious not to.

We repeat that we issued no statements, generated no hype. That was entirely the work of the FSB using the Army as its mouthpiece. So who set the ball rolling?

The answer as to why the FSB got so exercised is to be found in *Novaya gazeta*, Nos. 11 and 12. Using evidence from the criminal case and interviews with Military Prosecutors, Politkovskaya proved with facts and documents to hand that the shooting of six civilians, including a pregnant woman, and the subsequent burning of their bodies had been perpetrated by special operations troops of Military Intelligence. It is a unique case. Thanks to the courage of the Prosecutors and the public naming of the suspects, 10 military personnel have been arrested.

The FSB makes no attempt to refute these facts in its statement: it simply ignores them. The FSB is not concerned that this crime inflames and aggravates the war. The FSB is merely concerned that Politkovskaya did not have the requisite accreditation.

Actually, she did, and we print it here. Come on, Chekists! You will need to do better than this when preparing your disinformation.

In order to implement their highly intelligent campaign, the Chekists used some of our journalist colleagues as stooges. First the ultra-respectable *Vedomosti* carried an item to the effect that we had failed to provide a report to the Soros Foundation and that payment of our grant might be stopped. Why a serious business newspaper should suddenly start counting what by their standards is the small change in somebody else's pocket was baffling – until Shabalkin issued his announcement.

Statements were also distributed through Interfax, by then with our comments. At no point, alas, did our colleagues have qualms about printing private correspondence between *Novaya gazeta* and the Soros Foundation. You would think we were squandering taxpayers' money or the state budget.

How the correspondence was leaked is, however, a separate

issue. One copy is in the possession of the Soros Foundation, and the original was received by *Novaya gazeta*'s editor through the post.

Neither the Foundation nor the editor of *Novaya gazeta*, needless to say, passed this to the press; so somebody has been intercepting our post, opening our correspondence, trying to monitor the newspaper's activity, and perhaps, also, the activity of the Foundation. It is gratifying to report that they found nothing more substantial than a delayed report.

As in our case, only the FSB's failures enable us to see what they are getting up to on taxpayers' money. As usual, they are trying to suggest a link between articles which tell the truth about the Chechen War and Western intelligence services, Western money, and so on.

The FSB likes to show how well informed it is about other people's affairs, especially when they are none of its business and not within its remit. So it is far easier for them publicly to point out problems in Russia which don't exist, than to find terrorists like Khattab or Basayev. Or perhaps it is Politkovskaya and our delayed reports which are preventing them from being able to do that. Perhaps this is how they justify their professional incompetence. The replies to these and other questions will no doubt be obtained in court. Our lawyers are preparing to sue.

Don't be in too much of a hurry, Mr Shabalkin, to spoil your jacket by making a hole in it for that medal you hope to receive.

What Next?

4 March 2002

First the Editor of *Novaya gazeta* requested that I, Special Correspondent Politkovskaya, should write an irate open letter to Mr Shabalkin. I thought about it and declined. Just too boring. Then the Editor said we needed to write an irate open letter to Shabalkin's boss, Mr Patrushev, who runs the FSB. I thought seriously about this but again declined. Someone who can't catch Basayev and Khattab with a team of many thousands is not of the slightest interest to me. He can't even make me irate.

Then write to Putin! But instead I wrote a letter to Major Nevmerzhitsky, Commander of Reconnaissance of the Shatoy District Military Commandant's Office.

Major Nevmerzhitsky was a witness of the Shatoy tragedy – the murder and burning of the bodies of six civilians by soldiers of the Central Intelligence Directorate (GRU), which occurred on 11 January 2002 and was officially described by Khankala as an operation to capture the injured resistance leader, Khattab. It was this atrocity I was investigating during my February assignment in Chechnya. This so irritated the FSB that they embarked on the campaign of disinformation described above. Why did I address my letter to him? Because I felt like it.

Dear Vitaly,

See what they have been getting up to while we were trudging the tracks of Shatoy! They are saying we did it for money. Army Headquarters in Khankala claimed as much, and it doesn't really matter whose vocal cords they used. You were running around in the mountains; gazing down on the murder scene in horror from a cliff, trying not to fall off; discussing for days who had killed whom and burned their bodies; having to face 28 orphans. That kind of work, according to Officer Shabalkin, has a dollar value.

Of course we have nothing to prove to each other, and could now just keep quiet. But you actually saw what happened at Dai and Nokhchi-Keloy, and on the road to Barzoy where the bodies of two soldiers and an officer whom the Shabalkins of this world have no interest in have been lying in the river for over two months. You know that this is not about dollars.

At first I was very angry and thought that if Shabalkin had been in our shoes he would have had a different tale to tell. Then I calmed down and started to feel sorry for the man. 'They' in Khankala have a hard life: they have to run around like servants whose masters are in a bad mood in the morning because their boots haven't been properly polished. It's really not that easy to talk about places you have never been to and things you have never seen, and to make it look as if you are doing a great job and do know everything that's going on. You and I would blow our brains out rather than jump through hoops like those but Shabalkin, poor sod, plods on. So we are more fortunate, having seen everything with our own eyes and not having to pretend. Although we are not happier when we think about what it is we have seen.

How are things in Shatoy? Have they given up sending helicopters from Khankala to catch wounded Khattabs? How is Victor Malchukov getting on, the Shatoy Military Commandant who long ago saw the reality of what is going on around him, a man with haunted eyes? It must be difficult for you. I have an easier time here in Moscow, deflecting the attacks of idiots. It's a piece of cake by comparison with the mountains.

Anna Politkovskaya

Around me my family are grim-faced. I am flying out to Chechnya again, only I won't be meeting up with Vitaly. I have other plans.

The Saga of Anna's Assignment in Shatoy

14 February 2002

[On 11 January 2002, in what Army Headquarters officially described as an operation to capture the Chechen resistance leader, Khattab, soldiers of the Central Intelligence Directorate (GRU) murdered and burned the bodies of six civilians. Anna went to investigate.]

I take out the tape of my last assignment in Chechnya, and at the same time read through the newspapers and the news agency tapes.

Well, well. My colleagues seem to have been competing to see who could come up with the most unfounded stories. According to our esteemed Interfax news agency, I was detained on 9 February by the Shatoy District Military Commandant's Office during a special operation there because I did not have the necessary documents. It seems to concern nobody that there was no special operation in Shatoy, either immediately before, on, or after 9 February.

As I read on, the tone gets more caustic. It seems I escaped from the Commandant's Office and disappeared, thereby discrediting . . . I should be punished just where it hurts . . . The Press Office of the Joint Military Command in Chechnya fulminates that by my misconduct I have brought disgrace upon all journalists.

What actually happened was that on 8 February, the second day of my assignment, having made my way from Grozny to Shatoy, my first act, making no attempt at concealment, was to go directly to Sultan Mahomadov, the Director of the District Interior Affairs Office, and inform him of the purpose of my assignment: to investigate one of the most scandalous and tragic recent events in Chechnya, the extrajudicial execution and burning of the bodies of six civilians who were returning from Shatoy to their homes in the hill village of Nokhchi-Keloy on 10 January 2002. From the militia I went to the office of the District Administration and, as required, asked them to put a stamp confirming my arrival on my assignment papers. They duly did so.

From the District Administration I set off to the District Military Commandant's Office, to see the Commandant, Colonel Victor Malchukov. Why did I go to see him? Because, quite simply, I have known him for a long time, and respect his ability to talk to people in the villages, thereby resolving innumerable conflicts which arise between the Army and the civilian population.

We sat together and worked out a plan of how I could best do the job my newspaper had entrusted me with. The Colonel said that he had to fly to a meeting in Khankala the next morning, so alas there was a limit to the help he could give me.

My journalistic colleagues reported that I had been 'detained', and had 'escaped'. This was complete nonsense, although admittedly only in respect of 8 February, before the FSB piled in. By 9 February, it was already clear that the massacre near the village of Dai in Shatoy District by soldiers of the elite special division of the Central Intelligence Directorate of the Ministry of Defence had its roots, as people in Chechnya say, in Army Headquarters in Khankala.

At 11.00 a.m. on 9 February I had arranged an interview with Colonel Andrey Vershinin, the Military Prosecutor for Shatoy District, who is presently conducting a criminal investigation into the executions, and whose office is located within the headquarters of 291 Regiment, near the village of Barzoy, a few kilometres from Shatoy. The Military Prosecutor quite properly scrupulously checked all my documents, and then gave me a long interview in which he was as frank as it is possible to be while a case has yet to come before the courts. My sincere thanks to Colonel Vershinin. He is a terrific person to have in that job. We parted on friendly terms.

The surprises began immediately after this. During the interview, I discovered, my militia security officers had been questioned by FSB agents about me. What were they after? Why? Who gave them permission? Officers I did not know approached me, said they were well-wishers, and quietly advised me to get out of the regiment quickly, warning that preparations were being made to detain me, and that the FSB was categorically opposed to journalists sticking their noses into this case, which involved military commanders right at the top.

This was the moment when my 'disappearance' began; a change of cars, covering my tracks, searching for a place to sleep where no one would find me. There were many signs that this was far from a joke, and that it was vitally important to behave in just this manner. I very much wanted to stay alive and to get back home, in the face of a manhunt mounted by men armed to the teeth and with malice in their hearts. For this reason I had to dissolve in time and space, and not, as my press colleagues and the Khankala ideologists were shortly to write, in order to create a fuss and draw attention to myself.

Early in the morning of 10 February I slipped on foot into Starye Atagi, heavily disguised, avoiding checkpoints and the security sweep which was beginning in the neighbouring village of Chiri-Yurt. Moving very quietly, almost crawling on the ground, my main concern was not to attract any attention in order not to be killed. Escaping from Shatoy and from rabid FSB agents was only half the problem. Getting into Starye Atagi, which is now in the hands of the Wahhabis, was the next challenge. No federal soldiers or representatives of the new Chechen government walk the streets. They are very, very afraid of being killed. It's only journalists and human rights activists covertly collecting information who creep about like this, because journalists like me have no option, given how things have worked out in Chechnya, other than to keep a very low profile.

Perhaps you will think that this is playing at spies, that it amounts to militaristic thrill-seeking. Nothing of the sort. I hate this way of life. The situation created by the security agencies in Chechnya, and primarily by members of the FSB and Ministry of Defence, is so disgusting it makes me sick; a situation where a journalist's legitimate wish to be in possession of the full facts about an event results in direct threats to her life. What was I doing during those two days in Shatoy? My work, for heaven's sake, no more than that. Believe me, there is nothing more hateful than, in your own country, to feel that you are a target for shooting practice for parasites living it up, eating and drinking at your – a taxpayer's – expense. And then they have the gall to denigrate you.

Traditionally journalists do not write about how they get their facts. The reader's attention should be focused only on those facts themselves. That is entirely proper. Forgive me that today I have had to deviate from that ideal, reluctantly finding myself on the receiving end of a barrage of lies and conjecture.

A detailed report of my assignment in Shatoy will appear in the next issue. This will be the result of an investigation into the brutal murder of six civilians in Shatoy District, and I shall say no more about how I came by the facts. Only today, before I bring down the curtain, I will allow myself a few conclusions about the events which surrounded this inquiry.

In the first place, conditions for journalists working in Chechnya have been made completely impossible. I mean in terms of obtaining comprehensive information about an event.

In the second place, the unjustified, barefaced lies of the Army Command, passed on by most of the media without any attempt to check them out, are at the core of the world we now live in. More and more we are allowing ourselves to be brainwashed. It is a world where the Russian Army is encouraged to hunt civilians, including journalists, but not the terrorist leader Khattab.

And in the third place, many of my journalist colleagues, dancing to the tune of the state authorities and the Army top brass, are today prepared to do anything required of them, to report interviews without worrying about the truth, to write about scandals even when there are none, and all in order to avoid having to confront directly the fratricidal tragedy being perpetrated in Chechnya. That is what really matters about the mishaps which befell me on my last assignment, and which ended on 12 February.

Anna Politkovskaya

From the Editors

Novaya gazeta thanks General Victor Kazantsev, Plenipotentiary Presidential Representative in the Southern Federal Region, and many others for responding to our request to assist in the search for our special correspondent, Anna Politkovskaya.

We thank the Directorate of Personal Security of the Interior Ministry of the Russian Federation, and also the Secretariat of Presidential Aide Sergey Yastrzhembsky for helping to establish the whereabouts of our special correspondent after the incident in the Shatoy district of Chechnya.

Is Journalism Worth the Loss of a Life?

10 November 2003

Is journalism worth the loss of a life? Every time something like the events on the evening of 3 November in Ryazan happen – and in Russia attempts to kill journalists are no rarity – we, the servants and slaves of information, ask ourselves this question. If the price of truth is so high, perhaps we should just stop, and find a profession with less risk of 'major unpleasantness'? How much would society, for whose sake we are doing this work, care? In the face of that, each of us makes his or her own choice.

On 3 November 2003, at approximately 2104 hours, at the entrance to residential block No. 26, Zubkova Street in Ryazan, an attempt was made on the life of 30-year-old Mikhail Komarov, Deputy Editor of the Ryazan edition of *Novaya gazeta*. As he was returning home he was struck from behind on the head with a heavy blunt instrument. Komarov's reporting is well known in Ryazan, and in recent years he has specialised in investigative journalism, some of it delving into the commercial activities of the local oligarchs.

At night all the dormitory districts of Russian towns are as alike as identical twins. Their kinship is in the darkness which descends on them, in which you can kill a person, unseen and unhindered, and then escape without repercussions.

It is not yet late on 4 November, the day after the assassination attempt, but as usual you can't see a thing in the Ryazan suburb of Dashkovo-Pesochnoye. The district itself does not really seem to exist. Zubkova Street, 'Broadway', can only be sensed, immersed in the darkness of nonbeing. You can only feel that somewhere nearby is habitation. All the conditions for a successful hit are there. We grope our way along, guided by Valentina Komarova, Mikhail's mother, who is shocked by what has happened. She has two sons. The younger, Dima, is 20 years old and a promising footballer. Her elder, Mikhail, 'has turned out like his grandmother', Valentina explains, with a mixture of pride and fear. 'She was a truth-teller too. She survived the war and is still fighting to this day, although she is 80. She doesn't give in, and she's penniless. Misha is the same. How many times have I begged him, "Don't, son. Let them live their lives, and we will live ours." At work people kept telling me, "This is going to end badly." There, we've arrived. This is our entrance, No. 14.'

It was on these steps that two people in black woollen hats and leather jackets, the uniform of Russian hitmen, were waiting for Mikhail. The neighbours spotted them but, as is the way, thought nothing of it. 'As long as I'm all right, as long as it's not me they're beating up, everything is fine.' Here is the staircase the journalist crawled up, leaving a trail of blood, in order to escape his would-be killers. Today, just like yesterday, all the doors are firmly shut. The entrance is well adapted for murder, with dark corners in which you are your own rescue service, your own pyramid of power, prosecutor and militia.

Incidentally, the October District militia station is just round the corner. Actually, it is world famous because it was near here that, also in the darkness which is a friend not only of hitmen but also of the FSB, in the autumn of 1999 the Ryazan Directorate of the Federal Security Bureau was caught red-handed planting explosives in an apartment block just before the resumption of the Chechen War, the so-called hexogen 'sugar' training exercise.*

'Have you heard that somebody made an attempt on the life of the journalist Mikhail Komarov in your district yesterday?' I ask some young militiamen anxiously peeping out of the door.

'Yes. We've just seen it on television.'

'This kind of thing must often happen here, since you're taking it so calmly?'

'No, this is the first time,' Vitaly Vyazkov, duty officer at the station, says, not turning a hair.

---

* Apartment blocks in Moscow, Buinaksk and Volgodonsk were blown up, apparently by the FSB, with the loss of many Russian lives. The Chechens were blamed as a pretext for re-starting the war in Chechnya. An attempt to do the same in Ryazan was foiled, and was subsequently represented as a 'training exercise'.

Early morning on 5 November. On Wednesdays the October District Militia have an inspection parade. Some of the militiamen have not bothered to go to it and are smoking by the door, discussing the attempt to kill Komarov. 'He should have kept his head down,' a woman smoking a cigarette mutters. The others agree.

Their superiors arrive, the Acting Head of the District Militia, Alexander Naidyonov, and his deputy Yevgeny Popkov. 'We have nothing to say,' is their curt joint communiqué.

'Can you at least tell me whether you are instigating a criminal investigation? It is already 5 November.'

Colonel Naidyonov almost runs away from me, his eyes darting all over the place.

What's the problem? Isn't it straightforward: if there has been an attack on someone it should be investigated? Or might the militia's skittishness relate to the fact that in his statement Komarov named as his own prime suspect the Ryazan oligarch, Sergey Kuznetsov, one of the ten wealthiest locals, the owner of a large shopping centre and much else besides, about whose business methods Komarov frequently wrote?

This explanation seems to be confirmed when Investigator Mikhail Zotov, accompanied by Colonel Naidyonov, arrives to question the victim for the first time in the provincial neurological clinic. He is persistently curious to know why Komarov wrote so much about Kuznetsov. Was it, perhaps, Zotov suggests insistently, because he had been taking bribes to write 'good' articles about him and then, when Kuznetsov stopped paying, he started writing critically about him? This is what Kuznetsov is saying. No doubt everybody judges by their own standards. 'Give us what we want and we're on your side. Don't, and we're against you.' That is the sickening creed of the militia.

It is almost noon but the enforcers of law and order are in no hurry to get on with their work, and are plainly not on Komarov's side. We rush around Ryazan, putting together a criminal case: from the October District Prosecutor's Office to the Ryazan Provincial Prosecutor's Office, from there to the October District

Militia on Yesenin Street and finally, forcing our way into the office of the indignant Colonel Naidyonov, encounter a very amiable Georgian who will subsequently tell us, 'I am a Georgian, and accordingly the man has not yet been born who can bribe me.'

This is the Head of the Provincial Criminal Investigation Department, Militia Colonel Dzhansug Mzhavanadze, and he informs us with some ceremony that a criminal investigation was opened on 5 November at 11.30 a.m.

'What work is being done on the main line of inquiry, involving Kuznetsov? Are Komarov's articles being attached to the file, and his statement to the FSB two weeks ago that he was being threatened?'

'I am not at liberty to tell you about the means and methods we are employing to solve the crime.'

We fully understand, and carry on crisscrossing Ryazan to try to ensure that these do not turn into means and methods of covering up a crime. Oligarch Kuznetsov is everybody's daddy.

The oligarch is unflustered, and very democratic in his ways, as you would expect of a major financial supporter of the Governor of Ryazan.

'What sort of an oligarch am I?' Sergey Kuznetsov asks coyly. In an earlier life he was the Secretary of the District Committee of the Young Communist League. He radiates civilised behaviour, bonhomie and modesty. 'I borrowed $5,000 from my mother-in-law yesterday. I have invested my last kopeck in my business. I don't have a home of my own. I should have emigrated to Israel long ago. My mother, Galina Abramovna, is there and here I am struggling for a better life. I am a builder. By nature I am a creator. On the old rat-infested city rubbish tip I built a retail centre with 600 shops. I opened the best beauty parlour in Ryazan, which has an excellent surgeon. He gave my wife's breasts a lift, and removed my moles. Everybody without exception is pleased. Only Misha Komarov is dissatisfied. He writes endlessly that the plastic surgery operations are performed without a licence. He's just trying to settle personal scores with me. I am getting tired of his articles. I decided to teach him a lesson.'

'To teach him a lesson? Do you know that on 3 November someone tried to kill him? Just after he had left another court hearing against you?'

'You won't believe me but I've only just heard about it, immediately before our meeting.' The oligarch calls in the head of his security service, a large fellow in a black leather jacket. 'Have you been to the hospital?' he asks him.

The bodyguard relays in detail what the doctor told him about Komarov's state of health.

'Isn't it strange that the doctor has passed all this information – confidential medical details – to your Viking?'

Kuznetsov is pleased with the effect he is having and smiles masterfully.

'What confidential details are you talking about? I was treated in that very same neurosurgery department after somebody lobbed a grenade at me. But Misha never seems to learn.'

'What right do you think you have to "educate" Komarov as if you were his father?'

'In Ryazan I am everybody's father, and it seems to me I am having some success. Komarov thinks more carefully about what he writes, he weighs his words now. Personally I think *Novaya gazeta* is great. And don't be afraid for Misha; he has been hit on the head many times before because he doesn't know when to give way.'

We part, having got nowhere.

During the afternoon Victor Ognyov, the Deputy Prosecutor of Ryazan, makes a surprising announcement: he says a criminal investigation was launched yesterday, 4 November, at 1910 hours, rather than at 11.30 on 5 November as Colonel Mzhavanadze was assuring us just a couple of hours ago.

'The militia are saying something quite different. Who should we believe?'

'They simply did not know.' Ognyov imperturbably shuffles the papers in his file, where two separate directives about instigating one and the same case are visible to the naked eye. 'We intervened operationally so that everything would move along more effectively. First we appointed Skrynnikov, a junior investigator, but now at my request a more experienced official will investigate the matter (Mikhail Zotov, who was defending Kuznetsov against Komarov). We're about to send a special report on all this to the Prosecutor-General's Office in Moscow since, as you will agree, this is not a routine case. We are observing all the requirements of the Criminal Procedure Code.'

'But why is the charge merely "disturbing the peace"?'

'Because Komarov was neither killed nor robbed. There was no intention of killing him.'

'How can you be so sure? Do you know the person with the intentions?'

'We know if they had meant to they would have killed him, but they were merely giving him a fright. It will be a matter of minor physical injury affecting the victim's health for a short time.'

'He hasn't recovered yet!'

'You will forgive my remarking that there is no article in the Criminal Code relating to beating up a journalist.' Ognyov smiles sardonically.

Evening falls once more. Misha is lying in one of the narrow beds typical of an underfunded Russian hospital. His head is bandaged and he looks pale. His mother has brought in all the medicine, bandages and syringes he needs because as usual there are none in the neurosurgical department. No doctors or nurses in the evenings either, but luckily Valentina is a nurse herself. Komarov is holding forth to his neighbours about democracy, the duty of the mass media, and the need to be unflinching in the fight against corruption which spoils life for everyone. His neighbours listen sullenly, either because of their own ailments or because they have little faith in the victory of democracy or in the need to make the effort Misha is describing. Sitting on the edge of the next bed, Valentina lectures her son.

'Yes, I understand what you are saying, and I am not against your being a journalist, but you do need to be more careful.'

'We can't give in, Mum,' Mikhail answers with the passion of one who will brook no compromise in the fight for good. He is in a state of post-traumatic euphoria, ready for the worst, fearing nothing. 'Let them be afraid every week of what we are going to write about them, not we of them!'

'What are you going to do now, Misha?' I ask in parting.

'Carry on writing articles,' Komarov replies unyieldingly.

So, is it worth sacrificing your life for journalism? How does each of us make our choice?

Every successive attack on a journalist in Russia – and by tradition nobody ever gets caught – relentlessly reduces the number of journalists working because they want to fight for justice. The risks are very great and not everyone is up to the unremitting tension which accompanies this kind of work. As the numbers of one kind of journalist fall, so there is an increase in the number of those who prefer undemanding journalism, reporting which doesn't involve prying where you are not welcome.

Undemanding media cater for an undemanding public, ready to agree with everything it is told. The more there is of the former, the more monolithic the latter becomes, and the less opportunity society has of seeing what is wrong with the circumstances in which it lives.

In the last few months the situation has been deteriorating rapidly. It seems we are at a tipping point, and that soon the Government (the oligarchs, the FSB, the bureaucracy) will no longer be breathing down our necks, because they will have achieved what they want: there will be nobody left prepared to lay down their life in order to get at the truth about other people's lives. If there is no demand, there will be no supply.

[More than three years later, the criminals still have not been caught: neither those who attacked Mikhail Komarov, nor those who paid them to do so.]

The War in Chechnya

Chechnya Belongs to Russia, But We Don't Want the Chechens

31 January 2000

The crusted wounds look painted on. The shaven head of a semi-conscious child moves feverishly to and fro on an over-laundered greyish-brown institutional pillow. No groaning or whimpering, only a silence deeply unsettling in someone so seriously injured.

'She has small shrapnel fragments in her head, but don't waste your time on that,' the emotionless voice of a middle-aged woman instructs me from a dark corner of the ward. 'Much worse is that now she is an orphan. And take a look under the blanket!'

The shaven skull stubbornly continues trying to dispel its delirium. The little girl is five, her face jaundiced and sallow. Her name is Liana Shamsudinova, and from time to time her eyes flicker half open and stray disapprovingly over the ward without coming to rest on anyone. Her left hip is not covered by the blanket and is worryingly streaked with pus leaking from beneath an enormous dressing.

'You Russians count her as another resistance fighter,' the monologue from the corner goes on. 'The girl needs specialist treatment if she isn't to be crippled for the rest of her life, but she isn't going to get that here, and we don't get sent to clinics anywhere else in Russia, because we are Chechens.'

My invisible informant had correctly identified the most important issue that day. The setting was Sunzha District Hospital No. 1 on the Chechnya–Ingushetia border. Until recently every day saw a steady inflow of those most severely injured in the war zone in the security sweeps, raids, repeat raids and repeat security sweeps. Hundreds of people with amputated limbs: women, children, the elderly, Ingushes, Chechens and Russians. The wounds of most were neglected and festering because they had had to shelter two or three days in cellars waiting for the bombing to stop, unable to leave their villages. Then they had to wait as long again for soldiers at the checkpoints to relent and let them cross over into Ingushetia.

The result has been a wretched carnival of infection in the Sunzha hospital, destroying any remaining nerve endings. Along the corridors, spectral young girls swathed in bandages shamble with unfeeling, lifeless arms and legs. The nerves in some limbs have been severed, while others have succumbed to gangrene.

Who will pay for the intensive courses of treatment they will need for years to come? The same state budget which today is funding the war that crippled them in the first place? Where is our valiant state, conducting this war in accordance with its 'overall plan', expecting to find the money to provide artificial limbs for the hundreds of newly disabled it has created? Which of its plans contains the budgetary provision for that? Who is going to accept responsibility for the thousands of civilians whose health has been taken from them in the course of this fighting?

Millennium Celebrations Caused this Tragedy

I hate battle-pieces. In paintings, as in life, detail is what matters most. It is the detail which gives the measure of our humanity. How we react to the tragedy of one small person accurately reflects our attitude towards a whole nationality; and increasing the numbers doesn't change much. Little Liana Shamsudinova was born in 1994 in Martan Chu, Urus Martan District, and the recent details of her life are entirely typical of today's Chechnya.

Fleeing the bombing, her family lived from October to December 1999 in a refugee camp in the hill village of Assinovskaya. From mid-December the refugees came under increasing pressure from Migration Service officials, who did not want them concentrating in one locality and urged them to return to their home villages, assuring them that peace had returned and their area was secure. On 29 December Liana's mother, Malika Shamsudinova, finally fell for these lies, the family went back to Martan Chu, and just four days later Liana was orphaned. On 3 January 2000 at 8.20 p.m. their home on Pervomaiskaya Street suffered a direct hit from a tank shell.

There was no military engagement at that time in Martan Chu, but the soldier who fired the shell knew perfectly well what he was doing. He fired just for the hell of it. By current standards in Chechnya 8.20 p.m. is late at night. The federal command has ordained that absolutely everybody must remain in their houses. They are not even allowed out into their own courtyards to relieve themselves, on pain of being shot without warning. This actually happened in Novy Sharoy to Mahomadov, a refugee from Naur, who ventured out just as dusk was falling and was shot in his doorway by a sniper.

Liana's house was wilfully targeted by someone well aware that it was inhabited. A lit oil stove, that surest sign of life, was visible through the windows. There is every reason to suppose that the shelling was an expression of drunken exuberance on the part of the tank troops deployed on the outskirts of Martan Chu. There was no other firing on the village that night. The soldiers simply loosed off a shell and their unruly emotions were placated.

'They were celebrating the New Year,' Liana's aunt, Raisa Davletmurzayeva, surmises. This is what the villagers also concluded.

The result was that Liana's mother, Malika, was killed. She was 28 and was breast-feeding her youngest son, Zelimkhan. The shrapnel split her head in two, and the neighbours who ran to the Shamsudinovs' house found her body cooling, her breast exposed, and Zelimkhan pressed to it.

The little boy's position was unchanged in death, firmly clasped in his dead mother's arms. From beneath the remains of the roof the neighbours retrieved the bodies of Liana's elder sister, seven-year-old Diana, and, next to her, of her 18-year-old aunt, Roza Azizayeva, who had come to help about the house. The neighbours carried Liana out, alive and crying. There were no other survivors and today she is an orphan, her father having disappeared somewhere in Ukraine after going to Belaya Kalitva in search of work a year ago.

Since then Liana has not spoken to anyone, and she was certainly not going to speak in Russian to me. She has been in shock since 3 January, and only calls out from time to time in Chechen for her mother. In her lucid moments fellow patients have tried to communicate that her mother is dead. It is a Chechen tradition not to conceal misfortune, to teach children to be brave, even when a very young child is facing a lifetime of having to be brave.

'I will look after her of course,' Raisa tells me, 'but there is a limit to what I can do. In the Sunzha hospital we had to buy everything ourselves, hypodermic syringes, drugs, drip-feeds. She needs a lot of medical care. Where am I to find the money for that?' By now we are talking in a different hospital, in Galashkino, a tiny primitive facility with only 40 beds. Nearly all the wounded have just been transferred here from Sunzha, which is closed for a thorough disinfection. Contagion spreading from neglected 'Chechen' wounds had reached crisis levels.

Liana, although blameless, is also a carrier of infection, and now finds herself in the markedly worse conditions and reduced nursing care of Galashkino Hospital. The wards are cramped and overcrowded, there is little equipment, and it is freezing cold because the heating system is useless. With her major gangrenous fractures, Liana is unlikely to recover in such conditions. How can people survive when the Empire, sweeping aside all in its path, declines to rest its baleful gaze on those who happen to be in its way?

On 4 January the Shamsudinov family funeral was held in Martan Chu. In full view of the tank crews basking in the Caucasian sunshine, all the women and children they had murdered were borne to the cemetery. Not one of them even came to apologise for their New Year high spirits.

Similarly vile, but even more cynical behaviour was displayed in Shali. On 9 January the administration of this district centre assembled people in the central square to issue the first pensions and benefit payments from the Russian-installed government of Nikolai Koshman. There is a school facing the square and Zarema Sadulayeva, its Deputy Headmistress and maths teacher, had also gathered the children to finish giving out New Year and Kurban-Bairam (Eid ul-Adha) presents.

They had no idea that at that same moment resistance fighters were entering the far end of this very large village. A tactical missile came crashing down, not on the enemy detachment but straight into the crowded central square. The fighters melted away, but in the square many people died or were severely injured. How many? Dozens? Hundreds? There is a large discrepancy in the figures given for the simple reason that the surviving villagers could not dig graves fast enough and many buried their relatives together, so that there were fewer graves than casualties. It was another Guernica, comparable in horror to the infamous missile attack on the central market in Grozny last October.

The nightmare was repeated in Shali the following day. Ali-bek Keriev, Zarema's husband, took his severely injured wife away from the hospital, fearing that it too might be targeted. He asked his sister, a doctor, to come and care for her. Alas, 40-year-old Kisa was killed during an ensuing mortar bombardment, and since 9 January Ali-bek has been unable to sleep. He maintains a full-time vigil at his wife's bedside. On 13 January he managed to move her, pregnant and close to death, to the central hospital in Nazran but the outlook is not good. He can't bear to look at her dreadful wounds and watch her convulsions. She desperately needs powerful, intensive-care drugs but as usual they are in short supply. In his sleepless nights Ali-bek writes poetry, a personal appeal to the Being who may or may not be sitting on high observing everything that happens here below. All Zarema had done was to go out to distribute presents to children.

Whatever appeals may be addressed to the Almighty, relations between civilians and federal troops are just as soulless in Shali as in Martan Chu. There will be no inquiry into the killings in Martan Chu, the massacre of a family not meriting a criminal investigation. No prosecutor will question the shameless lies which tricked the Shamsudinovs into returning to their village. The implication is that the aftermath of the New Year crime is the personal problem of this luckless little girl and her Aunt Raisa, who now faces the task of trying to bring her up. Raisa views the future with unconcealed foreboding; in order to treat the child's injuries adequately she would need a lot of money for the proper drugs, a top-class clinic and consultants, things she is not going to find in Martan Chu or anywhere else in Chechnya or Ingushetia today. Be that as it may, the Empire refuses to make an exception: Chechens are not allowed beyond the borders of Chechnya and Ingushetia. Not a single general is to be found with the decency to admit that he bears any guilt for Liana's suffering, or that it is his duty to help her.

The situation is identical in respect of Shali: no half-witted gun layer has been blamed for devastating the central square, no criminal charges are being brought for the murder of civilians. Nobody has so much as apologised.

Madina and Alikhan: A New Generation Consigned to a Hospital Bed

Madina and Alikhan Avtorkhanov are cousins. Their mothers Khava and Aishat are sisters. Khava lived in Samashki and Aishat in Novy Sharoy in Achkhoy-Martan District. They were not far from each other, but the shelling left them separated by a whirlwind of deadly lead flying in all directions.

In this war family reunions take place outside operating theatres. The sisters met in the treatment unit of Sunzha Hospital. Khava was at the bedside of 22-year-old Madina, while Aishat was looking after her younger son, 18-year-old Alikhan. (Her elder son died during random shelling of their village during the First Chechen War.) Madina, only recently a beautiful young girl but now worn out by operations and pain, her parchment-coloured face and body a shadow of what they were, has almost certainly been permanently crippled by the injuries she sustained on 27 October. Some of her bone has been cut away and they need to find somewhere for her to have an operation, and then somewhere for her to convalesce because their house at 27 Kooperativnaya Street has been destroyed.

The history of Alikhan's illness is no less grim. One leg has already been amputated above the knee as a result of the curse of gangrene. For several days the soldiers refused to allow the wounded to be taken out of their village. He has already lost the big toe on his other foot and so far attempts to stop the gangrene from spreading have been unsuccessful. Alikhan is a quiet, thoughtful young man who holds Russia responsible for destroying his life on 23 October, the day he was injured. He has no plans for the future now. His only distraction is when one of the men visiting the hospital picks up his stump of a body and takes him for a 'walk' along the corridors.

Alikhan tells me that none of his classmates are still alive. He left school along with eight other boys and eight girls. All the boys have since been killed. He is alive, but crippled. Everybody was sheltering in their cellars during relentless shelling of Novy Sharoy. When things quietened down at around nine in the morning Alikhan's classmates quietly came together beside his house at 12 Tsentralnaya Street to discuss what they should do. Mortars were fired at them and all except Alikhan were killed. Who is going to provide the complex, expensive artificial limbs he now needs?

'Nobody, of course,' Alikhan says. 'I am a Chechen. I can just crawl from now until the day I die.'

'Why do you get so het up about them?' the officers demanded when I tried to find out who would be responsible for supplying the artificial limbs and treatment required after these wicked acts against the civilian population. 'They are not human beings, they are little furry animals. Don't worry, they'll soon give birth to plenty more new little furry animals.'

My present assignment to report on the war in the North Caucasus has immersed me in the suffering of our people, interspersed with this kind of insolent frontline and near-frontline cynicism. The war-zone slang is little better than what is going on there. They refer to Chechen men, even the resistance fighters, with the more or less respectable label of 'Chechies'. All other Chechens, particularly boys, children, and young people generally they call 'little furry animals'. Who does? The entire military and administrative infrastructure waging and servicing the present war. Even the hospital doctors have this wretched expression on the tip of their tongue. It is bad enough coming from sergeant majors, but a complete disgrace coming from the intelligentsia.

When this nightmare was inaugurated in September 1999, one did secretly hope in the depths of one's heart that the state would catch terrorists and refrain from waging war against everyone in Chechnya. Some hope! Today it is obvious that the policy from the outset was genocide. The genocide of one people, however, soon leads to the genocide of another, a truism borne out through the centuries by successive generations of invaders and those invaded. For the totalitarian empire being constructed in front of our eyes, punitive expeditions give life meaning. Today one group is sent to the guillotine, tomorrow a different one. The day after tomorrow it will be the turn of little Liana, and later still, we need have no doubt, it will be our turn.

Perhaps the genocide would be justified if the villains who grew rich by holding hostages to ransom and selling oil illegally were totally eradicated? There is no chance of that happening. The kidnappers are quietly resuming their business under a different guise. Petrol tankers from the liberated regions of Chechnya are again turning up in Plievo in Ingushetia. Refining continues at full tilt. The Chechen oil irregulars have sat out the cataclysm and are back in business.

But what about the so-called Wahhabis, the Islamist extremists? Perhaps they have been melted down by the flamethrowers, or have slunk away to caves in the mountains? Wrong again! On

18 January, Idris Satuyev, a Chechen refugee, Headmaster of the school in Alkhan-Yurt, was shot at point blank range by unidentified individuals in Maiskoye, Ingushetia, just for wearing a tie. 'I told them that had been my custom throughout a long working life in the school. My lifestyle is European and secular,' the headmaster wheezes. He has survived but is now very ill in the overcrowded Nazran Hospital, in Ward 3 of the accident department. Idris lies there dreaming of the only way out of his situation: to emigrate once and for all from our sixth of the world's land surface; no longer to be a Chechen obliged to live anywhere near us Russians.

How to Recruit a Disposable Women's Brigade

9 June 2003

[On 15 June 2003, 17 people died and 16 were injured as the result of an explosion on a bus transporting military and civilian personnel to the military air base at Mozdok. The attack was carried out by a female suicide bomber. On 1 August, as the result of another terrorist attack at the Mozdok military hospital, 51 people died and more than 100 were wounded.]

Once again, words flood from the television screen . . . 'suicide bomber', 'that bastard Basayev', 'Maskhadov knew', 'zombified by centres of international terrorism beyond the borders of Russia . . .' Instead of analysis, primitive ideological war cries: 'Enemies of the political process, trying to keep it from developing'; 'We will deal with Basayev and there will be no more suicide bombers'. Oversimplification of the problem to a level which only moves us further away from taking a sensible decision on how to deal with this new phase of Russia's Chechen tragedy.

So, what is really going on? What is happening to Chechen women in this fourth year of the Second Chechen War? Do they really need to be brainwashed and 'zombified' by centres of international terrorism?

No, actually they don't. No external input is required to make a Chechen woman decide to become a disposable terrorist bomber, because the work has already been done. A typical Chechen woman today really is a zombie: she has been turned into one by the grief in which she has been immersed for year after year, by the environment surrounding her family. She has been trained to be a suicide bomber not in foreign training camps but by the brutality shown by the warring sides towards the civilian population in Chechnya. This is what has engendered an overriding desire in thousands of mothers, wives and sisters to take their own cruel revenge for their disappeared sons, husbands and brothers.

She does this not because of the dictates of a Chechen form of Islam or the traditional *adats* or laws which govern life in her country, but out of despair. The Constitution adopted by referendum on 23 March has only increased the numbers queuing up to join the women's brigade for these special operations because there were high hopes that it might change something. Alas, the new Constitution has proved to be just so much paper. It has not stopped the Army's anarchy and is protecting nobody.

The number of civilian men and women 'disappeared' by the federals during the spring of 2003 has been far higher than during the same period last year. Worse, the authors of the fake political process leading up to 23 March unforgivably promised those searching for their abducted relatives that if they would just vote, some of the disappeared would return home; they would be released from prison. 'The Kremlin has given the go-ahead,' they lied. 'Just vote!'

Nobody returned, so let us not delude ourselves that the increase in terrorism since the referendum is a coincidence which Basayev is exploiting. It is all far more complicated than that.

Who is she, today's Chechen woman? The traditional upbringing of a Chechen woman is ascetic in the extreme. Her obligation is to endure everything without complaint. She should not speak of her personal feelings. For her, virtue is concealment, the ability to hide her feelings deep down, not to show them – not only publicly but even at home in front of her closest male relatives. All her turbulent emotions are bottled up. But can that last for ever?

The devotion and love of a Chechen sister for her brothers, and especially of a Chechen mother for her sons, is passionate and absolute. The strength of feeling is volcanic, and most Chechen women believe that with the loss of a brother, a son or a husband their own life comes to an end.

During the first and second years of the war these private volcanoes did not erupt. The Chechen women were waiting in the hope that everything would come right. They said they had faith that their menfolk would fulfil their traditional role. A Chechen boy is brought up to believe that a man's first duty is to defend woman and home. Unlike a girl, a boy can be spoilt; much can be overlooked by a woman in return for his willingness to die protecting her, if that should be required.

That is not what happened. The war dragged on, until finally all the traditions collapsed under the pressure of the style of war so mercilessly imposed by the federals. Chechen men found themselves having to be defended by the women. It was the women who haggled in bazaars in order to feed their families, and threw themselves under Army vehicles in an attempt to stop them kidnapping their men; while the men mostly stayed out of sight in cellars in order not to be abducted, 'swept' or blown to pieces.

This is how Chechen women were propelled into the foreground of the struggle. They were radicalised more quickly than the men hiding behind them, even if the men continue to believe they still have at least some measure of authority. The Chechen woman finally found a way of letting her powerful emotions burst out. The volcano erupted with molten lava whose bounds are only those it sets itself, vigilante justice as the only effective response to unbridled violence. Women rose up to defend their families, inflicting personal retribution on those they themselves pronounced guilty of murder. They chose to die rather than go on living, unable to defend their sons, brothers, or husbands.

★

I can already hear my opponents protesting, 'But Basayev claimed responsibility'.

Of course he did. He will claim responsibility for anything he can. The terrorist mantle of Salman Raduyev, who 'died' in prison, had to be inherited by somebody. Far more important is not who claims responsibility, but that there are women prepared to carry out the acts for which somebody else subsequently claims responsibility. There is no shortage of women prepared to blow themselves up, and their ranks are growing the longer the Army's atrocities continue.

But what about the Chechen men? After the suicide bombings in Znamenka and Iliskhan-Yurt on 12 and 14 May many spoke harshly against the women who carried out those attacks. 'They have humiliated us,' they said. 'They have shown us we are impotent.'

And so they did. They did humiliate the men and show them they were impotent. The reversal of traditional roles was complete. The women had independently dotted the i's. They would no longer rely on the men, discuss matters with them first, ask their advice. Instead, they would decide things for themselves, very quietly and privately, and the world would see only the result.

That's the reality, but everybody keeps prattling on about al-Qaeda, that lifebelt for failed politicians.

What is to be done now? We really cannot take seriously the security agencies' assurances that they are reinforcing checkpoints and sealing the administrative border of Chechnya, and that everything is 'under control'.

In the first place, nothing is under control other than the sloshing of black market currency through the checkpoints. In the second place, imposing even more severe restrictions will not stop women participating in terrorist attacks. In the third place, it is absurd to demand that Maskhadov should call upon the women to abandon these tactics: the women have reached boiling point because of the actions of many men, including Maskhadov. They will simply ignore him.

In the fourth place, finally and most crucially, the mind of someone bent on retribution functions extremely efficiently. You will not keep up with it or be able to guess which weak point it has identified. Checkpoints and checking everybody's documents will be ineffective against women carrying explosives on their person. 'We will pass through your checkpoints "pregnant",' some of them say. 'Your lot are not going to look under our skirts, and you can't keep a gynaecologist at every checkpoint.'

The only solution is to overhaul Russia's policy towards Chechnya. We need to take a step in their direction if we want to survive. This means a complete clampdown on the Army's anarchy. It means beginning peace negotiations (nominally between Maskhadov – if you can talk to Arafat you can talk to him – and nominally the Kremlin), under the watchful eye of authoritative international observers, in order to effect a rapid demilitarisation of the Republic, cessation of hostilities, and bringing of war criminals to justice. The sole result of the referendum was to tack the title of 'Acting President of the Chechen Republic' onto Akhmat-hadji Kadyrov. It is self-evident that Kadyrov, as someone incapable of anything other than feathering his own nest, should be removed.

The future political status of Chechnya? There will be time to think about that later. First, let's survive.

Nobody can doubt that it will take a hero to disentangle this mess, and heroes are currently in short supply. We need, nevertheless, to find such a hero, because we have already burned every other bridge.

The Soldiers' Mothers Go Off to Think About Proposals from the Chechen Side, But Will it Stop the Terrorism?

28 February 2005

The latest development in Russia's history is that in the sixth year of the Second Chechen War the first Russo-Chechen declaration of intent to restore peace in the North Caucasus has been signed in London. It is in English, and is not available in Russian. It is called 'The Road to Peace and Stability in Chechnya (the London Memorandum)'. The signing took place on 25 February 2005 when women representing the Union of Committees of Soldiers' Mothers of Russia, after several unsuccessful attempts to find somewhere in Europe to discuss a peace settlement with Maskhadov's representatives, finally came to London, the capital of the new Russian emigration. There they met with those whom Aslan Maskhadov had delegated to meet them on behalf of the Chechen resistance (Amina Saiev, Deputy Minister of Foreign Affairs of Ichkeria, Akhmed Zakayev, Maskhadov's Special Envoy in Europe, and Yaragi Abdullayev).

[The following account of the prehistory is taken from Anna Politkovskaya's article, 'The Struggle for Peace Is Deadly Dangerous', *Novaya gazeta*, 25 October 2004.]

On 9 October, a Saturday, when it usually becomes slightly quieter in the cramped Moscow office of the Union of Committees of Soldiers' Mothers of Russia and it is possible to think about something other than the immediate concerns of receiving soldiers, conscripts and their parents, Valentina Melnikova, a member of the Union's Coordinating Committee, and Ida Kuklina, a member of the President's Commission on Human Rights, sat down together. They discussed what is preoccupying nearly all the human rights organisations: the state authorities' manifest inability to cope with the Chechen crisis, the continuing acts of terrorism, and what the Soldiers' Mothers movement could do to change the situation. It was time to act.

Thus did the idea of writing an open letter to the field commanders of the Chechen resistance come into being. A further three days were spent revising and discussing it with members of the Committee, and on 13 October the following brief text was released to the news agencies:

We understand the cost of the armed violence in Chechnya; it involves immense and irreparable losses for the Chechen people. Hundreds of thousands have been killed or have disappeared without trace. There are refugees; ruins in place of cities and villages. Thousands of our sons, both soldiers and officers, have died. There have been hundreds of innocent victims of terror. A whole generation of young Chechens and Russian servicemen has been crippled by the experience of violence and lawlessness. Thousands of impoverished invalids are doomed to a life of penury. Tens of thousands of families grieve over the loss of those dear to them. Such is the cost of this war, which long ago exceeded the losses incurred during the Afghan War. Ten years of war have not brought the desired results either for you or for the federal authorities. Terror engenders antiterror, and vice versa. Neither in Chechnya nor in Russia do people feel safe.

Commanders of the Chechen armed groups! You will kill or be killed without end. You will not be able to change anything until you are recognised as negotiating partners. The Soldiers' Mothers appeal to those of you who truly seek the good of the Chechen people with a proposal to give peace a chance and open negotiations for a peaceful settlement. We are willing to travel anywhere, to meet those you authorise anywhere, in order only to halt this deadly race. In coming forward as the initiator of negotiations, we will make all necessary efforts to involve in the negotiation process representatives of the leadership of the Chechen Republic and the Russian Presidential Administration, inter-governmental and peace organisations, and influential and respected public figures. We await your reply.

Members of the Coordinating Council of the Union of Committees of Soldiers' Mothers of Russia, Valentina Melnikova, Maria Fedulova, Natalia Zhukova.'

The reply was not long in coming. The very next day Aslan Maskhadov communicated through Akhmed Zakayev, his envoy in Europe, that he and the fighters of the resistance welcomed the Soldiers' Mothers' initiative: for their part, they were willing to attend such a meeting. A day later, Zakayev rang Melnikova and their communications ceased to be only in writing. 'We agreed that the meeting should take place in a European country in November,' Valentina explains briefly.

The Mothers flew to London on 24 February. Their accommodation was decidedly acceptable: the Waldorf, one of central London's most luxurious hotels, near the famous Waterloo Bridge across the Thames. They came down to the hotel lobby at about 5.00 p.m., at first behaving like secret agents behind enemy lines. They were very nervous. On this note the meeting began between Ida Kuklina's group (and it was she, a colleague of Pamfilova and member of President Putin's 'Committee to Promote Civil Society', who was running the Mothers' show) and Zakayev's team. The meeting was held in the hotel's conference room from 5.00 p.m. until midnight. At first the Mothers demanded secret negotiations, which suggested that these representatives of civil society had secrets they wanted to keep from civil society. At 7.00 p.m., however, at the Chechens' insistence, observers representing *Novaya gazeta* and Radio Liberty were admitted. It was clear that journalists, unlike politicians, just wanted to see somebody at last agreeing to seek peace in Chechnya, and doing something to make it happen. Yet it soon became apparent why the Mothers were so reluctant to admit outsiders. They had come to London without any proposals other than that 'a Multi-Lateral Working Group should be set up to begin considering preliminary steps for the negotiating process', as Ida Kuklina put it.

'What, in your view, should be the mechanism for a ceasefire?' the Chechens asked.

'That is for the Working Group to decide,' the Mothers replied.

'But the Working Group cannot work while the war is continuing,' one Mother said doubtfully. 'We need a ceasefire. That is the main thing.'

'That is a matter for the Working Group, not us,' other Mothers corrected her.

'We would like to propose two groups of delegates, one from

each side, to establish their own ideas about the mechanism for a ceasefire, and then to bring them together.'

'No. Only a Multi-Lateral Working Group with everybody in it. With third-party observers.'

It was fairly pointless trying to discuss anything, and that looked decidedly odd. They had been moving towards this meeting for such a long time, and had presumably been preparing for it. Alas, I cannot write in detail about what was discussed at the Waldorf Hotel. The Mothers insisted I should convey only the gist, which I now do because it is particularly important for anybody who had high hopes for peace resulting from this meeting. The gist was that all proposals from the Chechen side were rejected. Not one made it into the final memorandum. As Ida Kuklina explained afterwards, 'We will take them back with us and consider them.'

'And what action will you take?' *Novaya gazeta* asked.

'I don't know,' Ida Kuklina replied.

'Why do you keep going on at us?' Valentina Melnikova added. 'We are ill old-age pensioners.'

'So as to be able to write about this.'

'Write anything you like.'

This too seemed very odd. What had been the point of seeking this meeting if there was no sense of urgency? They had evidently come to London for some other purpose.

In fact, at the Waldorf Hotel flaccidity alternated with bursts of hyperactivity. 'We cannot wait for Russian society to reach a consensus,' the Mothers declared. 'We have been at the forefront for the past 16 years. We do not wait, we act as the situation requires. The only place where people can come for help is to the Committees of Soldiers' Mothers.' That is an exaggeration. They are not by any means the only place people can go, even in Moscow. It was followed, however, by a truly absurd exaggeration: 'The generals will do what we tell them to.'

The Chechens were amazed. In that case, why had they not told them to stop the war long ago? Or was that not what they meant?

★

Zakayev's group tried consistently to hurry the Mothers along. They tried to persuade them of the need for momentum. Time was not on our side: they explained that radicalism in their ranks was increasing, which it might soon no longer be possible to contain. The overall situation in the North Caucasus was highly volatile. The Mothers, however, were not budging. One thing at a time. 'People are expecting a miracle from us, but there is not going to be one.' We heard that repeated again and again.

The Mothers' belief that taking things slowly was a fundamental principle of popular diplomacy was supported by the observers from European institutions: 'We are prepared to provide a venue for further meetings with the same participants somewhere in Strasbourg or Brussels, and we will continue the dialogue.' The European representatives who had flown in specially to London were Vytautas Landsbergis, the former President of Lithuania and today a Member of the European Parliament; and his Belgian colleague Bart Staes. Later, on 25 February, they were joined by Andreas Gross, a member of the Parliamentary Assembly of the Council of Europe (PACE); Lord Judd, former rapporteur to PACE on Chechnya, and Baroness Sarah Ludford, the main organiser of these Chechen–Russian meetings in London.

They broke up on 24 February having agreed the draft text of a joint London Memorandum which acknowledged the thousands of victims and the fact that the conflict cannot be resolved by military means.

Queen Anne's Gate is the name of a London street near St James's Park and here, on the morning of 25 February, the parties met in the presence of European observers for a concluding two-hour discussion and press conference, which as a matter of principle was to take place on neutral territory, in the British office of the European Union.

Baroness Ludford presided, firmly and constructively. The aim of the meeting was to finalise a joint statement, the London Memorandum: 'The Road to Peace and Stability in Chechnya'.

Thanks to the superhuman efforts of the Baroness, it did eventually materialise. The main reason why the London Memorandum was adopted in English is because this was the Baroness's native tongue and there was no time left to translate it. It was accordingly in the English language that the London Memorandum became part of the history of the Russo-Chechen War of the twentieth and twenty-first centuries.

Incidentally, as regards the Russo-Chechen nature of what is going on in the North Caucasus, and the complicated and paradoxical climate of the London meetings, the Mothers spent an inordinate amount of time attempting to lower the emotional charge of the Memorandum's language. They wanted to make sure that nobody officially labelled the war 'Russo-Chechen', but only, blandly and inoffensively, 'this conflict', in accordance with the Kremlin's official position to characterise it as an 'internal armed conflict'. The fact that the Memorandum will go down in history in a foreign language itself demonstrates that the conflict amounts to something more than an internal matter.

Queen Anne's Gate closed at 1400 hours Greenwich Mean Time on 25 February 2005. The greatest positive result was that a meeting had at least taken place. For the time being, that is all. The Mothers saw that the other side are not devils with horns, don't bite, are entirely reasonable and moderate. If on the 24th everything had got off to a nervous, edgy start, it concluded on the 25th with a joint photograph, although even that took some organising. It is to be hoped that these new insights will be taken back with them to the Kremlin. And then? Who knows?

Finally, who was paying for all this? People in Russia traditionally take an interest in that aspect whenever anything is happening in London. Was, perhaps, Berezovsky paying for this junket? Well, this time you can be reassured. I checked. All costs were paid by the European Parliament. The Mothers even handed its representatives their air tickets as proof of expenses. For that we owe the European Parliament a big thank-you, for saving us from damaging rumours.

The text of the proposals of the Chechen side, presented to the Soldiers' Mothers, was:

Step 1. Ceasefire and fight against terror. The opposing sides, via special representatives, create a mechanism for an immediate ceasefire without preconditions. The Chechen side is ready to cooperate in combating terrorism, both within the framework of bilateral relations and as a part of the international coalition to fight terrorism.

Step 2. Demilitarisation. After an armistice is reached, the removal of Russian troops from the Chechen Republic and the disarmament of the National Militia take place simultaneously. The functions of providing safety are transferred to a temporary peacemaking contingent in connection with this.

Step 3. Transition period. During the period between the ceasefire and elections, the state functions are assumed by a temporary coalition government, created under international control. In questions of providing safety the Provisional Government relies on the peacemaking contingent. (The 'Kosovo' option – AP) The legal basis for the creation and working of the temporary coalition government of the Chechen Republic of Ichkeria is the agreement of 12 May 1997. ('Agreement on Peace and Principles of Mutual Relations between the Russian Federation and the Chechen Republic of Ichkeria', concluded in accordance with the Constitutions of the RF and ChRI. – AP)

Step 4. Elections. Based on the Agreement of 12 May 1997, the Provisional Government prepares and organises direct democratic elections with participation of all political forces of the Chechen Republic under the observation of international institutions.

Step 5. Economic reconstruction. The European Union is called upon to grant large-scale, direct economic aid for the reconstruction of Chechnya.

The Secret of Maskhadov's Assassination. How and Why the Second President of Chechnya Was Killed

19 September 2005

In the Chechen Supreme Court in Grozny the trial begins this week of those who were with Maskhadov at the moment of his assassination.

Was he killed? Did he commit suicide? Was the body planted? Was it a planned operation or did they happen upon him by chance? It is still debated how and why it was that on 8 March 2005 in the village of Tolstoy-Yurt death came to Aslan Maskhadov, elected President of Chechnya in 1997 and 1999. With the outbreak of the Second Chechen War, it was Maskhadov who led resistance to Russian federal troops and who gradually became the personal enemy of Vladimir Putin.

Before 8 March any conversation with Russian soldiers in Chechnya about Maskhadov and Basayev would conclude with them claiming that everybody knew where Maskhadov was, only the order had not yet been received to bring him in, and that was the sole reason why neither of them was already in prison.

Does that mean that on 8 March the order was finally given? After the killing, both the federals and indeed everybody else started concocting increasingly bizarre and contradictory accounts. He had shot himself. He had ordered his bodyguards to shoot him. He had been killed in a different place and the body had been moved to Tolstoy-Yurt.

Novaya gazeta is in possession of the case files of Criminal Case No. 20/849, relating to the circumstances surrounding Maskhadov's assassination. The investigation was conducted by the same team from the Prosecutor-General's Office as the Beslan cases. Four individuals were held from March to September in the Vladikavkaz pre-trial detention facility and gave evidence in the Prosecutor's Office of North Ossetia. They are now in the dock in Grozny.

The four accused are: Ilias Iriskhanov, one of Maskhadov's bodyguards who arranged his accommodation in Tolstoy-Yurt; Vakhid Murdashev and Viskhan Khadzhimuratov, Maskhadov's bodyguards; and Musa (Skandarbek, according to his passport) Yusupov, owner of No. 2 Suvorov Street, Tolstoy-Yurt where Maskhadov stayed without leaving the house from 17 November 2004 to 8 March 2005). All four are charged under the Russian Criminal Code, Article 209, Part 2 ('banditry: membership of an established armed group'); Article 222, Part 3 ('illegal acquisition, storage, or bearing of firearms, explosive devices, military supplies, under the aegis of an organised group').

The main question is, why was Maskhadov killed in March 2005, and neither earlier nor later? The whole of the last winter of his life was spent in the expectation that peace feelers were about to be put forward. We now know this is not speculation but a fact.

From the evidence of one of the witnesses: 'He (Maskhadov) told me that negotiations with Putin were about to begin. On 23 January Aslan Maskhadov told me he had suspended the war on the Chechen side.' Similar testimony is scattered throughout the case. What were Maskhadov's hopes based on? Who instilled and fostered them right up until his last day?

We know the answer to that. Mainly it was Andreas Gross, a Member of the Swiss Parliament and former rapporteur on Chechnya to the Parliamentary Assembly of the Council of Europe, who visited the Republic under the vigilant monitoring of the Special Operations Executive of the Russian FSB, and accordingly became convinced by the winter of 2004 that he knew all there was to know about Chechnya. Also Akhmed Zakayev, resident in Great Britain, Maskhadov's Special Envoy in Europe. Also members of the Committee of Soldiers' Mothers.

Beginning in November, the very time when Maskhadov moved to Tolstoy-Yurt, Mr Gross began shuttling back and forth between European capitals and Moscow, preparing the ground for round-table discussions on Chechnya. He met a number of highly placed individuals, members of the Presidential Administration, and they assured him they were 'ready for peace'. The only condition they put to Gross was that he should cut out all undesirable contacts, by which was meant that his shuttle diplomacy for peace should exclude all those who had been insisting on peace from the inception of the Second Chechen War. Among those deemed unacceptable were most civil rights activists, including the author of these lines. Those who were acceptable were the officials of pro-Moscow Chechnya: Khanid Yamadayev, Alu Alkhanov, even Ramzan Kadyrov, and Mahomed Khambiev, the former Defence Minister of Ichkeria who had defected from Maskhadov to Kadyrov.

Gross was completely sincere and committed to the tasks for 'peace' which he had been set by Putin's Presidential Administration, and to the whole business of shuttle diplomacy entrusted to him. He told me all about it himself in Helsinki during those winter months. The main stopover in his shuttle trips was London, where he assured Akhmed Zakayev that this was the best way to proceed. Zakayev was in constant contact with Maskhadov and it was he who passed on all these hopes of peace and encouraged Maskhadov to believe that the long-awaited negotiations with Moscow might soon start.

In the meantime, the London negotiations of the Union of Committees of Soldiers' Mothers with representatives of one of the belligerent parties collapsed. They collapsed for the very good reason that the Soldiers' Mothers suddenly started adopting a hardline position in London, as if blithely unaware that failure was precisely what Moscow wanted from them.

This left Maskhadov with only one potentially promising, but in fact disastrous, way forward to peace: the 'path of Gross'. He took the bait. Reassured by Gross's blandishments, which he heard about from Zakayev and over the Internet, Maskhadov let down his guard and began regularly using a mobile phone. Russia had succeeded in killing his predecessor, President Dudayev, by locating him through his use of a mobile phone, and during all the previous years of the war Maskhadov had never touched one. Now his main method of communication became text messaging.

As one of the witnesses testifies: 'Aslan Maskhadov used his mobile telephone for sending text messages. When I asked him why he didn't ring anybody, he replied, "The whole world knows my voice. They would work out where I am instantly."'

It was through mobile telephone traffic that Maskhadov's whereabouts were established. More precisely, the intelligence services registered the fact that the source of the traffic was in Tolstoy-Yurt.

If we try to summarise what happened in the last months of Maskhadov's life, we find that he was weary of the war and of living in hiding. He did his utmost to achieve peace by making major compromises; he accepted the need to take extremely radical steps, and, to demonstrate his willingness, announced a unilateral cessation of military operations on 14 January, with an extension on 23 February. In other words, throughout the winter of 2004–5 Maskhadov was, on the one hand, being drawn into the Kremlin's games, but on the other was clearly outsmarting Moscow in the management of the peace process. 'Management' is perhaps not the ideal expression, but it best approximates to what was going on during the winter on the Tolstoy-Yurt–Moscow–Helsinki–Brussels (where Gross's round table was conducted)–London axis.

By March, Moscow was finding Maskhadov's activity intolerable and the process moved beyond Gross's control, even though he is an influential individual. 'Maskhadov's peace initiatives' were a constant topic of conversation in the political salons of Europe: the European Parliament, the Parliamentary Assembly of the Council of Europe. I know what I'm talking about because I was there. In the continent's highest diplomatic circles Putin began to recede into the background, acquiring the reputation of a man who 'would not compromise despite what common sense dictated', a man 'moving matters towards the next Beslan'. A moment came when Putin was clearly under considerable pressure from Western leaders as a result of Maskhadov's peace initiatives.

So, what are we talking about here? About the fact that Maskhadov's assassination was a direct result of his peace efforts last winter. He signed his own death warrant by seizing the peace initiative, if only briefly.

To all appearances, Maskhadov was very seriously preparing to declare a unilateral ceasefire, which he believed should be timed for the beginning of contacts between Akhmed Zakayev's group and the Soldiers' Mothers in London, as a sign of goodwill on the part of one of the warring parties. The ceasefire would be extended to coincide with Gross's round table in Brussels.

In order to achieve a real armistice, however, Maskhadov needed to reach agreement with the principal actor in the Chechen War, Basayev. Accordingly, on 13 November 2005 Basayev, summoned by Maskhadov, appeared at No. 2 Suvorov Street and stayed for six days. There is some lack of clarity about dates in the case materials, where it is asserted both that Maskhadov moved to Tolstoy-Yurt on 17 November, and also that on 13 November Basayev came to visit him there. Our information is that Basayev stayed in Tolstoy-Yurt from 13 December.

He stayed for six days, and the amount of time they spent together is very important. In the first place it refutes rumours that Maskhadov and Basayev never stayed in the same place, let alone for so long, in order not to be killed simultaneously. But the fact is a fact: they remained together in a very small residence.

From the testimony of one of the witnesses: 'He (Basayev) stayed for about six days in the old house (at that time the owner, Musa Yusupov, had two houses standing on a plot of 1,500 square metres: an old adobe house, and a new stone house). He and Maskhadov were together all the time and talked at length. When they were together they did not allow anybody else near.'

In the second place, those six days spent in conversation are clear proof that Basayev had no wish at all for a truce. Maskhadov did not let him off the hook and succeeded in bringing him round; Basayev deferred to Maskhadov and the truce was more or less observed by Basayev's men. As even the official media later stated, explosions in early summer 2005 were the work only of malcontents taking revenge. These had long been a third, and very serious, force in Chechnya, taking orders neither from Maskhadov nor from Basayev.

Agreement to observe a ceasefire was achieved between Maskhadov and Basayev. This raises an agonising question, to which for the present we have no answer: if Maskhadov was able to influence Basayev in this matter, why did he not do so over Beslan? Why did Maskhadov not use all his influence to prevent the seizure of the children?

As the evidence of one of the witnesses relates: 'Maskhadov also told me in conversation that the seizure of Beslan had been a mistake. He was very displeased about it.' A 'mistake'? Not a catastrophe?

Now, some accompanying detail about the last months of Maskhadov's life, which also tells us a lot. Would it have been possible for the federal forces to have arrested Maskhadov and Basayev earlier? Were they within their reach? Judge for yourselves, for instance, from the manner in which both were travelling around Chechnya last winter when, supposedly, everything had long ago been brought under control and, supposedly, operations were 'constantly being mounted to track down those guilty of the Beslan tragedy'.

This from the testimony of one of the witnesses: '17 November 2004. During the night we went to a meeting (with Maskhadov, near Avtury). We drove into Soviet Farm No. 4 at approximately 2130 hours. Some 200 metres from the bus stop we stopped the car, flashed the lights two or three times, and approximately two minutes after this a car standing at the bus stop drove off in the direction of Mozdok. (At the bus stop) stood Vakhid and Viskhan, who are distant relatives of Maskhadov, and Maskhadov himself.

Beside them were five or so large bags. They had at least three rifles and one sniper's rifle, black with a thick barrel. They also had three pistols. Maskhadov's was much longer than those of his bodyguards. The three of them were wearing green combat uniforms. In one of the bags I could see a military combat uniform.'

There follows a description of how all this baggage was casually loaded by Maskhadov and his bodyguards into the boot of the car and the back seat, and they headed off towards Tolstoy-Yurt. Through all the checkpoints, through localities riddled with nocturnal secrets and patrols. Avtury, where Maskhadov and his two bodyguards were standing at a bus stop, is completely under the control of one of the regiments of the Interior Ministry's troops, and there are legions of Kadyrovites there around the clock. Or at least, that is what the Kadyrovites claim. These details give support, if only indirectly, to the belief that in November 2004 no order had been issued to kill or even arrest Maskhadov. In late February 2005, however, it was.

Even more startling is the testimony regarding Basayev's trip to Tolstoy-Yurt to meet Maskhadov: 'Halfway to Farm No. 4 (again, in closely monitored Avtury) there was a vehicle. Some 200 metres before we reached it, the vehicle drove off and we approached Shamil Basayev. He was alone. Shamil Basayev had a plastic sack and a large sports bag. He was armed with a rifle. When I asked him what he had in the sack, he replied, "a sleeping bag".'

If Maskhadov's voice may not, in fact, be known to the whole world, Basayev's face is surely familiar by now to everybody on the planet. Here he was, standing at a bus stop, completely alone, with no mask, carrying a rifle and a sleeping bag.

Let us recall the official version of why Basayev supposedly could not be caught. He was said to be hiding all the time in the mountain forests, lurking in a network of caves, and if he moved he was invariably surrounded by a host of men armed to the teeth, so that to capture him would cost too many of 'our' lives. Does that mean that as of this date there were no orders for Basayev's arrest? We have no answer to that question.

Maskhadov spent almost four months in Tolstoy-Yurt, hemmed in virtually the whole time, at first in the old adobe house, but then from the end of December he and his bodyguards went down to the cellar. The case materials give its dimensions as 2 × 2 × 2 metres. A cramped vault.

From the testimony of one of the witnesses: 'They only came out of the cellar to pray namaz, at dawn and in the evening. Aslan Maskhadov, Vakhid and Viskhan (Murdashev and Khadzhimuratov) had three computers which opened like a book, and two video cameras. Maskhadov spent practically the whole day at his computer. They sometimes videoed themselves with the cameras. In approximately early February 2005, a man who appeared to be about 40 years old came to the house. He had a short beard and was wearing civilian clothes. In conversation with Maskhadov they called this man Abdul Khalim (Sadulayev, Maskhadov's successor. He just walked in, and equally easily left).

'On 8 March at about 9.00 a.m. armed men ran into the courtyard of No. 2 Suvorov Street shouting "Come out one by one with your hands up!"' They asked Musa Yusupov whether his house had cellars. 'I showed them the cellar area beneath my new house. Then they started conducting a search and in the old house found the entrance to the cellar in which Aslan Maskhadov, Vakhid and Viskhan were living. The soldiers blew up the entrance to the cellar and after that one of them shouted, "I can see a body." They shouted through the opening they had made to ask if anybody was alive in the cellar, and shortly afterwards took Vakhid and then Viskhan out of the old house.'

At the moment the entrance to the cellar was blown up, according to the case materials, Maskhadov was closest to it and took the full force of the blast. That is why he died instantly. His bodyguards survived only because Maskhadov died.

Do you remember the television images of the dead Maskhadov, stripped to the waist, lying on concrete in a courtyard? That was the Yusupovs' courtyard, despite all the official fairy tales suggesting it was Kadyrov's.

The Yusupovs' courtyard no longer exists. The adobe house collapsed during the operation on 8 March, and some four days later federals arrived, laced the Yusupovs' new house with ribbon explosives and destroyed all the evidence, thereby ruling out any tests or the possibility of an independent inquiry. One important question is: how sure were the soldiers that it was Maskhadov in the cellar?

Some three days before the operation they knew only that an important figure of some description was in this part of Tolstoy-Yurt. Maybe Basayev, maybe Umarov [Doku Umarov, a later President of Ichkeria], or maybe Maskhadov. That was all. By late in the evening of the seventh, however, from tracing the text messages it was evident that, with a high degree of probability, it was Maskhadov living on Suvorov Street. The information was sent to Moscow, and overnight a special Russian unit, answerable directly to the Director of the FSB, flew out. The reason why the culmination of the operation was not entrusted to soldiers of the Special Operations Centre of the FSB, which is permanently deployed in Chechnya, was simple: mistrust even within a single Ministry, and particularly of officers who are permanently stationed in Chechnya. The problem of the selling of information is acute.

The special flight of Moscow troops, and the fact that they were waited for in Chechnya for several hours without anybody else moving to the concluding phase of the operation, is further evidence that they knew it was Maskhadov they were dealing with. The Moscow agents who flew to Tolstoy-Yurt were a group of Russia's best commandos whose only task is to kill. And kill they did, because this time the order had come.

What resources did Maskhadov have for defending himself, if, indeed, he was intending to defend himself at all? What was found in the cellar?

It has to be said that there was precious little. He had a typical Chechen array of four assault rifles (between five men). Three of 5.45 mm calibre, and one of 7.62 mm. There were three homemade grenades, and one F1 grenade for blowing himself up. There should also have been the renowned Maskhadov Stechkin, his personal Army officer's pistol. The Stechkin, however, disappeared. We find the papers of the criminal case peppered with the investigators' questions about where the Stechkin had gone. Nobody kept an eye on it at the time.

Death, of course, is no laughing matter, but the morals among the Army in Chechnya, where looting has become ingrained over many years, make it difficult to suppress a wry smile. Even the operation to liquidate Maskhadov was not free of a spot of looting. To put it politely, the Stechkin was filched by the killers. Maskhadov had it when he was in the cellar but after the operation it was nowhere to be found. It's not difficult to imagine the details: the Stechkin is now hanging on a wall, or perhaps it is in a safe, belonging to a member of the FSB's special operations unit, and when he has had a drink or two its new owner shows off his trophy to his comrades-in-arms, or girlfriends, or, heaven knows, perhaps even to his children. The Stechkin will turn up at auction 50 years or so from now. It is the sort of thing that has happened often enough in the past.

So where does that leave us, in September 2005, as a trial begins at which the circumstances of the last months of Maskhadov's life will be under scrutiny, full as they were of peace initiatives, the Internet, and text messages bleeping from morning until night?

Basayev and Sadulayev want to hear nothing about peace. Their answer to the assassination of Maskhadov is only a long war, a parallel clandestine government, and explosions, armed conflict, and people dying on all sides every day.

And against this background, we have the constant bluffing by government officials about how wonderful it is in the newly Chechenised and Kadyrovised Chechnya. Mike Tyson, a semi-naked Miss Sobchak, an aquapark, a Disneyland, free parliamentary elections, Zhirinovsky and the rest of them posing against the backdrop of Grozny to which peace has supposedly returned. In fact they are all in a bunker, in a besieged city within a city, a government complex where they have now even built houses for the bureaucrats so they don't ever have to risk taking a step outside the confines of this stronghold. The reality – not the politicians' virtual reality – is that there is a total absence of even elementary control of the country, and an equally total absence of security for people who have nowhere to run to, and are forced to survive by fair means or foul.

Could not peace have been given a chance?

A Witness for the Prosecution Becomes a Witness for the Defence. The Zakayev Case: The Latest Sensation in a London Court

28 July 2003

There were few people in Court 3 of Bow Street Magistrates Court, London on the morning of 24 July 2003. Although hearings were resuming in the case of The Government of the Russian Federation versus Akhmed Zakayev, the Russian side had already indicated that the day would be of little interest, as they always do when there is to be cross-questioning of a witness for Zakayev's defence. This time there was a noticeable lack of members of our Prosecutor-General's Office, who are usually only too eager to come to London. Sergey Fridinsky, Deputy Public Prosecutor for the Southern Federal Region, charged with ensuring the extradition of Maskhadov's Special Representative, had decided not to fly in. Igor Mednik, Investigator of the Southern District Prosecutor's Office and second-in-command of the Zakayev case, had also decided to ignore Zakayev's defence witnesses.

How unwise. Mednik and Fridinsky would have been surprised to discover that a witness for the prosecution, a supposed victim of Zakayev, was instead appearing before Judge Timothy Workman as a witness for Zakayev's defence. In the case materials sent from Moscow and prepared by Investigator Mednik, Duk-Vakha Dushuyev figures as Zakayev's former bodyguard, who in December 2002 testified that in January 1996, on the orders of the individual whose extradition is sought, his other bodyguards had taken hostage two Orthodox priests, in Chechnya on a peacekeeping mission, in order to hold them to ransom. These were Father Anatoly Chistousov, who subsequently died in captivity, and Father Sergius Zhigulin, whose monastic name is Father Philip and from whom the court had already heard evidence.

Background

Akhmed Zakayev, born 1959 in Kazakhstan, graduated from the Department of Choreography of the Grozny College of Culture and Enlightenment and the Voronezh State Institute of Arts. From 1981 to 1990, actor with the Khanpasha Nuradilov Grozny Drama Theatre.

From 1991, Chairman of the Union of Theatre Workers of Chechnya and Board Member of the UTW of Russia.

From 1994, Minister of Culture of Chechnya.

From 1995, from the beginning of the First Chechen War, Commander of the Urus Martan Front. Subsequently Brigadier-General, Aide to the President of Ichkeria for National Security, member of the delegation preparing the Khasavyurt Agreements [which ended the First Chechen War in 1996].

Stood in 1997 for the presidency of Chechnya.

From 1998, Deputy Prime Minister. From the start of the Second Chechen War, commander of a special operations brigade.

In March 2000, wounded and evacuated from Chechnya.

From 2001, Special Representative of President Aslan Maskhadov.

A request to Interpol for Zakayev's extradition was issued by the Russian Prosecutor-General's Office. This led to his arrest for the first time on 30 October 2002 in Copenhagen. On 3 December 2002 he was freed by the Danish courts, which refused extradition on the grounds of inadequate evidence. On 5 December 2002 Zakayev arrived in London, where he was again arrested at

Heathrow Airport but released on bail three hours later. After a number of technical sessions, the hearing of the case began at Bow Street Magistrates Court in London on 9 June 2003.

A short Chechen advances towards the witness box to the right of the judge. His legs are unnaturally straight and he is forcing his recalcitrant feet forward, trying not to look at anybody and doing his best to conceal the difficulty he has in walking. This is Duk-Vakha Dushuyev. Though we are in London, the Second Chechen War has trained me to recognise the problem immediately: Duk-Vakha walks exactly the way many other men in Chechnya do who have survived the 'antiterrorist operation' but been left with limbs first fractured and then badly set.

'What do I have to swear on?' the witness asks the translator, reaching the stand, and his smile doesn't seem real. It is mask-like. 'On the Bible or the Quran?'

'As you please.'

Having taken the oath, Duk-Vakha explains that he was born in 1968, so he is only 35, although he looks nearer 50.

Barrister Edward Fitzgerald, QC, begins the cross-examination for Zakayev's defence:

'Did you testify against Mr Zakayev on 2 December 2002?'

'Yes.'

'Is this the testimony?'

Duk-Vakha is shown the case materials sent to London by the Prosecutor-General's Office and confirms to the court that this is the record of his own questioning in Grozny by Junior Judicial Counsellor Konstantin Krivorotov, Investigator of Particularly Serious Cases of the Chechen Prosecutor's Office. It reads:

'In approximately October 1996 I learned that it would be possible to become a bodyguard in the Ministry of Culture of the Chechen Republic. For approximately four months I took shifts guarding the building of the Ministry of Culture. In approximately February 1997 (name obliterated) invited me to work as

Zakayev's bodyguard. I agreed and from February 1997 to February 2000 was beside Zakayev virtually all the time. On one of Zakayev's visits to Urus Martan, I was tasked with accompanying him together with (obliterated). Even before this I had observed a white metal chain worn by (obliterated) on his trousers. I asked him where he got this chain, to which (obliterated) replied that he had taken it from an Orthodox priest who had worn an Orthodox cross on it. (Obliterated) told me that in 1995 two priests had arrived in Urus Martan to negotiate the release of Russian servicemen. Zakayev ordered that the priests should be kidnapped with the aim of obtaining ransom of $500,000 to finance weapons and equipment for the resistance fighters.

'Carrying out Zakayev's orders, (obliterated) recruited five or six members of Zakayev's bodyguard to take part in the kidnapping. In order to implement the plan successfully (obliterated) himself changed clothes and had his subordinates change into militia uniforms. I asked (obliterated) who could pay such a huge amount for freeing the priests, to which I received the reply that the Pope was prepared to pay $1 million, and also $500,000 had been promised by [Russian Orthodox] Patriarch Alexy II. I understood from his account that Zakayev failed to obtain the ransom. From the beginning of the counterterrorist operation, that is from 1999, Zakayev was in charge of the so-called Chernorechiye Front which offered armed resistance to the Armed Forces of the Russian Federation on the approaches to Grozny. During that period I was constantly beside Zakayev. We offered armed resistance to Russian troops until February 2000 when there was a mass retreat from Grozny. At that time Zakayev was paralysed. That is where I saw Zakayev for the last time.'

'Yes, that is my testimony.'

'You said then that Mr Zakayev gave orders to kidnap two priests?'

'Yes, I did.'

'Is that the truth?'

'No, it is not true.'

'So why did you do that?'

'I was forced to.'

'But why? What preceded this?'

'I lived in Grozny. Some time in November 2002 I and a comrade were stopped at a checkpoint. We showed our documents. Two armoured military vehicles were standing nearby. Armed men in masks jumped out of them, pinioned us, not explaining anything, handcuffed us, put bags over our heads, and threw us into the vehicles. One of the soldiers sat on me and they took us off. We drove for 20 to 25 minutes.'

'Where did they take you?'

'I don't know exactly, but I think it was Khankala. There I was lifted by the arms and dragged for some 30 metres. They told me to raise my legs, threw me into a pit and sealed it with a metal lid. They kept me there for about six days.'

'Were you interrogated during this time?'

'Yes, every day.'

'By whom?'

'I do not know exactly – I had a hood on my head the whole time – but they were Russians. Then I discovered they were from the FSB. I was dragged out of the pit and led to some premises. At the first interrogation they warned me that I should not use the words, "I don't know" or "No" because if I did they would immediately kill me.'

'Did they know you were acquainted with Zakayev?'

'Yes. They told me to tell them how I had fought with Zakayev in Dagestan, and also in the Islamic Jamaat battalion which Zakayev commanded. "You cut the heads off Russian soldiers!" When I said that had not happened, they said, "What difference does it make?" and began their torture.'

'How were you tortured?'

'With electricity, and they kicked me, and probably used truncheons. I could no longer see what with. At one of the interrogations they asked whether I knew Zakayev's telephone number. I said no. Zakayev was at that time already under arrest in

Denmark. They told me that they had telephone equipment and the telephone number. They tied me to the chair, attached something to my feet, one dialled a number saying this was a call to my friend in Copenhagen, and the electricity started. That went on every day. When this procedure ended they threw me back into the pit, and I was there the whole time.'

'In November?'

'Yes, it was already winter. It was cold. The pit was too small to stand up in. Your head was pressing against the metal hatch, and you also couldn't sit – there was water on the ground. Eventually I told them I would do anything they wanted. I could no longer stand the torture. You have to understand, I am human. Please understand.'

There is a shocked silence in the court. Everybody is motionless. The judge is no longer shuffling papers in front of him and, like everybody else, is looking directly at Duk-Vakha. Does he not believe him?

'They told me to sign a statement that Zakayev had ordered his bodyguards to kidnap priests. I told them, "I didn't know Zakayev then and I don't know what he did then." They said, "That doesn't matter. We know. All you have to do is sign." They warned me that if I should ever think of withdrawing my testimony, "We will skin you alive". Then they drove me to the FSB's Chechen headquarters in the centre of Grozny. There, for the first time, they took the handcuffs off and the hood off my head. I signed what they gave me.'

'Including the bit about the Pope?'

'Yes.'

'While you were signing were you being filmed with a video camera?'

'They told me beforehand to learn by heart the text they gave me to sign. They warned me not to hesitate in front of the camera when they started asking questions. I would be pretending to reply. They led me into a room. There were seven or eight soldiers there and two civilians. One of them introduced himself to me as being from NTV, from the programme *Top Secret*.'

'All this took place in the FSB building in Grozny?'
'Yes.'
'Where were you taken after the recording?'
'To prison in Grozny, but first to the court. They organised documents of some sort. I was in a very bad state, completely beaten up, covered in bruises, but the judge (in the Staropromyslovsky District Court) did not ask me anything, he just placed me under arrest for 10 days, to give time for my injuries to heal. After that they took me to the prison, but they wouldn't accept me because they said I would die there and they would be held responsible. They took me that evening to a different prison which did accept me and I was there for two months.'

'Did you know that your evidence against Zakayev had been televised?'

'Yes, the prison guards told me it had been shown on all channels. Two months later I was taken back to court. There was a member of the FSB, a Chechen, there. I know him, we went to school together. He warned me, "Do you know why they are freeing you now? So they can kill you and blame it on Zakayev. They will say he murders people who give evidence against him. If you want to live, get out of Grozny today." That's what I did.'

The British judge is very good at keeping his thoughts to himself. Judges are not expected to say much, just 'Yes' or 'No', and possibly, 'Mr Zakayev, the next hearing will be on such and such a date. If you are not here at 10 a.m. you will be arrested.' But the traditional British reserve was ruffled by this insight into Russian justice. The judge was moved to remark, 'This is an extraordinary situation, a dramatic turn of events.' He demanded a prompt response to a number of fundamental questions. For example, why had the Russian Prosecutor-General's Office been assuring the court that witness Dushuyev was in danger from Zakayev and that this was why his name had been obliterated in the extradition papers delivered to Britain, when in fact Dushuyev was in prison and hence in the custody of those making these claims? Had the Prosecution deliberately misled the court? The judge was outraged.

Misleading the court constitutes grave professional misconduct in Britain. The system works in a way which means that Zakayev has defence lawyers and the Prosecutor-General's Office has lawyers supporting its demand for extradition. They are appointed by the Crown Prosecution Service, which works with the Prosecutor-General's Office. If it transpires that there has been a deliberate attempt to provoke a miscarriage of justice, which the lawyers of the Crown Prosecution Service failed to detect through being unduly trusting of their Russian colleagues, they [the CPS] will face a disciplinary investigation and penalties. This would be a severe blow to their reputations which the profession would not forgive, a blot on their entire careers. Britain does not tolerate such games.

Accordingly, the lawyers of the Crown Prosecution Service were also thrown into disarray. They found themselves obliged to defend their own reputation, which was in jeopardy. What the court was now discussing was this sample of Kremlin justice, and the fact that even in Stalin-era trials such a thing had been unheard of. The lawyers humbly asked the judge to allow them an adjournment until 8 September, repeating, 'These are very serious charges. We are not prepared . . . We have no comment to make today . . .' The judge however insisted on a reply 'today, without fail', and gave them just two hours to contact Moscow (probably Fridinsky). When Judge Workman heard the replies he would decide how the trial should proceed.

Two hours proved insufficient and Judge Workman relented, agreeing to give the Prosecutor-General's Office until 1 September to provide explanations in writing, and warning that the case would resume on 8 September. He added unambiguously that hearings would continue for no more than four or five days, after which he would retire to consider his verdict.

What have we just witnessed? We have tried to spill out into Europe our corrupt legal practice of fabricating cases whenever and however the state authorities decree, and we have fallen flat on our faces.

The Russian State didn't get away with it in Britain. There was no way it could, because the British have no reason to allow this virus of ours to infect them. Who can blame them? But what of us now, the citizens of Russia, with our law enforcement gangsters ranged against us? The British will survive our invasion. They will merely note for the record the kind of people they are dealing with in the Russian legal system, and of course they will not extradite Zakayev.

But what about us? We citizens must make ourselves heard, not just keep our heads down. If you don't feel moved to defend Zakayev, then at least rise to your own defence. The State system poses a deadly threat. Anyone can be tortured. These are terrorist acts perpetrated by the regime against us all.

Chechnya–London: Another Courtroom Marvel in the Zakayev Case

11 September 2003

In London, in Bow Street Magistrates Court, at the hearings concerning the extradition to Russia of Akhmed Zakayev which resumed on 8 September, marvels of getting at the truth about the Chechen War through the law continued. This is something we rarely are treated to in Russia, hence our interest. On this occasion Mr Justice Timothy Workman was presented with information about the stranglehold in which the Russian Prosecution Service and other federal law enforcement institutions have the administration of justice in Chechnya, and why as a result of their stewardship we need recourse to the British legal system.

We remind our readers that the main event of the previous hearings in the Zakayev case on 24 July was the cross-examination of 35-year-old Duk-Vakha Dushuyev, formerly of Grozny, who was listed in documents of the Russian Prosecutor's Office as a witness for the prosecution, but in court in London under oath began giving evidence as a witness for the defence, relating how in November–December 2002 he was tortured in Chechnya by members of the FSB who demanded that he give false evidence against Zakayev, to which he agreed. It was precisely this plotline which on 8–9 September received a sensational new twist.

Investigator Konstantin Krivorotov himself proved to have been 'zombified' by the Russian Criminal Procedure Code. Junior Judicial Counsellor Krivorotov, Investigator of Particularly Serious Cases of the Chechen Prosecutor's Office, no matter what he was asked in the Bow Street court, even if a question was entirely specific and required only 'Yes' or 'No' as an answer, responded with a long lecture on the subject of the Criminal Procedure Code, explaining how wise and benign it was, what blessings it brought to those arrested and under investigation, and what vast opportunities it gave representatives of the investigative agencies for treating suspects humanely.

Only, nothing to the point. It was futile to try to stop Investigator Krivorotov when he was in full flood on the theory of Russian law. He became irate, demanded that he should not be interrupted, and even wagged his finger threateningly at the courteous British lawyers.

Why was that, you may ask? Quite simply, Investigator Krivorotov had a different task. He had been brought here to flannel, to confuse, and to divert the case from details, because the details of the saga of Duk-Vakha Dushuyev are potentially lethal to the extradition case.

But everything in its place. Krivorotov, the ardent supporter of the Criminal Procedure Code, found himself in London only because of Dushuyev's testimony. At the end of November 2002, when the Prosecutor-General's Office, demanding the extradition of Zakayev from Denmark, sent supporting documentation of very low legal quality and Zakayev was about to be released, Dushuyev was caught at a checkpoint in Grozny and taken, hooded, to Khankala. Under torture, he was offered his life in exchange for bearing false witness against Zakayev. He was taken to the FSB building on Garazhnaya Street in Grozny, next door to the Prosecutor's Office. Investigator Krivorotov wrote several statements which Dushuyev was told to sign. A television crew was summoned to the FSB building to record the 'voluntary confessions of Zakayev's bodyguard', which were then shown on NTV. Dushuyev was held in prison for two months on a charge routine in Chechnya – 'membership of an illegal armed group' – but this was then dropped on the grounds that he had supposedly confessed, and he was released. Dushuyev left Chechnya that same day and fled through a number of countries before deciding to find Zakayev's lawyers and admit what he had done. Such were the events which brought him, and consequently Krivorotov, before Judge Workman.

'Tell me, Mr Krivorotov, would Mr Dushuyev have been able to reveal any ill-treatment of himself during the course of the investigation? Before this hearing in London?' James Lewis, a lawyer acting on behalf of Investigator Krivorotov, asks a question which seems important to him. Mr Lewis is acting for the British Crown Prosecution Service, which is supporting (such is the way things are done here) the demand of the Russian Prosecutor's Office for extradition of Akhmed Zakayev.

'There is a clear procedure,' Krivorotov says, staying firmly in his theoretical realm. 'Dushuyev had several opportunities to state that impermissible methods had been used against him. In the first instance at the Preliminary Investigation, to me. The Criminal Procedure Code . . .'

The courtroom is verging on despair. Only Sergey Fridinsky, Deputy Prosecutor-General of the Southern Federal Region, who has publicly vowed to have Zakayev returned to Russia, looks pleased. Today he is present in London and smiles into his moustache with satisfaction when Krivorotov gets on his hobby-horse.

'What was Dushuyev believed to be guilty of when you brought criminal charges against him?' By now it is Zakayev's barrister, Edward Fitzgerald, asking the questions. He approaches in a roundabout way, and why this detail should interest him is unclear. 'Was it illegal to be Zakayev's bodyguard? After all, the government of which Zakayev was a member was recognised by President Yeltsin.'

'It is news to me that Maskhadov's government was recognised by the President.' For the first time Investigator Krivorotov replies honestly. He is genuinely taken aback. Nevertheless he rapidly regains his composure. 'Under the Russian Constitution there is no provision for the Minister of a self-proclaimed republic to have an armed bodyguard. Dushuyev was bearing arms at that time illegally. From 1999 Dushuyev was a member of an illegal armed group, the Chernorechie Front. That is why charges were brought.'

'In other words, anybody who resisted the Russian troops in 1999 is considered to have committed a criminal offence?'

'Of course,' Krivorotov shrugs, glancing expressionlessly at Fridinsky and barking out the sentences he has memorised. 'Anybody who opposes the federal troops is guilty of an act endangering society. In accordance with the Criminal Code.'

So the case proceeds, constantly returning inexorably to the central question to which Russia has no answer: what was and is actually going on in Chechnya from a legal point of view? Who is resisting whom there, and why? And how is the situation to be resolved?

This time Mr Fitzgerald is interrupted by Mr Lewis, to whose back the indignant Deputy Prosecutor-General Fridinsky has addressed a remark. Discussing the political aspect of the Prosecutor's Office's work is not permitted.

'Fine. Explain how Dushuyev was provided with a lawyer.'

Reader, you should know that Aisa Tatayeva from the Staropromyslovsky District Legal Assistance Service was brought to Dushuyev many days after Dushuyev had been held in a waterlogged pit in Khankala, from which he was periodically dragged for interrogation under torture. She advised him to 'tell them everything they want to hear'.

'Defence lawyers can be chosen by the accused, or appointed by the court. I knew where I could find Tatayeva at that moment, and she was summoned. That is, I personally invited Tatayeva.'

'How did you write the record of Dushuyev's interrogation? Did you write down everything he said?'

'I have my own method. I first listen to everything a person says, and then note it down, asking supplementary questions. Dushuyev came with an admission of guilt, I listened, and then wrote.'

The official version, sent to London over Fridinsky's signature on the eve of today's hearing, is that Khankala was never involved, that there was no torture, that Dushuyev had invented everything. He came to the Prosecutor's Office in Chechnya on 1 December 2002 of his own volition, wishing to confess his guilt in having participated in an illegal armed group, and the topic of Zakayev came up only by chance during his questioning.

'Well why, in that case, in the record which you compiled is there very little about what Dushuyev did, and a whole page about what Zakayev did, based moreover on hearsay? You were supposed to be investigating Dushuyev's crimes, were you not? This seems strange.'

Investigator Krivorotov again changes tack and heads for the thickets of the Criminal Procedure Code.

'Fine. But did you know about Zakayev's extradition case?'

'Yes. I realised that the record of Dushuyev's interrogation would be used in the criminal case against Zakayev.'

'Then why in that record is there no indication that the witness was himself under investigation?'

'What would have been the point of that?'

'You knew that Dushuyev would be filmed by a television crew? In the FSB building?'

'I supposed so. The relevant request had been received from the FSB Press Department.'

'In writing?'

'Verbally.'

'Dushuyev had been detained and was in your custody, and you handed him over to members of the FSB, and they took him to their own premises for filming. Is that correct?'

'Yes.' Krivorotov is losing patience. He again wags his finger at the court. 'It is Dushuyev's right either to talk to the press or not.'

'It did not occur to you that this filmed interview, where Dushuyev, on the basis of hearsay, accused Zakayev of serious crimes, of illegal arms trading, might harm Zakayev's case?'

'I don't understand the question.'

'Does it not seem strange to you that Dushuyev was your suspect but that the FSB had access to him when it wanted? How did the FSB even know that Dushuyev was with you? Did you report that to the FSB? And if so, why?'

'No. I did not report it.' For the first time Krivorotov looks as though he is telling the truth. 'When Dushuyev came to the Prosecutor's Office with his admission of guilt, he was accompanied by FSB officers, and accordingly I released him to the FSB for filming.'

QED. Thus did Investigator Krivorotov slip on a banana skin. This admission was fraught with consequences: it meant that all the official documents, including those signed by Deputy Prosecutor-General Fridinsky, were untrue. The court could place no reliance on them because they had been found to contain lies. Moreover, it was evident from them that Dushuyev was right when he claimed that the Prosecutor's Office in Chechnya did not work independently, that it knocked together whatever procedural papers were required, and thereby in effect legitimised the torture to which people were subjected by the FSB.

'I do not consider it substantive where Dushuyev came first, to the FSB or to us.' Krivorotov has suddenly realised what he has said. He explains that the majority of those arriving with an admission of guilt go first to the FSB, and then the FSB brings them to the Prosecutor's Office to formalise their confession. But the more he goes on, the more obvious is the lawlessness perpetrated in Chechnya with the blessing of the Prosecutor's Office.

'Do you really not know that people are tortured by the FSB in order to obtain the evidence they want?' Although Barrister Fitzgerald is calm, it is evident that he already knows he has won.

It had seemed at times, at the hearings on Monday and Tuesday, that this was a dead end. One side said one thing, the other the exact opposite, and how could it all be reconciled? How could one find the highest common factor which alone would make the dead-end submissions comprehensible to the judge, and hence also relevant to the issue of deciding on extradition? Investigator Krivorotov's inadvertent admission that it was precisely the FSB who had dragged Dushuyev in to him had been brilliantly engineered by Fitzgerald. A subtle, virtuoso victory over falsehood.

'I don't know anything about torture.'

Krivorotov is invited to familiarise himself with the official conclusions of the European Committee on Torture on precisely this issue. The investigator is forced to claim that he does not see what is going on right next door to him, but only a minute passes, and once again we see the man mesmerised by the Criminal Procedure Code:

'We in the Prosecutor's Office are under an obligation to take legal action where facts such as these come to light.'

Of course you are, but the whole point is that for years you have been ignoring it!

Thus it was that Investigator Krivorotov became a witness for the defence, and hence against any possibility of extradition. Why? It had been been proved in court that the law enforcement agencies functioning on the territory of Chechnya are totally arbitrary and lawless. That is why Krivorotov could treat his listeners in a London courtroom only to long explanations about how things are supposed to be. He knew only too well how they are supposed to be, but he also knew that how they are bears no relation to that. Poor wretch. Anything goes, and nothing seems wrong. Barbarity becomes the norm.

At precisely 1300 hours Greenwich Mean Time Judge Workman interrupted Investigator Krivorotov with the magic words, 'One hour for lunch'. By tradition, nothing on earth takes precedence over the lunch hour. The same inflexible rules, however, require that a witness whose cross-examination has not been completed should not discuss matters relating to what he is being cross-questioned about with anyone. This meant that while everybody else was having lunch, Investigator Krivorotov stood as lonely as a statue at the courtroom door, smoking nervously. Deputy Prosecutor-General Fridinsky walked past him from the Italian restaurant across the road. Others involved in the case made their way back for the afternoon sitting. One couldn't help feeling sorry for Krivorotov, and an exceptionally humane impulse prompted your correspondent to go over and offer him a sandwich. Lord, how he recoiled! 'No!' He shook his head as if he had been offered an arsenic sandwich. 'But I have two. I have more than I need.' 'No!' Investigator Krivorotov blushed and turned away, as if we did not know each other. Something wasn't right.

The Prosecutor-General's Office Loses: Legal Costs will be Met by the Russian Taxpayer

17 November 2003

People can have entirely different perspectives: love Zakayev or hate him, support the Kremlin's atrocities in Chechnya or fight them, rejoice at world leaders' love of Putin or be horrified by it, but on 13 November 2003, shortly before noon Greenwich Mean Time, the entire Russian nation was given a good and deserved kicking by Europe. The Prosecutor-General's Office had been asking for it for a long time. In Bow Street Magistrates Court, in the case of The Government of the Russian Federation versus Akhmed Zakayev, Mr Justice Timothy Workman delivered an outspoken and uncompromising judgment, beyond anything the most wild-eyed optimists had dared to hope for when they assured us that Zakayev would not be extradited.

The refusal of Judge Timothy Workman to extradite Zakayev was based first on the grounds that Russia lacks an independent judiciary, so there can be no confident expectation of a fair trial;

second, on the fact that racism flourishes in our country; and third, because what is going on in Chechnya is not a rebellion or an 'antiterrorist operation' but a full-blown civil war instigated by the Russian Government itself in contravention of its obligation to avert wars, to extinguish them, and not to foment them within its borders.

The verdict was announced not in the ordinary magistrates' courtroom where the case had been heard but in a lofty ceremonial hall with something resembling a throne set at a considerable height. On this the judge seated himself. The translator promised on oath not to lie, and Mr Justice Workman began:

'The Russian Federation seek the extradition of Akhmed Zakayev in respect of some thirteen allegations of conduct which, had it occurred in the United Kingdom, would have amounted to the offences of soliciting persons to murder, three counts of murder, two counts of wounding with intent to cause grievous bodily harm, one count of false imprisonment and six counts of conspiring with others in a course of conduct which would necessarily involve the commission of offences of murder, wounding and hostage taking.

The judge continued:

'I am quite satisfied that the events in Chechnya in 1995 and 1996 amounted in law to an internal armed conflict. Indeed, many observers would have regarded it as a civil war. In support of that decision I have taken into account the scale of fighting — the intense carpet-bombing of Grozny with in excess of 100,000 casualties, the recognition of the conflict in the terms of a cease fire and a peace treaty. I was unable to accept the view expressed by one witness that the actions of the Russian Government in bombing Grozny were counterterrorist operations.

'Having satisfied myself that this amounted to an internal armed conflict which would fall within the Geneva Convention, I reach the conclusion that those crimes which allege conspiring to seize specific areas of Chechnya by the use of armed force or resistance are not extraditable crimes because the conduct in those circumstances would not amount to a crime in this country. On that basis I propose to discharge counts 7, 8, 9 and 13.'

The next section of the ruling bears the highly eloquent title 'Abuse of Process'. This is more to do with the professional methods of the Russian Prosecutor-General's Office, whose representatives were conspicuous by their absence. Rumours were circulating yesterday that Sergey Fridinsky, who was in charge of the campaign to extradite Zakayev and who had given the President his word that he would be returned, had been warned by the Crown Prosecution Service that an adverse ruling was likely, as a result of which the whole lot of them had decided to absent themselves from their public humiliation.

One can see their point. The evidence of prosecution witnesses was found not to be reliable. It is worth recalling who was in this group which Fridinsky had assembled: Akhmar Zavgayev, a Senator representing Chechnya, currently preparing to enter the Duma; Yury Kalinin, Deputy Minister of Justice responsible for the prison system; Konstantin Krivorotov, Investigator of the Chechen Prosecutor's Office; Yury Bessarabov, Professor of Law at the Research Institute of the Prosecutor-General's Office; and Stanislav Iliasov, Russian Government Minister for Chechnya. These individuals should not continue to occupy their posts after such public disgrace.

'The alleged offences on which Mr Zakayev is sought occurred in 1995 and in 1996. The offences would have been apparent to the Authorities at the time, and two witnesses assured me that they made statements to the Prosecution shortly after the event. It was not until some six years later that a decision was made to arrest Mr Zakayev, and it was not until 25 October 2002 that the Russian request for his arrest was circulated by Interpol. Throughout 2001 and 2002 Mr Zakayev acted as a peace envoy, travelling extensively, but his whereabouts were apparently known to the Russian Authorities. Indeed, on 18 November 2001 Mr Zakayev travelled to Moscow Airport in an attempt to negotiate disarmament. He met with senior Government officials who had themselves been reassured that there were no proceedings anticipated against Mr Zakayev. The existence of the decision to arrest Mr Zakayev taken two months earlier appears to have been overlooked. Mr Fridinsky, the Russian prosecutor in this case, has explained that they had no idea that Mr Zakayev was going to attend a meeting in Moscow. Whilst I do, of course, accept that Mr Fridinsky may not have known, I find it surprising that a warrant for such serious crimes alleged to have been committed by such a well-known person should not have been noticed by the Russian Immigration Authorities.

'In addition to the delay in arrest, it is apparent that there has been delay in the investigation and preparation of the Prosecution's case. Although two witnesses told me that they had made statements soon after the events, those statements have not been produced or provided to the Defence. With one exception (an unnamed witness) who made a statement on 13 March 2000, the other 11 witnesses made their statements after Mr Zakayev was arrested. In respect of four of those witnesses, their statements were not taken until after the extradition request to Denmark had failed. Note that in the request to Denmark it was being alleged that Mr Zakayev was involved in the Moscow theatre siege and that he had murdered Father Sergius (now known as Father Philip). Both allegations were later withdrawn, and indeed Father Philip has given evidence before me.

'I have also noted that the Kremlin denied the existence of any criminal proceedings against Mr Zakayev when in fact a warrant was still extant. I have noted that the Russian Government continued to negotiate with Mr Zakayev despite the existence of the warrant, and that there was no attempt to extradite Mr Zakayev until the moment of the World Chechen Conference and the Moscow theatre siege. I have also noted the statements of the Russian foreign minister likening Mr Zakayev to Osama Bin Laden.

'When those factors are added together the inevitable conclusion is that it would now be unjust and oppressive to return Mr Zakayev to stand trial in Russia.

'I found that the evidence given by Mr de Waal, Mr Rybakov and Mr Rybkin was truthful and accurate, and from their evidence I am satisfied that it is more likely than not that the motivation of the Government of the Russian Federation was and is to exclude Mr Zakayev from continuing to take part in the peace process and to discredit him as a moderate. I therefore find as a fact that the Russian Government are seeking extradition for purposes of prosecuting Mr Zakayev on account of his nationality and his political opinions. I take the view that Mr Zakayev is entitled to the benefit of the protection provided by Section 6(i)(c) [of the European Convention on Extradition].

'With some reluctance I have to come to the inevitable conclusion that if the Authorities are prepared to resort to torturing witnesses there is a substantial risk that Mr Zakayev would himself be subject to torture. I am satisfied that such punishment and detention would be by reason of his nationality and political opinions. I therefore believe that Mr Zakayev is entitled to the benefit of Section 6(i)(d) and should not be returned to face trial in the Russian Federation . . .

'I am therefore discharging the defendant.'

That is an end to it. The judge is silent, the courtroom animated. People are trying to congratulate Zakayev, but the case is not over yet. Edward Fitzgerald, Zakayev's defence lawyer, rises to his feet. His concerns extend beyond the law to the financing of all this. Who is going to pay the legal costs? The judge calmly accepts the bills and invoices as is the way in Britain. This means it is clear who is going to pay. The costs of a court case which has lasted almost a year will be payable by the losing side, that is, by you and me, since it is we who employ the officials of the Prosecutor-General's Office, officials who have failed to learn to work in accordance with the law but excel in carrying out political orders, as the London court has demonstrated.

Each has received his just deserts. Zakayev is free, his passport will be returned to him in the immediate future, and he will again be able to travel at will throughout the world. Representatives of the Crown Prosecution Service of Great Britain who, in accordance with the British judicial system, represented the Russian Prosecutor-General's Office, have strongly advised Mr Fridinsky against thinking of lodging an appeal because it would have no prospect of success and could lead only to an even more shaming outcome; all the charges have been rejected as without a basis in law, meaning that no new evidence would be accepted. The Russian Prosecutor-General's Office has egg all over its face.

These, however, are only details. Three important truths were established in London on 13 November. The first is that, for the first time in many years of a monstrous war, the federal authorities and the Chechens have been communicating with each other in legal language rather than the language of armed conflict, security sweeps, ambushes and explosions. The forum for this was a British court which demonstrated that it was concerned only with hard evidence and had no interest in political expediency.

The second is that it has been established in a court of law, not in the newspapers or on television, not in the drawing rooms of the establishment or at conferences, after lengthy examination of the evidence for and against now marshalled in several volumes, that, as most of us already knew but were unable to prove, what is happening in Chechnya is not an 'antiterrorist operation' but a war.

The third is that, after the London court ruling, it is impossible to go on pretending that our country is on the road to democracy. There are no reforms; instead we have authoritarianism, subservient courts, torture in places of detention and racial harassment. The framework of international relations is collapsing because it has been shown in court that the system the Russian regime talks about simply does not exist. Russia is a radically different country from the one which the politicians pretend exists. We have a brutal war, racism and violence as the means of resolving all issues.

That is the end of the story of the London court proceedings in respect of Akhmed Zakayev. The Government wanted to show the world how cool we are and how we stand for truth, but succeeded only in showing our true nature. The Russian Government is the laughing stock of Europe because it has no substance, only wild pretensions.

The fact that the court ruling was going to go against the Russian Prosecutor-General's Office became clear in Sheremetievo-II, the Moscow airport from which I was flying to London to hear the verdict.

I handed over my passport. The young frontier guard tapped at his computer for a long time and finally said,

'You have problems.'

'What kind of problems?'

'You know yourself.'

'No I don't.'

What had popped up on his screen was that the bearer of this passport was to be detained and subjected to general unpleasantness and all manner of additional and humiliating searches.

'Why?'

'That's a military secret,' he replied. One would have liked to think he was joking but there was no hint of a smile.

The woman in charge of the shift arrived, a pretty girl, Yuliya Demina. She took away various things that she had no right to take: my passport, my ticket. She ordered me to stand in a particular place and not to move, and then she went away. She was gone for a very long time and the plane was about to leave. The young guardian of the border came out of his booth and prattled on again about 'problems' which 'you know yourself'.

'Are you going to have problems coming back in?'

'What do you mean?'

'You might not be allowed back in, for instance.'

It's the usual approach in this, the era of the Second Chechen War. You can become nobody at any moment, especially if you have witnessed something. No laws are required to do that, as was proven in London, where I was permitted to fly to at the very last moment.

Nord-Ost

Nord-Ost: *The Price of Talks*

28 October 2002

My personal involvement in this crisis began at about 1400 on 25 October. At 11.30 I had spoken on my mobile phone to the hostage-takers for the first time and they agreed to a meeting. At 13.30 I arrived at the headquarters of the security operation. Another half-hour was spent getting everything co-ordinated: some unknown person was resolving matters behind doors which kept slamming.

Finally, I was led up to a protective cordon of trucks, someone said, 'Give it a go. Perhaps you can do it', and Dr Leonid Roshal [Head of the Disaster Medical Centre] and I made our way to the entrance. It was very frightening.

We went into the building. We shouted, 'Hello! Anybody there?'

There was no response. It felt as if the building was completely deserted.

I shouted, 'It's me, Politkovskaya! It's Politkovskaya!' I slowly started climbing up the right-hand staircase. The doctor said he knew the way. In the first-floor foyer there was again silence, darkness, and it was cold. Not a soul. I shouted again, 'It's Politkovskaya!' Finally, a man appeared from behind what had been the counter of the bar.

His black mask wasn't on properly and I could see his features clearly. He was not aggressive towards me, but hostile towards the doctor. Why? I don't know, but I did my best to calm a situation which was becoming heated. 'What are you up to, doctor, helping your career along?' the man in the mask taunted. Dr Roshal is 70 years old, an Academician, and has already achieved so much that he really doesn't need to worry about his career.

I said as much, a bit of an argument started, and it was time to lower the temperature again since otherwise . . . Otherwise it was obvious what could happen.

The man with the ill-fitting mask went off into the depths of the darkened foyer, still muttering, 'Why do you say you treat Chechen children too, doctor?' There was some further fairly incoherent nastiness which amounted to suggesting that mentioning that he also treated Chechen children showed he didn't think they were the equal of other children, perhaps even that Chechens are not human beings.

It was a familiar tune and I interrupted it, not because that was a particularly clever thing to do but simply because I had had enough. I said, 'All people are the same. They have the same skin, the same bones, the same blood.' This less than original thought unexpectedly had a conciliatory effect. I asked permission to sit on the only chair in the middle of the foyer, 5 metres or so from the bar, because my legs had turned to jelly.

Permission was immediately granted. My shoes slipped on some disgusting red mess trampled into the carpet. I looked down cautiously at this ghastliness, anxious not to seem to be taking too much of an interest, but even more anxious not to put my feet in congealed blood. Thank God, it was only some kind of dead dessert, possibly fruit and ice-cream. I trembled a little less.

We waited 20 minutes or so while the leader was sent for. While we waited there, heads in masks appeared over the balcony occasionally. Some of the masks covered their faces properly, others only did half the job.

'Was it you who helped the people in Khotuni against the paratroop regiment?' the heads ask.

'Yes.'

The heads are satisfied. Khotuni, a village in the Vedeno

District, turns out to be my safe-conduct pass. If I have been there I am worth talking to.

'Where are you from?' I ask the man from the bar counter.

'Tovzeni,' he replies. 'Many of us are from Tovzeni, and from Vedeno District generally.'

There follows a lot of confused coming and going by men in masks, the sign of a tragedy in the making. Time just passing by, disappearing into nowhere, fills me with idiotic foreboding. The leader still hasn't appeared. Perhaps they are going to shoot us here and now.

Finally, a person in combat fatigues comes out, his face completely covered. He is stocky, and with exactly the deportment of Russian special operations officers who give serious attention to their physical fitness. He says, 'Follow me.' My legs again turn to jelly, but I wobble after him. This is The Leader.

We end up in a dirty service room by a ransacked buffet, behind which is a water tap. Somebody walks behind me and I turn. I realise this looks nervous, but what can I do? I haven't had much experience of talking to terrorists under conditions as tense as these. The leader brings me back to cold logic.

'Don't look behind you! You are talking to me, so look at me.'

'Who are you? What should I call you?' I ask, not really expecting a reply.

'Bakar. Abubakar.'

By now he has pushed the mask up to his forehead. He has an open face with high cheekbones, also very typical of our military. He has a rifle on his knees which he puts behind him only at the very end of our talk, when he even apologises. 'I've got so used to it I no longer feel it there. I sleep with it, eat with it. It is always with me.' Even without this explanation I already understand everything.

'How old are you?'

'Twenty-nine.'

'Have you been fighting in both wars?'

'Yes.'

'Did you sit it out in Georgia?'

'No. I never left Chechnya.'

Bakar belongs to a new generation of Chechens who for the past 10 years have known nothing but a rifle and the forests. He left school, and life in the forests became his only option. A destiny devoid of choice.

'Shall we get down to business?' I suggest.

'OK.'

'First, the older children still in there. You need to let them go. They are only children.' Sergey Yastrzhembsky, Aide to the President of the Russian Federation, had asked me to raise this with them as my main priority.

'Children? There are no children in there. In security sweeps you take ours from 12 years old. We will hold on to yours.'

'In retaliation?'

'So that you know how it feels.'

I return to the subject of the children many times, asking for them to be allowed at least some relief, for me to bring food, for instance, but the answer is a categorical no.

'Do you let ours eat in the security sweeps? Yours can do without too.'

I have four other requests on my list: food for the hostages, items of personal hygiene for the women, water, blankets. To anticipate, I get agreement only to bring water and juice. I will be allowed to bring them, shout from downstairs, and then I will be let in.

'Can I come several times? I can't carry much in one go. There are so many hostages. Perhaps you will allow me to bring one of the men.'

'OK.'

'Do you mind if that's another of our journalists?'

'No. And also somebody from the Red Cross.'

'Thank you.'

I start asking what it is that they want, but politically Bakar is all at sea. He's a simple soldier and no more. He explains what this is all about, at considerable length but not at all clearly, and from what he says I identify four points. The first is that Putin must 'give the word' – declare an end to the war. The second is that within 24 hours he must demonstrate that these are not empty words, for example by withdrawing troops from one of the districts.

'From which district? From yours? Vedeno?'

'What are you, a GRU agent? You're interrogating me like a GRU agent. That's all I've got to say, go away!'

It is impossible for me to go away at this point, although I very much want to. I hear myself almost pleading, which is completely the wrong tone, of course:

'Please understand, I need to know what it is you want. And I need to know exactly. Otherwise . . .'

From time to time I trip over myself. I am racking my brains over an intractable problem: how can I ease the plight of the hostages as much as possible, since the hostage-takers have at least agreed to talk to me, but not lose my credibility in their eyes? And I am making a mess of it. Quite often I can't think what to say next, and blurt out a lot of nonsense, just hoping not to hear Bakar say 'That's it!', whereupon I would have to leave empty-handed, having failed to negotiate anything at all for the hostages. As we approach the third point of 'their' plan, Boris Nemtsov [chairman of the Union of Right Forces political coalition] phones Bakar on his mobile. The resistance fighters took it from one of the hostages, a *Nord-Ost* musician, and now they are using it for all their conversations.

While he is talking to Nemtsov, Bakar becomes very agitated. Afterwards he tells me Nemtsov is trying to trick him. Nemtsov said yesterday that the war in Chechnya could be ended, but today, 25 October, the security sweeps have been renewed. Then I ask, 'Who will you believe? Who would you trust if they told you that troops were being withdrawn?'

Only Lord Judd, it transpires, the Council of Europe's rapporteur on Chechnya.

We get to 'their' third point, which is simple: if the first two demands are met, they will release the hostages.

'And yourselves?'

'We will stay behind to fight. We will behave like soldiers and die in battle.'

'But who in fact are you?' I ask, scaring myself with my audacity.

'The Reconnaissance and Sabotage Battalion.'

'Are you all here?'

'No. Only some of us. We had a selection process for this operation and chose the best. If we die, there will still be others to continue our struggle.'

'Do you accept Maskhadov's authority?'

He is thrown by this, and again becomes extremely irritated. His rambling explanation is best summarised as, 'Yes, Maskhadov is our President, but we are fighting on our own.'

This is confirmation of my worst fears: the group is one of those acting independently in Chechnya. They are waging their own very radical war autonomously. By and large they have no time for Maskhadov, considering him insufficiently hard-line. I continue:

'But you do know that peace negotiations are being conducted by Ilias Akhmadov in America, and Akhmed Zakayev in Europe, who both represent Maskhadov. Perhaps you would like to contact them now? Or let me dial them. Yours is the same cause.'

'What for? We don't acknowledge them. While we are dying in the forests they are slowly conducting their negotiations because it is not their heads the rain is falling on. We are fed up with them.'

There is no real fourth point to their plan, other than some strongly felt remarks of Bakar's own: 'People have been asking to come here as suicide bombers for a year and a half', and 'We have come to die'. I have no doubt of that. These are doomed men and women prepared to die, and to take with them as many lives as they see fit.

The mobile phone rings again. Bakar listens. It is a phone call from home, from the Vedeno District of Chechnya. He starts shouting and raging: 'Don't ring here any more. Ever. This is the office. You are interfering with my business.'

'May I talk to the hostages?'

'No.'

But five minutes later, he says to a 'brother', sitting almost behind my back, 'OK, bring one.'

He goes and brings from the auditorium a terrified, pretty girl called Masha. The hostages have had nothing to eat and she is so frightened and weak that she can't speak.

Bakar is irritated by her mumbling and orders her to be taken away. 'Bring another one, older.' In the interim, Bakar tells me how noble they all are. They have so many pretty girls in their power – and Masha really is very pretty – but they have no desire. All their strength is being kept for the struggle for the liberation of their land. I understand him to mean that I should be grateful for their not having raped Masha.

We speak briefly about morality and ethics, if these are the right words.

'You won't believe it, but morally we feel better here than at any time in the past three years of the war. We are finally doing something. We feel entirely at home. We feel better than ever. We will be glad to die. The fact that we will go down in history is a great honour. Don't you believe me? I can see you don't believe me.'

Actually, I very much do believe him. This kind of talk has been heard among Chechen fighters for a year already. Resentful of the virtual Maskhadov's inaction, many resistance units have sat through an entire winter in the forests and have now had enough. They can't come out of the forests, they can't fight. They need something to do, but there are no orders from their Commander-in-Chief. As this mood has grown, units have either fallen apart or become radicalised, in effect embarking on parallel wars over which Maskhadov has no authority.

The 'brother' brings another pretty girl in a state of extreme nervous exhaustion.

'I am Anna Andriyanovna, a correspondent of *Moskovskaya Pravda*. Everyone outside must please understand, we are already expecting to die. We realise that Russia has abandoned us. We are a second *Kursk* [a submarine which sank with the loss of all hands shortly after Putin became President]. If you want to save us, come out to demonstrate in the streets. If half of Moscow begs Putin, we will survive. We can see clearly that if we die here today, a new slaughter will start in Chechnya which will rebound on Russia and cause new carnage.'

Anya talks incessantly. Bakar is getting edgy but she doesn't notice. I am again very much afraid that he will decide to be masterful. Finally she is taken away and we agree that I shall organise things at once and bring some water into the building. Bakar unexpectedly adds, 'And you can bring some juice.'

'For you?'

'No, we are preparing to die; we are not eating or drinking anything. For them.'

'And perhaps some food? If only for the children.'

'No. Ours are starving, so let yours starve too.'

I go outside. I find that Dr Roshal has already left. It begins to pour, damn it, just at the wrong moment. 'I haven't even got an umbrella,' I think. 'I look like a wet hen.' Well, you have to think something.

We have a whip round among everybody standing nearby. The journalists are the first to dig deep, and the firemen. Somebody runs to the nearest shop to get juice. We find that the representatives of the state have no change available at this moment. That seems odd, but there is no time to think about it, only the realisation that we must move as quickly as possible before the hostage-takers change their minds.

The juice is brought back. Roman Shleinov (a colleague at *Novaya gazeta*) and I take two packs each in our arms and try to walk. On our right is an Interior Ministry officer, on our left an FSB officer. They are arguing. The one from the Interior Ministry has orders to allow us in since this is aid for the hostages and represents an opportunity to prolong contact with the outlaws as long as possible. The one from the FSB has orders not to let us through.

They quarrel. The rain pours down and we stand there like

idiots in full view of all the snipers, just waiting, it seems to me, for someone to start shooting. Finally the FSB agent agrees: 'Go on, then.'

We take one batch and then another. Darkness falls; the gunmen had told us to bring it before dark but a criminal amount of time passes before the state manages to come up with juice for the next batch.

The third time, they allow a group of male hostages out to meet us. I'm afraid to say anything to them in case the hostage-takers start shooting. I just say 'Hello', and they reply. They are allowed out in single file. A young man in evening dress and a white shirt passes me. Presumably he plays in the orchestra. He whispers tersely, 'They have told us they will start killing us at ten this evening. Pass it on.'

The next time I just nod silently to him, making eye contact, to let him know I have told the relevant authorities. They are leading the hostages down the steps to meet us, perhaps intending to make a point of showing how well they are treating them. Picking up his crate of juice, my musician whispers on the way back, 'Understood'.

The gunmen suddenly start becoming very nervous. They shout and pace up and down. A hostage calls from above, 'Bring some disinfectant. We really need it. We did ask for it.' He is driven back. I ask permission to bring the disinfectant, but am met with a complete refusal.

'At least some food? Just a little? For the children? Please . . .'

'We are dying of hunger, let them die of hunger too. Go away.'

This day in history comes to an end, to be followed by the assault. Now I keep asking myself whether we did everything possible to help avoid those deaths. Was it a great victory to have 67 hostages killed (excluding those who died after they got to hospital)? Was I any help to anyone with my juice and my last-ditch efforts? I believe I was, but that we could have done more.

Too much is now behind us, and a great deal still lies ahead. The tragedy of *Nord-Ost*, for which there were of course reasons, will not be the end. From now on we will have to live in constant fear when our children or old people go out of the house. Will we ever see them again? It will be just the way people in Chechnya have been living these last years.

There are only two alternatives. The first is finally to recognise that the more excessive force we use there – the more blood, killings, abductions and humiliations – the more people there will be in Chechnya who want revenge at any price; the more recruits there will be to the ranks of those wishing to die in retaliation.

And since this war will be fought not on a battlefield but amongst us, involving completely innocent people – you and me, and all of us – we can be sure that there will be another *Nord-Ost*, and that nobody anywhere can feel safe, whether going out or staying in their own flat. A cornered fighter will devise ever more ingenious means of retribution.

The second option is fraught with difficulties, but is at least a move in the right direction. We need to start talking to Maskhadov, a man clinging to what little remains of his power. Otherwise we are doomed to conduct negotiations like those over *Nord-Ost* within a framework of hopelessness, with innocent lives at stake.

57 Hours

4 November 2002

The last few days have passed in a feverish delirium. Moscow is burying the hostages. Today, just like yesterday, just like tomorrow. It is unbearable. The faces of the dead are calm, not contorted, as if they had simply fallen asleep. And actually that is just what they did, because Russia failed to administer the gas [used prior to the assault] in the correct concentration.

I make it a rule not to write reports from funerals but this will be an exception. Lena, my old, dear friend, is burying her son Andryusha and her husband Sergey. On 23 October the three of them went to the theatre together. They were seated together, waited together for help to come, but only Lena survived.

The coffins of Andryusha and Sergey are side by side in the church, with a narrow passage between them. There are so many people you couldn't push your way through. Nobody makes any speeches, there is no politics, only Lena walking up and down this passage, murmuring from time to time. When she stops walking she rests a hand on each coffin and tries not to collapse. She lowers her head between the coffins and so resembles a bird with outspread wings, or somebody wounded struggling to get to their feet.

I too am terribly, irredeemably guilty for what has befallen Lena, and only I know why. It is too late to do anything about it.

After the funerals I fly to Paris for a few hours and very soon regret having done so. The television station France 2 has invited me to take part in the country's most popular Saturday evening programme. I agreed only because people were telling me how little the West understood what is happening in 'the East'.

On the show, compered by French television celebrity Thiérry Ardisson, a well-known French singer was to perform immediately before me. I didn't write his name down and can't remember it now. There was also the Minister of Health from the Chechen Government when Maskhadov was in power, Umar somebody. Torrents of words poured forth about the Chechens, and how long and tirelessly they have been fighting for their freedom. The singer thought it was terrific, as did the presenter. It only left a very short time for me to say . . . Well, to say what, now that I had this prime-time opportunity?

I spoke badly, briefly, and not at all to the point. It was a disgrace, of course, because if you are given an opportunity to state your viewpoint, you should be ready to do so. No matter how hard I tried, though, I felt completely alien in this environment. We were on different wavelengths. Nobody in the audience wanted to hear about what, having just come from all these funerals, mattered most to me – the victims, the dreadful consequences. The Ichkerian Minister of Health (who really had nothing to do with anything, and who seemed rather at sea) found himself the focus of a whirl of emotional exclamations from admiring, ecstatic Frenchwomen of the same, far from young, age as me. Their superficial, romantic nonsense left me feeling nauseated, because they were as blind to the reality as . . . well, as we are. Only for them, Chechens are all good, and for Russians they are all bad.

I flew back to Moscow. The World Chechen Congress took place in Copenhagen immediately after the assault, and was subjected to an unprecedented barrage of protest from the Kremlin, which cancelled visits and summit meetings. (Moscow had to make do with the arrest of Akhmed Zakayev as a booby prize from the Danish Government.) On 1 November the Moscow participants of the Congress, in accordance with its concluding resolution, laid a wreath where the *Nord-Ost* victims had died.

They invited me to join them, but I didn't. The first reason was simply that, on principle, I avoid marching in columns and have never laid anything anywhere as a member of a crowd. The second reason was even simpler; I was still on the plane. There was, however, a third and most important reason, which I am sad about and unsure how to express, but which I think I need to explain.

Something wasn't quite right about this wreath-laying ceremony. It wasn't because, as so many people now believe, 'the Chechens are to blame for everything'. Even less was it because I personally have anything against Chechens. Of course I haven't.

But I really didn't like the way most of the Chechens I know behaved during those 57 hours when everything was on a knife edge, when at any moment the *Nord-Ost* audience might have been blown sky high, when a message from influential Chechens addressed to those under Barayev Junior's command would have carried far more weight than anything anybody else could say. That, at least, is how I felt. They said nothing. No statement came, and now their silence is a historical fact. That is the other reason I was so upset by those nauseating Frenchwomen.

Only Aslambek Aslakhanov, a Chechen and a Deputy of the Russian Duma, went in to talk to the terrorists, despite the fact that his act could have had extremely unpleasant consequences for him: he is, after all, an Interior Ministry general, and unambiguously a 'federal' in the minds of those who took the *Nord-Ost* audience hostage. But Aslakhanov went in, despite his own young children at home. He went in, and that too is a matter of record.

But where were all the others? Where was businessman and politician Malik Saidullayev? Where were the Umars? (I've forgotten their surnames too, and really can't be bothered trying to rediscover them.) I mean that rich Umar somebody who owns a hotel near Kievsky Station in Moscow. And what about Bislan Gantamirov, sometime Mayor of Grozny? And Salambek Khadzhiev? And so on and so forth, ad infinitum?

None of them spoke out; not even Kadyrov, whom most of the Moscow Chechens are so busy buzzing around when he comes from Grozny that you start having dark suspicions about vested interests on both sides. In his old age, Kadyrov has covered himself with ineradicable shame by valuing his own life higher than the lives of 50 completely innocent spectators of the *Nord-Ost* musical. The terrorists invited him, as the Chief of Chechnya appointed by Putin, to visit them in exchange for 50 hostages but he didn't go, subsequently claiming he 'hadn't heard about it'.

During these 57 hours, the Moscow Chechens were whispering in corners. That was completely inadequate. They didn't even decry Kadyrov, or attempt to persuade him to go down in history as a man who saved the lives of 50 women and children. For 57 hours the so-called Chechen diaspora, almost to a man, went underground, some of them turning up only in Copenhagen.

My own feeling is that this leaves a bad taste. It just wasn't the way these people ought to have behaved. Perhaps I am completely wrong and I will be told later that the Chechens were terrified of the consequences, and that their main priority is to survive in a society now bristling against them even more than before, and so on and so forth.

No doubt that is all true, but can you really rank fears? The diaspora seemed heedless of the fact that the hostages were even more terrified of what seemed like their imminent inevitable death; and that for more than 100 of them (and we still don't know how many more) those 57 hours facing death were the last hours of their lives. That is why today we are attending funeral after funeral where the priests lose their voices because even their highly trained vocal cords cannot cope with so many services.

So, should we sympathise with the fears of the Chechen diaspora? Absolutely not. You will have to excuse me, but I totally reject their fear. Everybody involved was scared, including those who mounted the assault and those on the receiving end of it. So let us come back to our initial question: why did the Chechens behave as they did during these 57 hours?

Because they are cowards. Faced with their own younger generation who have turned into uncompromising radicals the whole lot of them bottled out. They slunk away. And perhaps, too, they considered it all beneath them. They think they are so elevated, but now we can see how low they are.

That too is a fact of history. The myth of the incomparable fearlessness of the Chechen nation has been relegated to history, to the period before 23 October 2002.

In Chechnya security sweeps are proceeding incessantly. People are being tortured, suffering just as much as before. Villages have been blockaded. The zone behind the Chechnya barrier has once again been turned into a training ground for the Army. On this side of the barrier things are better, but not much.

One Member of the Nord-Ost Terrorist Group Survived: We have Found Him

28 April 2003

Six months ago there was a terrorist act at the *Nord-Ost* musical. Since then we have puzzled many times over how such a thing could have happened. How did they get into Moscow? Did someone allow it? Why? Now we find there is a witness, who was also a member of the terrorist group.

At first there was only the bare information that one of the group of terrorists who took the audience hostage was still alive.

We checked the information out, repeatedly analysed the list of Barayev's group published in the press, made enquiries, and tracked him down: a man whose name is indeed officially listed with those of the other terrorists.

Were you a member of the Barayev group who took the Nord-Ost audience hostage?
Yes, I was.

Did you go into the theatre with them?
Yes.

I read an ID document with 'PRESS' on its cover in capital letters on a dark background: 'Khanpash Nurdyevich Terkibayev. *Rossiyskaya gazeta*. Special Correspondent. Pass No. 1165.' Signed Gorbenko. Sure enough, *Rossiyskaya gazeta* does have a director of that name.

What topics do you write about? Chechnya?
No reply.

Do you go in to work at the newspaper? What department do you work in? Who is your editor?
Again, no reply. He pretends not to understand Russian very well, but how can you be a special correspondent of the country's main government newspaper if you don't speak Russian? Khanpash's narrow, mongoloid eyes, not much like those of a Chechen, register incomprehension. He is not putting it on, he genuinely does not understand what I'm talking about. He is no Russian journalist.

Was this pass given to you by someone as cover?
He smiles slyly:
I would not mind writing. I just haven't had time yet to think about it. I only received this pass on 7 April. See the date? I don't need to go into the office, I work in the President's Information Service.

Under Porshnev? What job do you do?
(Igor Porshnev heads the Information Service of Putin's Presidential Administration, which should make him Khanpash's immediate superior.) Even Porshnev's name produces incomprehension in *Rossiyskaya gazeta*'s 'special correspondent'. Khanpash has no idea who Porshnev is.

When necessary I meet [Presidential Aide] Yastrzhembsky. I work for him. Here is a photograph of me with him.

Sure enough, here is Khanpash photographed with Sergey Yastrzhembsky. Sergey is looking past the camera and appears displeased. Khanpash, on the other hand, now sitting in front of me in the Sputnik Hotel on Lenin Prospect in Moscow, is looking straight into the lens, as if to say, 'There! That's us.' You can tell from the photograph how palpably unwelcome it was to Yastrzhembsky, and deduce that it was insisted upon by the man now telling me his complicated life story, punctuating the narrative with numerous photographs which he pulls from his briefcase. 'That's me and Maskhadov, me and Yastreb, me and Maskhadov again, me and Arsanov, me in the Kremlin, me and Saidullayev, me and Gil-Robles (the Council of Europe's Human Rights Commissioner).

I look more closely, and quite a few seem to be rather inexpert photomontage. (They were subsequently checked by specialists and this was found to be the case.) 'What's the game?' I ask. Khanpash again looks uncomprehending, rummages in the briefcase and pulls out 'me with Margaret Thatcher and

Maskhadov', to show how familiar he is with the London scene. It is 1998, Maskhadov is wearing a tall astrakhan hat, Thatcher is in the middle, and Khanpash is on the other side. Intriguingly, Maskhadov looks as he did before the war, while Khanpash looks as he does today. Odd. But he is already showing me another photograph of himself with Maskhadov during the present war. Maskhadov is wearing combat fatigues, his beard is very grey, and he looks terrible. Khanpash doesn't look too chipper either. This one is genuine.

Aren't you afraid of walking around Moscow with photographs like these? In Chechnya they would shoot you on the spot for the one with Maskhadov. Here they will plant firearms on you and put you in prison for years.
He replies, 'I am in with Surkov.' Khanpash begins to sound boastful. 'After *Nord-Ost* I visited Surkov. Twice.' (Vladislav Surkov is the influential Deputy Head of the Presidential Administration of Russia.)

Why?
I was helping him to work out a Chechen policy for Putin. After *Nord-Ost*.

And were you able to help?
Peace is needed.

That's an original thought.
I am currently working on peace negotiations for Yastrzhembsky and Surkov. The idea is to negotiate with the fighters hiding in the mountains.

Is that your idea or the Kremlin's?
Mine, supported by the Kremlin.

Negotiations with Maskhadov?
No. The Kremlin will not agree to negotiate with him.

With whom, then?
With Vakha Arsanov [former Vice-President of Ichkeria, repudiated by Maskhadov]. I have just had a meeting with him.

Where?
There.

But what are you going to do about Maskhadov?
He needs to be persuaded to give up his powers until there is another presidential election in Chechnya.

Are you involved in that too?
Yes, but I haven't been asked to do that, I'm just doing it on my own.
Actually, there may not be an election.

But if we do, nevertheless, live to see an election, who would you put your own money on?
Khasbulatov or Saidullayev. They are a third force. Not on Maskhadov, not on Kadyrov. That's what I think. After *Nord-Ost* it was me who organised negotiations between the Deputies of the Chechen Parliament and the Presidential Administration, with Yastrzhembsky.

Yes, that surprised a lot of people, when Isa Temirov together with other Chechen Deputies turned up openly in Moscow, spoke at the famous press conference at the Interfax news agency, and called on people to vote in the referendum. That was a blow against Maskhadov, although previously they had been for him. So you were behind that?
'I was,' he replies proudly.

And did you vote afterwards in the referendum yourself?
'Me? No.' He laughs. 'I am from the Charto family *teip*. They call us Jews in Chechnya.'

Would it be accurate to say that the Nord-Ost tragedy was intended to have the role the Budyonnovsk hospital hostage-taking played [in 1995, a turning point which eventually led to the ending of the First Chechen War], *only this time to end the Second Chechen War?*

This is not an idle question. It is crucial. Khanpash has a finger in every pie of Russian politics. He knows everybody, he's accepted everywhere. He's capable of engineering all kind of twists and turns in the North Caucasus. If you need to bring Maskhadov into play, he will lead you to Maskhadov. You want to exclude Maskhadov? He can fix that too. So, at least, he tells me. But his profession, he says, is acting. He graduated from the Drama Faculty of Grozny University. Never mind that there never was any such faculty, and that he can't remember the name of his acting teacher, this enables him to claim he is friends with Akhmed Zakayev. 'We worked together in the theatre.' In the First War he acquired a video camera and started working in television. He accompanied Basayev on the Budyonnovsk raid, but was not imprisoned for taking part in it. On the contrary, he was amnestied in April 2000.

Where did you get the papers for the amnesty?
In the Argun Office of the Chechen FSB.

This is an important detail. The Argun FSB section has been one of the most dreaded throughout this war. At precisely the time Khanpash was receiving an amnesty from them, almost everybody else who fell into their hands was being dispatched into another world. Khanpash is the first person I have met who survived being in their hands, and he was even given a certificate of amnesty for his Budyonnovsk involvement.

Between the two wars Khanpash, as a 'hero of Budyonnovsk', became a leading consultant to President Maskhadov's Press Service. He had his own television programme on Maskhadov's channel, *The President's Heart*, later renamed, *The President's Path*. That said, he was obliged to leave Maskhadov's entourage even before the Second War, but when military operations resumed he was back, and again became a furious jihadist. It is astonishing, but right under the noses of the federal troops and every imaginable Russian intelligence agency, in the midst of heavy fighting when everybody else was running for cover, Khanpash managed to make a television programme whose title can be roughly translated from the Chechen as, 'My Homeland Is Where Jihad Is'.

Admittedly, neither then nor now did I believe that.

What do you mean? Your homeland is not where jihad is.
That was just the name of the programme.

I heard Maskhadov has turned you away again recently?
Not Maskhadov, his representatives abroad, but I don't trust them. Rakhman Dushuyev in Turkey told me that he had received a cassette from Maskhadov saying the President no longer wanted me to call myself his representative, but I did not hear the cassette myself, or talk directly to Maskhadov. I recently had no trouble meeting Kusama and Anzor (Maskhadov's wife and son) in Dubai. They accepted me. I ate and slept at their house.

Dubai, Turkey, Jordan, Strasbourg. You seem to be travelling all the time. How do you get visas?
I know all the Chechens. I travel to all countries and call on everyone to make peace and unite.

You travelled to Dubai from Baku?
Yes.

You turned up there after the terrorist act in Moscow in October and asked Chechens living there to help you? You told them you were one of the participants in the Nord-Ost *hostage-taking who had survived, and now urgently needed contacts in the Arab world in order to escape pursuit?*
How do you know that?

Chechens in Baku told me, and I read it in the newspapers. Your name is on the list of terrorists who were in Nord-Ost. Incidentally, are you suing over that?
No. Why should I? I just asked Yastrzhembsky, 'How did that happen?'

What did he say?
'Just ignore it.'

The most recent upward spiral of Khanpash Terkibayev's vertiginous political career in politics is indeed associated with the disastrous events of 23–26 October 2002, when the hostage-taking at the *Nord-Ost* musical caused the loss of many lives.

Had you known Barayev Junior for long?
Yes. I know everybody in Chechnya.

So did they have any explosives in there?
No, of course not.

After *Nord-Ost*, Khanpash really did become a confidant of Putin's Presidential Administration. He held every authorisation he needed to enable him to move unobstructed from Maskhadov to Yastrzhembsky. He negotiated on behalf of Putin's Administration with Deputies of the Chechen Parliament to get them to support a referendum. He obtained guarantees of immunity for the Deputies so they could come to Moscow. It was none other than Khanpash who, as leader of their group, took them to Strasbourg, to meet senior officials of the Council of Europe and the Parliamentary Assembly, where the Deputies did everything required of them at the behest of Dmitry Rogozin, Chairman of the Duma Foreign Affairs Committee.

Naturally, the question arises, why did they choose Khanpash? What services had he rendered? How had he demonstrated his loyalty? Because without such proof he could not possibly have become involved in all this. We come now to a retelling of the most important part of our long conversation.

Khanpash appears to be the man for whom everybody involved with the *Nord-Ost* tragedy has been looking so diligently. He is the insider who made the terrorist act possible. Information in the possession of *Novaya gazeta* (which he doesn't deny: he is vain), indicates that Khanpash was an agent sent in by the intelligence services.

He entered the building with the terrorists as a member of their unit. He claims he secretly enabled them to travel through Moscow and to the *Nord-Ost* venue itself. It was he who assured the terrorists that everything was under control, that there were plenty of corrupt people, that the Russians had again accepted bribes, as they did when high-ranking resistance fighters were able to break out of the encirclement of Grozny and Komsomolskaya. They needed only to make a lot of noise, he told them, and there would be a second Budyonnovsk, enabling peace to be secured. Then, when they had fulfilled their mission, they would be allowed to escape. Not all of them, but many. 'Many' turned out to be only Khanpash himself.

He left the building before the assault began. He had a map of the Dubrovka Theatre Complex, something possessed by neither Barayev, who was in command of the terrorists, nor even, initially, by the special operations unit preparing the assault.

How come? Because Khanpash belongs to forces far higher in the militia and security hierarchy than the Vityaz and Alpha special operations troops who were risking their lives to storm the building.

Whether he was telling the truth about the map is not, actually, all that important. Khanpash would lie for a kopeck, as his faked photographs demonstrate. Those who could confirm or deny certain details of his story, like where his firing position was, have, to all appearances, been eliminated or are less garrulous. Do I believe there was more than one agent sent in? I think it is entirely possible.

What matters is that if there was an insider operating in *Nord-Ost*, the authorities knew about and were involved in preparing a terrorist act. It doesn't matter why. The main thing is that they (which section of them?) knew what was going on long before the rest of us did. They set up their own people for a terrible ordeal, knowing what was going to happen, fully aware that thousands would be permanently affected and hundreds killed or injured. The regime stage-managed another *Kursk* disaster. (Remember the messages sent by the unfortunate hostages from the occupied auditorium? 'We are like a second *Kursk*. Russia has forgotten us. Russia does not need us. Russia wants us to die.' Many outside the hall were indignant and thought this completely hysterical, but in fact they were accurately describing the situation.)

The question remains, then, why was this done? Why were all those people killed six months ago?

The first step is to work out who was responsible. Who, within the regime, was in the know? The Kremlin? Putin? The FSB? – the classical triad of modern Russia?

The state authorities are not a monolith and neither are the intelligence services. It is definitely not the case that most of the officers working in the operational headquarters beside the Dubrovka Complex were only pretending to be trying to avert the tragedy, in the full knowledge that the whole thing was a put-up job. Most of them were entirely committed, like the Vityaz and Alpha Units, like the rest of us.

But if Khanpash was in there, there is no escaping the fact that some dark nook of the state authorities did know and was only going through the motions of sympathising during those three days of insanity. This completely alters the complexion of those events.

So who were the intelligence agencies who knew? Certainly not the special operations soldiers who carried out the assault. If they had known the depths of the duplicity, there might simply have been a repeat of 1993 when the units refused to mount an assault [on Yeltsin's White House at the behest of the leaders of the anti-Gorbachev putsch], and the ending might have been completely different.

Neither was it the officers of the FSB and Interior Ministry, who planned the operation to rescue the hostages in all good faith. It was not they who infiltrated Khanpash into the terrorist group and subsequently fixed him up with a job.

Khanpash was not going to tell me who it was, but clearly the FSB and Interior Ministry were only acting out somebody else's script.

In the Second Chechen War methods such as these have been used extensively by military intelligence. In the so-called death squads it is officers of the GRU, the Central Intelligence Directorate, who make the running. The extra-judicial killing of their fellow citizens there is their stock-in-trade. Against these blood-soaked leaders neither the FSB, nor the Interior Ministry, nor the Prosecutor's Office, nor the courts can lift a finger. It is the practice of GRU units to exploit Chechen criminals and also their own victims, like those widowed by the death squads, as convenient fodder for achieving their aim of intimidating the whole of Russian society.

So was it the GRU, or someone as yet unknown? I have no answer, but it is vital that we should find out.

Why did those people die? Why such an unbelievable death toll of 129 lives?

That is what we get when we lift a corner of the curtain, when we hear the story of a double agent, a provocateur of our days so uncannily like Yevno Azef.*

People died, but the provocateur is alive and well. He is the political insider. He has his snout in the trough, looks good, and, most importantly, is still in business. In a few days' time he will be going back to Chechnya. What will he be cooking up this time?

'I need 24 hours to meet up with Maskhadov,' he boasts.

'Just 24 hours?'

'Well, OK, two days.'

Khanpash is forbearing towards naive people like us.

---

* A Tsarist police spy who organised deadly terrorist acts, even assassinating the Tsar's uncle to entrap his colleagues in the Socialist Revolutionary Party.

A Scheme for Protection Against Witnesses: Managed Terrorism in the Land of Managed Democracy?

22 December 2003

The information agencies tapped it out: 'Khanpash Nurdyevich Terkibayev has been killed in a car crash in Chechnya.' In the course of what we now know to have been his short life, the 31-year-old from Mesker-Yurt was to play many roles, of which the most important was unquestionably his complicity in the *Nord-Ost* hostage-taking in October 2002.

Who was Terkibayev? At first appearance, he was the last surviving witness from among the hostage-takers at the Dubrovka Theatre Complex. Officially listed as one of the terrorists, he claimed to have entered the building on 23 October last year as a member of Barayev's unit. In reality, as Terkibayev himself told me, and as is indirectly confirmed, he was a turncoat, an informer who once inside first fed information to the secret services, then left the building shortly before the assault.

Khanpash Terkibayev had previously been a journalist for Maskhadov, presenting the President's television programme between the two wars. After *Nord-Ost* he was a member of President Putin's Administration, on whose behalf he led a delegation of Chechen Deputies to the European Parliament in Strasbourg in April 2003. He would also show to anyone interested to see it his press pass as a special correspondent of the official newspaper *Rossiyskaya gazeta*. He was, in short, the servant of many masters.

The pinnacle of Terkibayev's career was undoubtedly *Nord-Ost*. His was a horrifying tale which proved that Khanpash genuinely did move in the circles he described and that, accordingly, the atrocity was stage-managed by at least one of the Russian secret services. Simultaneously, another Russian secret service and several special operations divisions were combating it, culminating in the use of a secret chemical weapon against Russian citizens.

In May this year our newspaper published an interview with Terkibayev who at that time was still firmly in the saddle. From his revelations it was clear that the *Nord-Ost* tragedy was advantageous to the highly original regime known as 'Russian managed democracy'.

What happened after our interview? We called on the team investigating *Nord-Ost* to question both Terkibayev and the author of these lines on the subject of Terkibayev. On one occasion the investigator actually did come to *Novaya gazeta*'s offices. In his record of the visit he wrote whatever he fancied, as is now common practice, a so-called free paraphrase. His interest in Terkibayev did not extend beyond the fact that, after our report, Basayev was threatening him for his treachery.

Terkibayev lived for much of this year in Baku, where things got so bad for him that he had no option but to move. Sooner or later Basayev's people would have eliminated him, so he moved to Chechnya. This was a step born of desperation, putting his head in the tiger's mouth. The federal forces now had no time for him, and he had no other source of support. The car accident followed.

What is the most important aspect of this? Historically, as everybody knows, double and triple agents end up getting murdered. For us, however, this only makes things worse. Terkibayev never was questioned, and accordingly one further fragile link in the chain leading to the truth about *Nord-Ost* has been broken. He took with him information which ought to be known to everyone in Russia, the answers to fundamental questions about *Nord-Ost* to which we, thanks to the efforts of those at the top of the political pyramid, have no answers. Who supported Barayev's unit in Moscow? (We are not talking here about corrupt officials issuing visas, although, ironically, some are facing trial this very week.)

How did Barayev's people get into Moscow at all? How were preparations for a terrorist attack in Moscow made? Who was Terkibayev's controller in the secret services, and in which one?

Why was there an assault? Why were negotiations which had some prospect of success in getting the hostages released terminated? Who was involved in taking such criminal decisions?

If we reduce these questions to their lowest common denominator, they indicate something we all suspect but cannot prove: that this was a managed act of terrorism in which Barayev was manipulated, and in which the female suicide bombers in black who accompanied him were dupes.

One important detail for anyone interested in receiving accurate information is that not only was Terkibayev not questioned by the members of the official *Nord-Ost* inquiry, he was even ignored by the members of the Public Commission of Inquiry, which does exist, although it is so inactive that it might as well not.

The timing of the car accident is also revealing: Terkibayev might have been about to open his mouth. The CIA was taking an interest in him. CIA agents were (quite properly) conducting their own inquiry into the death of an American citizen who had been among the audience, and had been signalling that Terkibayev was of interest to them as a source of evidence. (This may also have been a reason for Terkibayev's move from Baku; in Baku he was accessible to the CIA, while in Chechnya he was probably not.)

Where does that leave us? 'The agent must not be allowed to talk', and Terkibayev has been duly silenced.

That is the main surmise about the causes of the car accident. Nobody will ever be able to prove that it was a genuine accident. Even if it was, nobody would believe it.

More generally, in the now eternal absence of Terkibayev the unquestioned and liquidated, I personally will never believe that the secret services are not involved in organising terrorist acts. They have done everything they could to torment me with the belief that they are. If there is another hostage-taking, the first question that will spring to mind will be, who is behind it? Which of those supposed to protect us are actually orchestrating the terrorists?

One Month Before the Nord-Ost *Inquiry Ends, the State Authorities Bury Answers to the Main Questions, and Throw Truth to the Winds*

19 January 2004

At the end of a two-hour meeting [between the head of the official investigation into the *Nord-Ost* hostage-taking and victims and relatives], I had to intervene and remind Mr Vladimir Kalchuk about the truth of the Terkibayev affair.

His reaction was bizarre. He told me to get lost and to stop writing to him, otherwise he would 'hint' to the *Nord-Ost* victims that my son's mobile telephone number had been discovered in the memory of the phone the terrorists were using, 'and then we will see what they will do to you. They may well be interested to know exactly what kind of personal links you have with the terrorists, you and your son . . .'

In view of this, I will have to persist with my reminders to Mr Kalchuk. First, negotiations needed to be conducted during the siege, which I did. Second, the person I chose to help me was indeed my son, Ilya Politkovsky, and help me he did, courageously, conscientiously and openly trying to save, among others, the life of his close friend, Ilya Lysak, a musician in the *Nord-Ost* orchestra. Lysak was inside the occupied auditorium and used his personal connection with my family in order – equally courageously and heedless of the possible consequences – to facilitate negotiations. It was he, who today is still extremely ill, who handed his mobile telephone to the terrorists, and they used it to talk to me and my son, to agree the exact time I would enter the occupied building. They also used it to talk to Sergey Yastrzhembsky, the President's Aide.

I am sure the overwhelming majority of people would have done the same in the circumstances. Apparently the individual entrusted with leading the inquiry into the *Nord-Ost* tragedy would not.

Russia: A Country at Peace

[As the following pieces illustrate, a recurrent theme in Anna Politkovskaya's articles is the regime's application of state resources to bolster its stranglehold on power rather than to deal with the huge and pressing problems of the population it rules.]

The Tunguska Meteorite Landed Right in the Middle of Russia, and So Did We

25 December 2000

Yielding to the desire to find a contrarian way to start the new century, our newspaper decided to leave its mark somewhere nobody has left a mark before. Apart from the Tunguska Meteorite.

On 22 December, the day of the winter solstice, we arrived at the very spot which, since the demise of the USSR, has been the geographical centre of the Russian Federation, the Evenki Autonomous Region. There, in the main square of the township of Tura, the capital of Evenkia, we erected a suitable monument designed by the Moscow artist, Dmitry Krymov.

Admittedly, the square in Tura doesn't yet have a name, so if you do decide to visit it you will have to ask a passer-by where the monument to the centre of Russia is. Anybody will be able to point it out, though, because everybody in Tura, apart from infants and the very ill, came to the opening ceremony. Oh, and also those who went instead to the local Palace of Culture for a concert by Dmitry Kharatian and Alexey Buldakov. At *Novaya gazeta*'s invitation they made the more than seven-hour indirect flight from Moscow to provide a top quality celebration of the unveiling of the monument.

Ivan Bakhtin, the Deputy Governor of Evenkia, told us that even half a day before the celebrations in Tura nobody really believed the monument would be erected, or that the visitors from Moscow would arrive, or that there would be a fireworks display, and a concert, and presents.

'Why was that?'

'Because today's temperature is 48 degrees below zero, which for us is considered warm.'

But now, what our readers really want to know is what the centre of Russia is like. There is no escaping the fact that it is highly symbolic. What gives meaning to life here, in all its variety, is the struggle for survival. If you want to live, you need to be focused. Relax, and you die. If you want to eat, make sure you shoot plenty of game in season. If you want felt boots and a fur coat so as not to freeze, barter the pelts of bears, reindeer and sable you have killed for clothing. And never be on your own. If you are alone and you have a fall, you are dead. The world is ordered in a primitive but strict and logical manner, as befits a symbol.

We learned that it is a stone's throw from the centre of Russia to the pole of cold. The snow was not just very abundant, it was all you could see. Fir and pine trees do not survive, and even birch trees eke out a dismal dwarf existence. The local taiga is exclusively larch so the larch tree should be the symbol of this symbol of Russia, ginger-red and recalcitrant, not the blond, languid birch.

There does seem to be a vast supply of land rich in diamonds, oil and gas. The trouble is that first you have to get here.

There are no cities at the centre of Russia, only townships, villages and factories. There is no gas in the houses, although there is plenty underground; no water, no drains, no avenues or embankments, neither along the Podkamennaya River nor over the Nizhnyaya Tunguskaya. Both rivers flow this way and that the length and breadth of Evenkia. Nobody has thought of trying to build anything we would recognise as a respectable road. There are no railways, no metalled roads, only an all-season dirt road 14 kilometres long which links Gorny Airport and Tura. All the other 'highways' are passable only in the winter. Hence the work routine of the local administration consists of just three things: first, keeping the winter roads in good order; second, monitoring the forces of Mother Nature as she constantly destroys them; and third, starting all over again. If you let your mind wander and stop monitoring the infrastructure every day, you will soon be unable to move at all. Your world will contract to the size of your own inner world and you will exist in a snowbound cell.

Who, you might ask, is capable of enduring such hardship? The answer is, only 20,000 citizens of Russia. Here, in the very heart of Russia, a meteorite fell in the early years of the departed century. It became known as the Tunguska Meteorite. And now we are here too.

A Hostage of the Russian Federation

8 September 2005

Anybody who watches the national Russian television channels saw the item. It was claimed that Adam Chitayev, a former resistance fighter with a federal warrant out for his arrest, had been detained in Ust-Ilimsk, Irkutsk Province. He was supposedly guilty of abducting both Russian servicemen and members of international missions, and was said to have been masquerading as a schoolteacher of English.

Russia has long been trained to believe this sort of thing. If a Chechen has been arrested, that's as it should be, or if it's not quite as it should be, then it's better to be safe than sorry. Nobody gave a damn about Chitayev. Hundreds of criminal cases relating to so-called international terrorism are cooked up like Siberian pelmeni dumplings the length and breadth of the country, on the principle of the more the merrier, and anyway you can't tell the innocent from the guilty. Naturally, the arrest of some Chitayev or other was regarded as only proper, as what the law enforcement agencies are there for. But only by anybody who doesn't know who Adam Chitayev is and, more broadly, who the Chitayev brothers are. In Strasbourg an increasing number of people do know. That, in fact, is where the answer is to be found as to why a man who was not hiding from anybody was suddenly arrested in faraway Ust-Ilimsk, only for it to be announced to the whole of Russia that he had been hiding.

The Chitayevs are appellants in *Strasbourg* v. *The Russian Federation*. What is more, they have almost won. This summer the procedure of having a case considered by the European Court of Human Rights, which takes many years, ended in an interim victory, a so-called 'Decision on the Admissibility of Appeal No. 59334/00'.

The story of the Chitayev family is one to which *Novaya gazeta* has returned several times. Their fate was not unusual by Chechen standards in 2000. It befell many people, but very few decided to seek redress through the courts.

Arbi, born in 1964, was an engineer who had always lived in Grozny. Adam, born in 1967, was a schoolteacher. Like many Chechens he lived in Kazakhstan for a long time before returning to Chechnya in 1999, immediately before the war. Together with his wife and two small children he moved in with his brother in Grozny. 'In autumn 1999 armed clashes began in Chechnya between Russian troops and Chechen rebels,' the European Court ruling reads, and, in accordance with the rules of Strasbourg, it is based on documentation which confirms every word. 'Grozny and its suburbs were the target of large-scale attacks by Russian soldiers.'

Arbi's flat in Grozny was destroyed (as is confirmed by a certificate, attached to the case files in Strasbourg, from one of the apartment management boards in Grozny). 'The plaintiffs, together with their families and possessions, moved to their father's house in Achkhoy Martan. On 15 January 2000, members of the Interior Affairs Temporary Office (temporarily occupied by militiamen from Voronezh Province) conducted a search of the plaintiffs' house. They took with them a new cordless telephone in its packaging.'

On 18 January one of the Chitayevs went to complain to the Interior Affairs Office and to demand the return of the telephone. It actually was returned, but on 12 April retribution followed. There was another search and more looting, but also an arrest, followed by yet more looting. Things went from bad to worse, despite the fact that everything of any interest had already been stolen: a video, a printer, televisions, a computer, a heater, and 'two files of documents'. Interestingly enough, a list of the stolen goods was provided to Strasbourg over the signature of one Vlasenko, an officer of the Achkhoy Martan Interior Affairs Temporary Office.

Arbi and Adam were arrested. On 14 April their father, Salaudi, went to find out what had happened to his sons and was himself arrested, officially for violation of the curfew. He was released five days later. The brothers were held in the Interior Affairs Office for 17 days.

> They were fettered to a chair by their handcuffs and beaten. Various parts of the body, including their fingertips and ears, were subjected to electric shocks; their arms were twisted; they were beaten with rubber truncheons and plastic bottles full of water; they were suffocated using adhesive tape, polythene bags and gas masks; dogs were set upon them; and pieces of skin were torn from them using pliers. Plaintiff No. 1 (Arbi Chitayev) had a gas mask put on his head which was pumped full of cigarette smoke. Plaintiff No. 2 (Adam Chitayev) was brought into a room and told he must confess to being a resistance fighter and taking part in kidnappings. When Plaintiff No. 2 refused to sign the confession, he was gagged with tape and beaten on the back and sexual organs. Simultaneously, another person pointed a rifle at him and threatened to shoot him if he moved.

On 28 April the Chitayevs, along with others detained in the Office, were taken away blindfolded and told that they were going to be shot. In fact they were dropped off at the Chernokozovo pretrial detention facility where

> They were forced to run to an interrogation room, bending down and with their hands on their heads while the guards beat them on the back. In the interrogation room were an iron table and chair and there was a hook on the wall. They were kicked, and beaten with rifle butts and hammers on various parts of the body, concentrating on their kneecaps; straitjackets were put on them which were attached to the hook so that they were hanging from it, and beaten. Their fingers and toes were crushed using hammers and door jambs; their hands and feet were tied together behind their backs (the 'sparrow' position) . . . The detainees were not allowed to pray under threat of further beatings.

The Chitayevs were lucky. They emerged from Chernokozovo in October 2000, having passed through all the circles of hell which are customary there but at least they were alive. They were outraged by their illegal arrest and torture, which made them rare among survivors of Chernokozovo, and this in itself testifies to their firm belief that the Russian regime had no grounds whatsoever for impugning them. The Chitayevs were not and never had been members of the Chechen resistance. It also mattered that they are educated, serious, socially active and progressive. Their indignation took them first to the Russian legal institutions – the Prosecutor's Office and the courts – and then, when they were unable to raise any interest in their sufferings there, on to Strasbourg. Arbi and Adam Chitayev lodged official complaints, and Arbi took the difficult decision to emigrate from Russia, seeing no possibility of continuing to live in a country where such humiliations were possible. We met him abroad, where he was not enjoying exile and finding it difficult to make a living, but at least feeling safe. Four years on, remembering the details of his months of detention as he looked out of the window at life in Europe, he was shaking as if he had Parkinson's disease. Adam, however, decided to stay, moved to Siberia, and got a teaching job. In Strasbourg, meanwhile, the case, with the slowness which seems to be essential, edged up the queue of many thousands of appeals of his suffering compatriots, towards examination.

The Chitayev brothers knew that Chechen appellants to Strasbourg were in a uniquely dangerous situation. Before hearing any verdict, very many of them would be murdered by 'masked members of unidentified security agencies wearing combat fatigues', as they are routinely described.

The Chitayevs did not, however, withdraw their appeal. On the contrary, they responded conscientiously to every inquiry from the European Court of Human Rights, wrote supplementary explanations, and were very active. Neither did the Russian state authorities leave them in peace. They were threatened with criminal cases, arrests and retaliation. The more vigorously the Chitayevs defended themselves, the greater the pressure which was brought to bear on them.

On 30 June 2005 their case was finally considered in Strasbourg. You read the court record with a sense that something is missing. Everything the Chitayevs allege has documentary confirmation: all our government's replies to inquiries from the Court of Human Rights about the degrading treatment of the Chitayevs are bald, unsubstantiated assertions, mere fantasy along the following lines: 'On 12 April when the plaintiffs' house was inspected eight military greatcoats and four military jackets were found ... video recordings of interviews with Shamil Basayev, a videotape of the documentary film *Nokhcho Chechnya: Day of Freedom*, photographs of Arbi Chitayev with a rifle.'

The suggestion is that here was a hotbed of resistance fighters and abductors of soldiers, never mind that the greatcoats belonged to the Chitayev brothers themselves, of whom there are four; or indeed that these are Soviet-era military greatcoats dating back to the days when the brothers were serving in the Soviet Army.

The result of this approach does not reflect well on Russia: a 'decision on admissibility' is effectively a ruling in favour of someone whose appeal has been accepted for consideration. The basis and approach of the future verdict is already evident in the decision on admissibility, as is obvious in the Chitayevs' case. The Chitayevs will win their case against the Russian Federation because it has failed to provide any justification either for their arrest or for the looting of their home.

Every stage of the deliberations in Strasbourg has been followed by the Russian authorities, indeed an official government representative has been present at every hearing, including the last one on 30 June. While they still had time, before the final verdict, the regime resuscitated their criminal case against Adam, Arbi being beyond their reach. Here we again find the eight military greatcoats and tape of an interview with Shamil Basayev. A warrant was issued for Adam's arrest and locating him was not difficult as he was not hiding, indeed living at his officially registered address. Not merely a law-abiding citizen, but one tenaciously determined to have the law respected, Adam was arrested and sent under convoy to Chechnya.

This is barefaced retaliation for his appeal to Strasbourg, the state's attempt to get even with someone who is not prepared to behave like a sheep.

Planet Earth: The World Beyond Russia

[Anna Politkovskaya did not only criticise the Putin regime and Russia's 'security forces'; she was not uncritical of the West. Nevertheless, she admired civilised and enlightened attitudes when she encountered them there, and hoped they might be transplanted.]

The Secret of Claridge's. What Did the Prime Minister of Great Britain and Novaya gazeta's *Columnist Talk About Over Lunch?*

14 May 2001

London, 30 April 2001. The city was unwelcoming. People waiting for spring were still faced with driving rain, a cold, bitter wind, a never-ending twilight, an autumn that couldn't be shaken off despite the May tulips lining the avenues in the park.

The weather was a fitting background to the task I had set myself: having flown to the British capital, how was I to get the answer to a question I wanted to ask Tony Blair, Prime Minister of this influential island kingdom? Why, for some time now, has he been on such good terms with President Putin? What are the qualities in Putin he finds so appealing?

Any Russian journalist knows that to get an interview with a head of government you need the patience of a saint. In Moscow, miracles do not happen – such is the nature of the Kremlin – but in London on the morning of 30 April I received a personal invitation to the traditional annual lunch of the London Press Club, founded in 1882, with the Prime Minister of Great Britain. Remarkably, I had not made a huge effort to get this invitation.

I was just handed it. For 12.30 at Claridge's, a grand old London hotel. So why not go?

The miracles did not end there, at least in the view of this citizen of the Russian Federation. At 12.20 there was nobody at the entrance to Claridge's other than an elderly commissionaire wearing a heavy grey wool uniform and a high Dickensian hat. It is customary for the commissionaires of very expensive London hotels to be grey-haired elderly gentleman who would have been retired long ago in Russia.

The commissionaire opened the door of my taxi and suggested that, if I was coming for the lunch with the Prime Minister, I would find it more convenient to use a different nearby door. I knew what he was up to. He was surreptitiously directing me to a queue where the British security services would filter would-be guests. They have their own, Irish, terrorists to worry about, after all.

So I marched through the main entrance, and soon realised I had got it wrong. All the aged commissionaire had wanted was to show me a shorter and more convenient route to the Prime Minister. I returned specially to my starting point to check and, while I was at it, looked around to see which rooftops the snipers were on.

There were none. Neither were there any lantern-jawed, shaven-headed security guards with searching scowls, or the bleeping metal detector frames through which anyone in Russia is obliged to pass if they are likely to be within a kilometre of anywhere the President might show up.

At 12.45 Tony Blair arrived. At 12.50 the gong sounded for lunch. At 13.00 promptly we took our seats. My table was next to the Prime Minister's. We tucked in to the starter, duck in aspic with milk sauce. Not bad but, to be honest, not that special either. Mr Blair was chasing it across his large plate, just like me.

The diners got on with their duck, and the gentlemen, all of them what in Russia we would call 'directors of the media', made no attempt to disturb the Prime Minister's meal. Nobody ran up to him to ask questions while he was pretending to enjoy the starter.

At 13.19 Dennis Griffiths, the Chairman of the London Press

Club, introduced Tony Blair to the guests and invited him to speak. What he had to say was intriguing, but for the most part consisted of declaring his love for the press and joking about the fact that he was wearing spectacles for the first time in his life.

A ripple of laughter ran over the tables and people clapped.

At 13.35, while Blair was still speaking from an improvised podium, orderly rows of waiters glided into the room bearing enormous plates. This was the main dish. Everybody got the same: a small piece of extremely tender braised or boiled pink salmon, with three tiny potatoes, a couple of sprigs of sweet basil, and a modest pile of kidney beans.

Blair, who as everybody knows recently had a fourth child, sat down and set about his salmon in exactly the way the hard-up father of four children would in Russia. The Prime Minister got through his diminutive piece of pink fish rapidly and with obvious relish.

He was now free, and I mounted my attack. The path to him was straight and clear, obstructed only by the remains of the first course and Blair's press secretary, Alastair Campbell, a former popular columnist of one of the London newspapers. Alastair, however, was eating his fish, and everything was in place.

The response of the Prime Minister of Great Britain to my inquiry regarding the nature of his affection for Putin was brief but comprehensive. He replied, 'It's my job as Prime Minister to like Mr Putin.' And that was that. What more was to be said? The chef's job is to cook the fish; the doctor's job is to remove an appendix; the job of one head of state is to demonstrate how much he likes another head of state. It's as simple as that.

At 14.10 speeches by members of the Press Club began and continued until 14.45. Blair listened politely. At 14.50 he quietly left, as had been previously announced in the programme. There were no standing ovations or elaborate farewells. It was all very understated and British.

At this point dessert was brought in: tea or coffee and a piece of chocolate praline gâteau with coffee-flavoured custard. The Prime

Minister was leaving but turned to the tables one last time. He glanced sadly at the unattainable plates of gâteau which the waiters, seemingly oblivious to the head of their government, were carrying past.

Everybody has a job to do, and nobody should try to stop them. That really is the British attitude. If a waiter is bringing diners their gâteau you get out of his way, even if you are the Prime Minister.

Who in Europe Will Take Responsibility for a War in Europe?

16 August 2001

Here we are, almost at the furthest end of the Old World. A very high bank over a brooding black Norwegian fjord, and a small township climbing up this fjord cliff. It is small, self-contained, wonderful, and feels rather carefree. It is called Molde. Molde does not trifle with lakes or seas; what dominates here is the mighty Atlantic Ocean itself. You could get in a boat and sail to America – the whole world is on your doorstep. Within the borders of Russia few people are aware of the existence of Molde.

Molde, however, is not entirely what it seems. There are people in this town whose whole lives were turned upside down by all that has been going on in Russia.

High above the fjord is the town cemetery, a neat, quiet, sorrowful place, and as unnerving as any cemetery where life meets death irrevocably, leaving only a gravestone in place of a once living, rebellious human soul. I heap red roses on the earth around a severe, grey Scandinavian stone which, at the cemetery's very highest point, looks out towards the ocean. Facing the infinity of the Atlantic, the words chiselled into the stone read, 'Død Tsjetsjenia. 17.12.1996'.

That means, 'Died in Chechnya'. Ingeborg Foss, a 42-year-old Norwegian nurse who lived in Molde and left this quiet Atlantic coastal town on 4 December 1996, died together with five nurses and doctors, three of whom were Norwegian, in the Chechen village of Starye Atagi on 17 December. She was ten days into her Red Cross mission, working in a hospital which had been set up there.

'Ingeborg rang me twice from Chechnya,' Sigrid Foss, Ingeborg's 82-year-old mother tells me. 'She said it was very frightening.'

'Did you ask her to come home? Did you try to persuade her? Did you insist, as a mother?'

'No,' Sigrid replies. 'It was her destiny.'

Brief, to the point, betraying no sense of hurt, but what a scree of emotion there is in the heart of this woman, her face incised with wrinkles. Love of her daughter, grief at her passing, but also pride that Ingeborg proved so reckless for the sake of people she did not know but who were nevertheless ill. And, of course, the pain of irredeemable loss.

Long before Chechnya, Ingeborg had dedicated herself to working for the Red Cross. She had worked in Nicaragua and Pakistan but when the Red Cross offered her a contract in Bosnia, she suddenly refused, saying, 'I have an aged mother. I can't.' Nevertheless, she made up her mind to go to Chechnya. The Red Cross assured her that conditions were not as bad as people were saying, and that everything would be fine.

Sigrid catches constantly at her grey braids of hair, blown about by a strong wind which has sprung up here in the cemetery, high above the fjord. She is barely able to hold back the tears. Her eyes redden and her eyelids droop, and then she squats down and lays a hand on the dark brown fjord soil by Ingeborg's gravestone. She steadies herself for a few moments before catching her grey hair again. She pushes it up, away from her eyes in defiance of the wind, and the gesture seems to help her gather what remains of her strength. They say here that the older women of Norway do not cry. It is not their way. They are strong, indomitable, familiar with suffering, and do not usually give way to tears. They lived through the Second World War, when Norway endured a brutal occupation, with partisans, a resistance, fighting, and many dead. Most later lived through great poverty and hunger, and it was only when they were very old that Norway became rich and was able to provide them with decent old people's homes and good pensions.

Sigrid is one such Norwegian woman. You can tell that she is by nature very tough, like anyone who lives with the wind and the sea and who is used to seeing their family sail out, never to return. She is fully aware of what someone standing beside her in the cemetery may be thinking.

'Yes, losing my daughter has put ten years on my age,' she nods, swallowing a lump in her throat in order to continue the simple story of her family. All her life Sigrid taught Norwegian and English, and of course brought up her own children, but her husband was a doctor. Sigrid lost first him, and then the daughter who had decided to follow in his footsteps.

Sigrid proudly shows me a certificate, Order No. 589, dated 11 December 1997, issued by President Aslan Maskhadov, awarding Ingeborg the highest decoration of the Chechen Republic. That award and a grave are all that Sigrid has left after the death of her daughter.

'Do you feel Russia has wronged you?'

'No. My grudge is against the Red Cross.'

Sigrid Foss says that she believes the organisation in whose cause her daughter died was over-ambitious.

'At that time, between the two Chechen wars, the Red Cross wanted to establish a hospital against all the odds, as if to say, "Look at us! We can do something nobody else can do! The Russians are too frightened, and the Chechens don't have the means." Their ambitions led them to assure Ingeborg there was no great danger, when in fact it was deadly.' Sigrid was told this by the Norwegian doctor who by a miracle survived, and who accompanied the stretcher bearing Ingeborg's body back to Molde.

'A stretcher? Not a coffin?'

'That's right.'

For Sigrid, 1997 and 1998 passed under the initial shock of

bereavement, but then she wanted to establish the truth. Gradually, however, things took a bizarre, heartless turn. As if it was not enough that Ingeborg's life had been cut short, Sigrid found she had no way, because of everything going on in Chechnya and Russia, to find out who exactly was responsible for her daughter's untimely death.

What is left for someone whose child has predeceased them? Given that it is impossible to right the terrible wrong that has happened, they do at least want to know what that was. Alas, to this day Sigrid Foss does not even know whether there is an inquiry into the murder of her daughter in Starye Atagi, let alone whether it is making progress.

Everybody has forgotten her: Russia, because her daughter was helping the Chechen population to survive, and at present that is unfashionable in Russia; Chechnya, because Chechnya has no time for anything other than trying to survive.

'Two years ago we had a phone call from the Norwegian Foreign Ministry. I was told they had no information. They did not even know whether an investigation was being conducted in Russia. I couldn't make out who our Foreign Ministry was in touch with in Moscow about the murders in Starye Atagi. The Red Cross was no better. They sent me a letter a year ago saying there was no news. In five years you are the first person from Russia to remember Ingeborg and come to visit her grave.'

'But what about Norwegians?'

'No Norwegians have come either.'

'Død Tsjetsjenia.' Norway, Molde, Russia. I say goodbye to Sigrid Foss. Do you still think the world is vast? That if there is a conflagration in one place it does not have a bearing on another, and that you can sit it out in peace on your veranda admiring your absurd petunias?

Our greatest problem today is that this most basic and long-established truth has to be reiterated as if it had just come into existence. Neither that modest grave in Molde, nor the thousands of graves all over Chechnya, have acted as a wake-up call for

Europe, which continues to slumber as if the war being fought within its bounds was not already in its twenty-third successive month; as if Chechnya were as far from Norway as it is from the Antarctic.

For all that, Chechnya is no less a part of the Old World than any of its other territories. Mr Kruse, a correspondent for Norwegian state television who has worked in Russia for many years, exclaimed in some surprise during our conversation to the effect that, 'Oh, but Russia is a different part of Europe. You can't apply the usual criteria. Even war criminals in Russia are not really war criminals. You can hardly blame the present fate of Milošević on Russia's leaders, given its great spiritual heritage and sheer geographical scale.'

Alas, this is an all too typical European attitude. Russia has today been categorised as a maverick territory where, with the tacit agreement of the heads of the European states, the European Parliament, the Council of Europe and the OSCE all lumped together, it is apparently acceptable for citizens to live under laws quite different from those which apply to the rest of the European continent, laws which the rest of Europe couldn't imagine living under in its worst nightmare.

That is why I gave Mr Kruse a hard time. I asked him why he thought it was all right for a Chechen woman to be killed for no reason, just because passing soldiers were in a bad mood, but not for the same fate to befall a Norwegian, or Swedish or Belgian woman. How was a French woman any different from a Chechen woman, or a Russian woman who happened to belong to a 'great power'?

It isn't all right, of course, but many people in Norway are taken aback by questions like that. It is obvious that Chechen women are no different, but that does not square with Europe's self-contradictory desire not to fall out with Putin while retaining a semblance of civilised values.

All my conversations, meetings and interviews – in the Norwegian Foreign Ministry, with reporters, at the Nobel Institute in Oslo, with the future Prime Minister Kjell Magne Bondevik, even in the Norwegian Human Rights Centre (there really is such an office block in Oslo, where most of the human rights organisations operating in Norway are accommodated under one roof) – only served to further persuade me of something I already knew: Europe has no stomach for opposing the war in Chechnya. Europe is mired in double standards when it comes to human rights. One standard applies to most of Europe; it is distilled, splendid, civilised and tidy. For Russia, where democracy was born only a decade ago, there is another, naturally less distilled and pure. For the rebellious enclave of Chechnya, however, there is no standard at all, a void. Europe effectively condones the existence of a territory where atrocities go unpunished, and pretends that the war being waged there does not concern Europeans. There are few protests, no sanctions are imposed on Russian officials, and crimes that would never be tolerated in the rest of Europe – killings, extra-judicial persecution and executions – are seen as unproblematical in Russia and Chechnya. Indeed, there is even tacit acceptance of the monstrous notion that one particular nation should bear collective responsibility for the actions of a few of its members.

Applying double standards is a dangerous game. Europe has been here before, with infamous consequences. In 1933 the Führer of a new Germany was also 'democratically elected'. Europe was frightened by his speeches but, until they could no longer be ignored, paid them no attention, preferring to look to its own prosperity and pleasant morning coffee. With Europe turning a blind eye, two nationalities – the Jews and the Gypsies – were held collectively responsible for the deeds of particular individuals. What was the consequence? The consequence was 1945, with millions dead, millions burned in crematoria, and Europe in ruins.

It all started so simply. A particular gentleman with psychological problems took it into his head that one nation was great and the rest were less great, and that some, indeed, should be annihilated. Are we really to say that things are different now? That the

Kremlin sometimes gives Chechens honours and medals and even promotes them to top positions and is doing something for them? Hitler did all that too, as a smokescreen for Europe's benefit. There were 'good' Jews, 'honest' Gypsies were paraded now and again, and sometimes there were even 'civilised' Slavs to be discovered, so that Europe wouldn't be upset, would not become alarmed too soon. Europe pretended to swallow all this, but that did not save countless men, women and children from dying subsequently at the hands of the people of that 'great' nation.

To return to the present. The double standards Europe applies to Chechnya are gradually infiltrating Europe. What did Ingeborg Foss give her life for? Why does nobody in Europe, not even in Norway, not in the OSCE or the European Parliament think it matters that an aged Norwegian mother knows nothing about how or why her daughter died, or that the investigation of the deaths of six doctors and nurses in Starye Atagi has ground to a halt? (That nothing is being done has been confirmed by the Prosecutor-General's Office of the Russian Federation.)

So what is modern Europe's moral code? A pretence? Self-delusion for some and a convenient fiction for others who don't want it to get in the way of pan-European fraternisation between the major powers to crush those who are weaker?

Russia is in the grip of war fever, Europe reacts sluggishly, and here is the result: Ingeborg Foss, a young Norwegian woman, died in Chechnya and now her old mother, Sigrid Foss, is alone in the world. Just like Aishat Djabrailova from Gudermes, who lost her husband and her sons in the Second Chechen Slaughter. Like Lyudmila Sysuyeva from Tyumen Province who received an official form advising her of the death of her only son, followed shortly afterwards by a sealed zinc coffin, and who now doesn't know whom to turn to. We are in close proximity to each other: from Oslo to Moscow is just two hours by air, and another two hours will take you from Moscow to Chechnya. Europe is tiny.

This generation of politicians, to whom we gave the right to rule, have failed us. They act in their own interests, not in the interests of Europe.

As we said our farewells, Sigrid told me, 'The fact that you remembered Ingrid has given me a few more years of life.' Behind us the Atlantic roared and the seagulls cried out. 'People need answers to the questions which most concern them while they are still alive,' she added. 'That may be the most important thing those in authority can do.'

The Other Anna

[Anna Politkovskaya has been described as 'steely'. She was not; she was matter-of-fact. These articles show her humanity, a sensitive conscience, a willingness to engage with the unfamiliar, and regret that her homeland was not a more enjoyable place to live.]

The Joy of Paris

1 June 2000

So much has been said about Paris that it is embarrassing to join the chorus. But it can't be helped, I really want to. This city has such powerful magic that your tongue, that wretch which betrays your innermost feelings, is untied and puts to sleep protesting reason. You want to shout that you too have been happy here. Even if it's banal, cliché-ridden, even if it's already been done to death by everybody, including the greatest and most brilliant people on the planet, you still want to say it your way, even though you recognise the pointlessness of the enterprise.

So, I'm in Paris, it's late May and the chestnuts are in bloom. The next five days are mine, all mine.

The reason for being here is that a collection of reports from Chechnya and Ingushetia, published in *Novaya gazeta* between September 1999 and April 2000, are being published here. This is very pleasing because it puts our regular readers, from Chukotka to Kaliningrad, ahead of the Parisians, those legislators on every aspect of fashion. The publisher who has lavished so much loving attention on *Novaya gazeta* (not without the prompting of Alexander Ginsburg, former political prisoner and dissident, who is today a champion of human rights, friend of Solzhenitsyn, and a Parisian), is not only very large, popular, and well known in Paris, but boasts the aesthetically pleasing name of Robert Laffont. There, in just those two words, those four syllables which flow into each other, France is rendered into sound. The uvular trill of the 'r', twice. The lily-like 'la' where a tender 'l' merges with a kiss from lips delicately forming that special 'a' to produce a sound close to the la-la-la of a toothless babe.

However, the imposing Robert Laffont was not until tomorrow morning. My first night in Paris was to be spent in a café. Where else? But how are you to pluck the very finest pearl from such a gleaming pile? In Paris, a city of freedom and a certain frivolity, the only way is to advance boldly and see what happens. The very first Parisian café we managed to select entirely at random ('Should we go in here?' 'Oh no, much too crowded!' 'OK, then, down the street there to the right?' 'How about this one?' 'Let's find a seat') was called by coincidence 'Le Select'.

It was perfect. We found ourselves in the centre of Montparnasse, both the district and the Boulevard, and accordingly in a haven where the artistic elite of the entire world came to alternate resuscitation with inspiration. As we soon found out.

If we had known where we were headed, we might have been more circumspect. At the next table was a boisterous party of stereotypical Parisians: quasi-actors, quasi-artists, of differing ages but all with a suggestion of the eternal student at their greying temples. They were having a great time, oblivious to the joys or sorrows of anyone around them. There was little space between the tables and the rooms were very narrow, the furniture ancient. The interiors were perfectly preserved from the early 1920s. It is wholly impermissible to make any changes to the historical appearance of Parisian cafés. They are museums of the spirit of Paris.

The atmosphere, too, had been preserved. A young girl-artist, very proud of herself – like all Parisian girls – and instantly tipsy, eager to find happiness with a young boy-artist sitting some distance away, headed rapidly towards him through a historic, narrow space and sent a bottle on our table flying. There was water everywhere, in my handbag, on our clothes, in our shoes. So what did this select, impulsive fledgling of Montparnasse do about it?

Well, actually, nothing. Women in Paris are very proud indeed and have their noses in the air while managing simultaneously to seem entirely available. Our artistic mademoiselle politely, but not too politely, cooed 'Pardon' and quickly found the joy she had fluttered in here to find, in the company of her Pierre, who was perhaps an as yet undiscovered Derain, or Matisse.

The names, of course, are deliberately selected. Derain, Matisse, and indeed Picasso, Cocteau, Max Jacob, Henry Miller, Scott Fitzgerald, and Hemingway himself had sat at these same little tables at which the early twenty-first-century Montparnasse avant-garde had given us a good soaking.

What more could a former Soviet citizen want in order to be happy? At this moment in life, nothing, unless to feel their backside in contact with the tattered armchair which had been scuffed by the threadbare trousers of the young Hemingway as he sipped the same cocktail as you. He was select, and you are select.

The waiters of Le Select, incidentally, are men of advancing years, if not just plain old. And yet, how proud they are, standing out even among the proud Parisian crowd. In vain will you seek to attract their attention, for you are no Picasso. Your predicament, however, is that you don't want to rise irately from your seat and storm out, having lost patience with the arrogant *garçon*. For some reason you understand and forgive, for you are still only in the foothills.

The waiter eventually deigns to come over to you, a debutante here still far from conquering Montparnasse. He brings you the water you requested long ago, naturally in a 1920s tumbler. The glass is thick and coarse, without a hint of gentility, and openly proclaims its primary function as being not to get broken too soon. The clientele have always been a bit rowdy. Give them half-decent glasses and you would have been permanently in debt, even if some of them did go on to become Nobel Prize winners, the *crème de la crème*, champions of the world.

You have to sympathise with the glasses. As he bangs mine down on the table, the waiter does not favour his non-regular customer with so much as a glance. The party next to us are 'his'. He and they belong here, guffawing, flirting, twining themselves around each other, even though one brings the coffee and another pays for it. Naturally the *garçon* can only look down on me.

He is haughty, but not actually rude. He even appears partly to forgive me for being a nobody in Montparnasse. You get a strange feeling from your mute contemplation of this old Parisian professional's game. You catch yourself trying to be noticed by him, supercilious though his glance will be, and are glad when you see he has forgiven you. You want to jump up straight away and pursue the bluebird, to stand out from the crowd, if only for an hour, but most certainly to be a hero. Such, they say, are the antics provoked by Montparnasse. We may not be the greatest on its slopes but neither are we going to be the least.

But now, farewell, proud Le Select! You may not have known it, but in fact we were not such nonentities. Tomorrow we too would begin our conquest of Paris. The 'pre-publication marketing' of our book was about to begin. What in Russia we would call the hype. How was it? Bruising. Russian public relations firms have no idea: from an early breakfast to a late supper inclusive there were press conferences, interviews, parties, presentations, conversations. By evening I was hoarse, and the next morning everything began all over again. There was a whirl of journalists who for some reason were interested in the book, some of whom had even found time to read it. The timetable was rigorously adhered to: I was whisked from one interview to the next, with no deviations from the agreed programme. Between meetings with journalists there was an orientation talk with my publisher Malcy Ozonna about things I must under no circumstances forget to say. Marie Gigault from *Le Monde* was to be told one thing, Thierry Brandt from the Franco-Swiss newspaper *Le Matin* something else, the magazine *Elle* something else again.

For all that, the frenetic pace did not dissipate the emotional charge. Everywhere kind words cascaded down, love, warmth, admiration, respect – a positive tsunami. Life was suddenly something to enjoy, surrounded by interested people. These were feelings long unfamiliar in Russia where people do not love you for your articles. On the contrary, most hate you for them.

The French intellectuals involved in promoting the book were clearly puzzled by my increasingly obvious embarrassment as this carousel of kindness continued. 'Isn't it just the same in Russia when somebody has written and published a book?' 'It is not at all the same in Russia.' 'What do you mean? Has your book not been published in Russia?' 'Of course not!'

They were amazed. They shrugged their shoulders. For the first time they looked at me uncertainly, unable to believe it. I did not try to explain. What would be the point? These were trivial details. I looked about me instead, taking in what really mattered – how the Parisiennes were dressed.

You have only to stand in the bustle of Place de la Madeleine for ten minutes to understand that there is no answer to this question. The essence of Paris is that the women dress as they please. The men too. And they think as they choose to, and put on their make-up in the morning as they see fit. This kind of life is called freedom. Liberty. You live as you please, however you like.

Moscow had been only a transit airport on my flight to Paris. The starting point of the journey which brought me to the capital of France was Ingushetia and Chechnya: refugee camps; foothills; forests; soldiers desperate to go home; hungry people crying; the routine horror of life in our homeland where everybody lives as best they can, just trying to survive. That is why 'my' Paris seemed such a sweet, heavenly treat. It was like the taste in your mouth after wormwood, when a single chocolate has the impact of kilograms of honey.

' "Why are you not sleeping?" "Paris will not let me sleep." ' Sometimes we hum that song to ourselves as we struggle towards the light through the routine austerity of life in Russia. And do you know what? It wasn't true! I slept very soundly in Paris, for the first time in all the months of the war, without sleeping pills, without shivering. Nobody was yelling at me, goading me, telling me I was a traitor. Everybody liked me. Everybody admired me. May you enjoy the same experience.

That was the joy of Paris, the private property of one Russian journalist who dares to testify to it. It was a joy all the more poignant because immediately before it I had to dare to do quite different things. My book will go on sale in the bookshops of Paris on 4 June 2000. Its publishers have decided to call it *Journey to Hell: A Chechen Diary. The Daring Testimony of a Russian Journalist.*

What You See at the End of the World

June 2006

I was recently in Australia at the annual Sydney Writers' Festival and couldn't resist a little tourism. Having failed to resist it, I now can't keep quiet about what I saw. The following are just the jottings of a tourist.

I have never seen a chapel or a naval base like these, although I have seen plenty of both. I had been told I must see a really curious place of worship, only it was in a naval base. Admittedly, it was an old Australian base, but still . . . So there I was at the checkpoint with my knees knocking, long conditioned to the knowledge that checkpoints are bad news. You don't get through them, or, if you do, only under guard.

In the goldfish bowl sat a cheery, suntanned officer who glanced casually at our passports and did not stick a rifle in our backs and tell us to get out. He was delighted that somebody was interested in visiting his base. 'Have you come to see the chapel?' he asked. 'Do you know how to get to it? You want to drive there? Of course. No probs.'

He groped somewhere behind him and let us through. A recently democratised Soviet citizen's brain had difficulty coping with such free and easy behaviour: how could we be admitted to a naval base without having the car inspected, without even a look in the boot? What if it was packed with explosives? You even get checked nowadays if you want to drive into the Luzhniki Sports Complex in Moscow, just to relax and smell the flowers. This Australian officer, so woefully lacking in vigilance, continued whistling to himself, loafing in his chair, his body language totally at variance with my expectations.

At last we reached the chapel. Picture it: Australia is at the end of the world, you can't go any further, and this naval base is right at the end of the end of the world, on a stunning, high promontory jutting out into the Pacific Ocean. It hovers above it. Our chapel was at the very end of this end of the end. When you enter you are suspended above the ocean, and moreover the chapel's far wall, behind the altar, is made of glass. When you look at the altar it is like praying to the expanse of the ocean and the lofty, amazingly blue sky above the sea. Your prayer is to that great Ocean of Peace to protect and preserve you. A chapel in a naval base is built not for open-mouthed tourists, of course, but for those putting out to sea, and sometimes never returning.

This is a chapel which discriminates between faiths no more than the waves, which are wholly indifferent to the religious affiliation of those they swallow. Red-headed, fair-haired, curly-haired, hook-nosed, the Pacific engulfs them all impartially.

No doubt the chapel has a nominal affiliation, and I can probably guess which, but as you stand before the altar looking out to the end of the world, this place feels pagan. All those ingenious interventions placed between man and nature, this sect, that cross or another, or no cross at all, dissolve and become meaningless. You are communing with the sea, even if out of habit you call it the Almighty. You ask it not to take you, and there is no philosophy beyond that, not a hint of that universal human error of recent times, the belief that we are the all-conquering rulers of the earth.

Otherwise, the chapel is simple, like a plainly constructed hut. In addition to the rear wall, the façade is glass, and if you spin around you feel that both you and this cliff jutting out into the ocean are floating in the sky. The chapel is furnished with benches, their cushions embroidered with naval insignia, and on the walls are lists of those who did not return, and a cross. I was going to ask the officer at the checkpoint about the denomination but thought better of it. What do the specifics of faith matter?

The cheery sentinel waved us goodbye, and our incursion onto the territory of a military site was over. I am no uncritical admirer of the West who imagines that everything is better and purer there than in Russia, but I have to admit that it is far more common there to encounter something warm and human.

Sydney is a mixture of a city, which makes it seem strange by comparison with anywhere else. The centre appears on the one hand to be pure London, but on the other pure New York. With that wonder of the modern world, the Sydney Opera House, looking out towards the harbour like the open lid of a shell, the central area resembles New York; with the exception of the Opera it is a concrete jungle of skyscrapers with narrow avenues between them. Fairly comfortless, highly urban, as linear as anyone could wish.

But it is only superficially New York. When you start reading the street names you are amazed: everything is just like in London: Hyde Park, King's Cross, the station and the adjacent district. There is a Paddington, and even an Oxford Street, and it too is very long. The names of London streets and places have been transplanted, with only a light admixture of local exoticism. King's Cross Station in Sydney, for example, is located in Woolloomooloo, an Aboriginal name Londoners could not imagine in their worst nightmares.

The Aborigines, admittedly, are in short supply. Woolloomooloo there may be, but Aborigines, the indigenous inhabitants of Australia, there are not. Search as you may, you will find none in the streets of Sydney.

Australia was born in tears and did not hold out the prospect of an easy life. In the late eighteenth century there was a crime wave in London, and England, running short of prisons, hit on the idea of finding an island on the other side of the earth where it could dump its criminal elements, with the Exchequer bearing only transportation costs. Once the criminals were there they could be left to survive as best they could, a way of thinking similar to the Tsarist regime's view of the island of Sakhalin.

Captain Cook was given the commission by his government and duly performed it. Soon convict ships were sailing to the distant land he had discovered, the convicts were disembarked, and their survival was then very much up to them. There were already people on the island who bore little resemblance to Captain Cook, strange, dark-skinned people talking mumbo-jumbo. They named them Aborigines and set about brutally exterminating them, regarding them as little better than animals. Later they began sending the younger sons of lords to the British island, allotting them enormous territories in Australia to cultivate for next to nothing. Some Aborigines considered that these territories belonged to them, by the grace of Mother Nature and not of the minor aristocracy.

The offspring of the British upper classes accordingly took to destroying anybody who tried to defend his lands. There were occasional truces which held for a time, and Aboriginal women had babies by the younger sons and the British staff who served them. It was accepted that half-castes were taken from the Aboriginal women and brought up as British.

Those times are, of course, long gone, and today's Australians try their utmost to right the historical wrongs of their conquering forebears, but if they have had much success it is not very noticeable: I didn't spot a single Aborigine in Sydney. People told me to wait because one elderly Aborigine sometimes played his didgeridoo at the central harbour.

'One?'

'One.'

In all the evenings of my visit not even that one Aborigine appeared. On the harbour front Chinese musicians played passionate Latin American music which flowed out into the tourist shops, and there were heaps of Aboriginal bits and bobs: gift boomerangs, knick-knacks made of kangaroo hide, paintings in traditional colours and motifs on a variety of surfaces. Alongside sat photographs of the artists: smiling Aborigines. So many photographs, so few live Aborigines. One wondered anxiously whether they had all died.

There is a permanent exhibition of Aboriginal art in the National Art Gallery of New South Wales in Sydney with some 200 works dating from the 1950s to the present day, a period when there were no longer any conquerors, and the descendants of those cruel people were trying to atone for their sins. For all that, the most common subject of Aboriginal painting is conquerors killing Aborigines. Another is the family trees of Aboriginal tribes, certifying their right to their lands. The Aborigines draw all this in a unique manner: everything appears to be viewed from above, and the impression is that there are multiple visual planes. The kangaroos are flattened too, as if they are dead and have been dissected. The same goes for lizards, and koalas, and Aborigines themselves.

If you stand at the harbour waiting for the Aborigine to play his didgeridoo, you will observe a remarkable scene. White-collar workers, business people who work in the city centre, stream out into it straight from the ferry at the harbour quays. Here people come to work in the morning, and in the evening go home on the little ferries and steamers. A ferry moors in the morning at Central Quay, and city workers in dark suits and clutching laptops pour from it as if an underground train had just come in. The city is built around the harbour, with people living on the shore and working in the centre. The roads around the harbour are narrow and suffer from traffic jams, but nobody has yet devised a way of causing traffic jams in the Pacific Ocean. What's more, the ferry is cheap, and always arrives on time.

I naturally boarded the ferry, and it set off. The first stop, still in the city centre, was the Rocks. That is the name of a district, and is the point where Captain Cook landed. There he stands today, a statue by his own toy-like house, which is built of the typical reddish-beige local sandstone.

The ferry takes us further, to the quays in the dormitory suburbs. Such-and-such Street, only it is a quay. Rose Street, only that is a pier. There are signs like we have at bus stops, and a shelter in case of rain. Around the quays low houses grow into the cliffs, small stores and completely wild countryside. Ten minutes on the morning ferry takes you to New York with its soul-destroying pace of life, but on the way home you can meditate on the water flying by the side of the boat, the crests of the waves, the seagulls, the surf, and you must already be feeling better. Psychotherapists cannot be much in demand in Sydney, where the citizens have the ocean, and the major urban transport arteries lay themselves over it. There is nothing to build, and nothing to constantly maintain. What would Moscow's Luzhkov find to do if he were Mayor of Sydney?

You can also take the ferry to the theatre, the museum, and the colonial-style Governor's residence.

The ferry also takes you to the zoo, which in Sydney is called Taronga Zoo. Who or what was Taronga? None of the local people could give me an answer. Well, fair enough. The main thing is, I saw an echidna, a funny little animal, quiet and retiring, with a long nose and quills. Not the world's most beautiful animal, perhaps, just as not all people are Apollo Belvederes, but why do Russians say damningly, 'You are not a mother – you are an echidna'? I observed the ways of the Australian echidna for a long time but couldn't work that out. It just snuffled everything around with its long nose and did nobody any harm.

In Taronga, naturally, there are a lot of koalas. They look like little cuddly bears, almost completely grey, but with a beige shimmer, and they sleep 20 hours out of 24 in trees, according to the sign, in uncomfortable postures: the back of their furry neck pressed against one branch, their backside against another, and the rest of their body dangling down. They sleep sweetly, so that must be how they like to be. How important it is not to impose our own ideas of comfort on other people.

And then, of course, the kangaroos. How could one visit Australia without seeing a kangaroo? Unfortunately, the kangaroos seemed rather unfriendly. They were probably afraid. They would look at you, but very anxiously. You could go into their pen and they would hop alongside, not agile bipeds but on their two rear paws, and not too close. Along with the kangaroos, an insolent beauty lives in Taronga: the emu. She sashayed over and promptly pecked the back of my head, which was at just the right level, with a beak the size of a small shovel. She was clearly asking for food, but all the signs in Taronga shout: Do Not Feed The Animals! So we parted with the emu not on the best of terms.

The cockatoos in the Sydney zoo are very handsome, striking, multicoloured, and friendly. They are almost the size of eagles, but the best cockatoos live on the Sydney central embankment, enormous, white with black patches, and move in flocks over short distances, from one of the enormous trees which surround the opera to another, kicking up a fuss among themselves, like our crows, and paying no attention at all to people.

Well, that is it. After the zoo I had to fly for 22 hours, for the most part over seas and oceans, with two stops, in Singapore and Dubai. In total it took over 24 hours to get back to Moscow. It wasn't much fun, but I don't regret it. To have been to the far end of the earth, which you always knew existed, is very invigorating and a good inoculation against the great-power mentality drummed into us in Russia. How can we be the epicentre of everything if you can fly for 24 hours from Moscow and still find there is more world to see?

Afterword

Dear Anna,

I want to tell you about our lives without you. Where are we now? At what point in history? One thing is clear: not where we ever wanted to be. In the more than ten years you have not been with us, we could have already been living in another country, turned from the Gulag Empire into a normal European state, as many of our neighbours have done. But, as Stolypin famously put it, 'In Russia, every ten years everything changes, and nothing changes in 200 years.' I am sick and tired of this quote, but it contains so much despair that is so familiar to us that I want to repeat it.

Do you remember the 1990s – 'dashing', bloody, holy? Do you remember what romantics we were? Criminally romantic we were, and we must admit it today. It was naive of us to believe that if books by Solzhenitsyn, Shalamov, Grossman appeared in our bookshops – books that had previously meant a prison sentence for those who read them – if we had free newspapers and different parties, not just the Communist Party, this would be the beginning of a normal life. We would be like everyone else. We would join the rest of the world, stop scaring everyone with our Iskander rockets. Rallies, a hundred thousand strong, gathered in the squares, we walked about and chanted: 'Freedom! Freedom!' It seemed to us that this eternal Russian dream, this wonderful creature so lovingly nurtured in our kitchens where we used to gather and dream, was about to become reality, that literally tomorrow we would be free. No one at the time could possibly know that a former convict, who spent his whole life in a prison camp, cannot just come out of the camp gates and become free overnight. He cannot be free because all he knows is his prison camp, all he can do is live inside his prison camp.

How many illusions we had then! We naively believed that as soon as we removed that henchman Dzerzhinsky from his granite pedestal, that would be enough and the whole country would breathe freely. And so they published Solzhenitsyn and Rybakov and everyone read everything. My friends and I, any intelligentsia household, often did not own a decent coat but we all had large libraries. Now our children and grandchildren do not know what to do with all these books and thick magazines; they do not need them – they put them in the rubbish.

Yes, we ran around the squares and shouted: 'Freedom! Freedom!' Yet no one knew what it meant. And then it began ... Plants, factories, research facilities, enterprises were closing down – and what could we do with all that freedom? No one had imagined that we would be free but destitute. Everyone wanted to be a master, not a servant. Even today, if you walk into an expensive shop and ask for a little extra attention it is taken as an offence, a sign of condescension. Yet everyone has only recently emerged from socialism, where everyone was poor, but equal in their poverty.

I think, Anna, you must have already seen those TV images: 'new Russians' eating black caviar, boasting gold urinals in personal jets and the largest yachts in the world, all while people somewhere in Ryazan or Sakhalin, without any work or money, look on with hungry eyes. No one thought about the people. Ideas were cherished, not people. Now we are surprised that our people's heads are a real mishmash of red and white: right-wing and left-wing ideas. Because no one had ever talked to them; no one took pains to explain anything to them from TV screens. Now it is Putin who talks to them; he has learned from our mistakes. But it is not about Putin alone. Putin says what the people want to hear; I would say that every Russian is a little Putin. I am talking about the collective Putin: we thought that it was the Soviet power that was the problem, but it was all about the people. The 'Sovok', the Soviet mode of thinking, lives on in our minds and our genes. How quickly has the Stalinist machine set to work again . . . With what knowledge and excitement everyone is once again denouncing each other, catching spies, beating people up for being different, unlike everyone else . . . Stalin has risen! Throughout Russia they are building monuments to Stalin, putting up Stalin's portraits, opening museums in Stalin's memory . . .

You passed away, Anna, with the belief that we had won the coup. Yet the years that we have lived without you have clearly shown that the coup had only hidden for a while, taken other forms, only to come back victorious. If anyone were to put on a T-shirt with Stalin's picture or with the word 'USSR' on it in the 1990s, they would be made fun of. Now it is considered okay. There are dozens of books about Stalin lining our bookshops: books about Stalin's women, about the great generalissimo during the war, about the wine he loved, about the cigarettes he liked to smoke. It is quite incomprehensible how people at the same time grieve for their innocent loved ones murdered by Stalin and express their love for Stalin. Nostalgia for everything Soviet. Russians want to have a Schengen visa, a foreign car, even if a second-hand one, and hold on to their faith in Stalin.

The hardest thing you would find to accept is that Russians have learned to kill their brothers; they have learnt to hate. I could tell you how a Moscow taxi driver kicked me out of the car when he found out that I was from Western Ukraine, that my mother was Ukrainian and that I loved Ukrainians.

'Crimea is ours!' he yelled at me.

'No, it is not yours, it is Ukrainian.'

'Donbass is ours!'

'No, it is Ukrainian.'

I am not sure if your heart, Anna, could endure this pain as well. Undoubtedly, you would have gone to the front line in Ukraine, undoubtedly you would have written your honest reports from there. If in the past bodies of soldiers in zinc coffins were brought back from Afghanistan and were buried secretly at night, today they bring back the so-called 'Cargo 200' from Ukraine and Syria. But there is also a terrible difference. When I was writing my book *Boys in Zinc* about the war in Afghanistan and would go to meet a mother waiting for a coffin with her son's remains, she would greet me with the words, 'I shall tell you everything! Write the truth.' Today, mothers are silent, they talk in whispers. Only one of them admitted to the newspaper reporter, 'I shan't tell you anything, because they will not pay me compensation for my dead son. I want this money to buy an apartment for my daughter.'

Where did this happen? When? When did we turn back, sink back into the darkness of madness, fear and hatred of the Stalin years? We are still afraid to openly admit it to ourselves. But it is so. There is a war on . . . In the former Soviet Union, dozens of journalists have been killed, every year new names appear on this blacklist. Life in Russia is still in limbo between chaos and a prison barrack. It is not an accident that I often hear people in my circle talk about reading books on 1930s Germany or the final years of the Russian Empire, on the eve of the Russian Revolution. Ask yourself: why? Well, there are so many terrifying similarities with our life today. Some talk about the Third World War, others about the return of fascism.

Freedom is a long road . . . This is what we have learnt since your departure. We really need you, Anna! We have learnt from you that there can be no compromises in a war; even the smallest compromise makes you an accomplice. It would be much harder for all of us without everything you had managed to say and do. Without your belief that it is not hatred but love for humanity that will save us. Thank you for having been here and still being here.

SVETLANA ALEXIEVICH

VINTAGE CLASSICS

Vintage Classics is home to some of the greatest writers and thinkers from around the world and across the ages. Bringing you not just the books you already know and love, but new additions to your library, these are works to capture imaginations, inspire new perspectives and excite curiosity.

Renowned for our iconic red spines and bold, collectable design, Vintage Classics is an adventurous, ever-evolving list. We breathe new life into classic books for modern readers, publishing to reflect the world today, because we believe that our times can best be understood in conversation with the past.

A Note on Our Sustainability Commitments

We create Vintage Classics red spine paperbacks with the environment in mind.

We have minimised the carbon impact of our books by using low-carbon FSC™-certified paper. Our covers use minimal finishes and we are working towards making all our books recyclable. All red spine editions printed in the UK use 100% renewable energy.

For more information on our sustainability commitments, please visit greenpenguin.co.uk.

Discover more in **VINTAGE CLASSICS** red spine

Brave New World	Aldous Huxley
To Kill a Mockingbird	Harper Lee
Catch-22	Joseph Heller
Native Son	Richard Wright
The Handmaid's Tale	Margaret Atwood
The Gulag Archipelago	Aleksandr Solzhenitsyn
The Master and Margarita	Mikhail Bulgakov
Beloved	Toni Morrison
Stoner	John Williams
The Sailor Who Fell from Grace with the Sea	Yukio Mishima
The Savage Detectives	Roberto Bolaño
The Joy Luck Club	Amy Tan
Autobiography of Red	Anne Carson
I Who Have Never Known Men	Jacqueline Harpman
Oranges Are Not the Only Fruit	Jeanette Winterson
Disgrace	J. M. Coetzee
My Left Foot	Christy Brown
Sugar	Bernice L. McFadden
Death and the Penguin	Andrey Kurkov
Persepolis	Marjane Satrapi